TRAILING CLOUDS

Trailing Clouds

Immigrant Fiction in Contemporary America

David Cowart

CORNELL UNIVERSITY PRESS

ITHACA AND LONDON

First published 2006 by Cornell University Press
First printing, Cornell Paperbacks, 2006

Printed in the United States of America

Library of Congress Cataloging-in-Publication Date

Cowart, David, 1947–
 Trailing clouds : immigrant fiction in contemporary America / David Cowart
 p. cm.
 Includes bibliographical references and index.
 ISBN-13: 978-0-8014-4469-2 (cloth : alk. paper)
 ISBN-10: 0-8014-4469-1 (cloth : alk. paper)
 ISBN-13: 978-0-8014-7287-9 (pbk. : alk. paper)
 ISBN-10: 0-8014-7287-3 (pbk. : alk. paper)
  1. American fiction—Minority authors—History and criticism. 2. American
fiction—20th century—History and criticism 3. Immigrants in literature.
4. Emigration and immigration in literature. I. Title.
PS374.I48C69 2006
813'.5099206912—dc22

                                                            2005037545

Cornell University Press strives to use environmentally responsible suppliers
and materials to the fullest extent possible in the publishing of its books. Such
materials include vegetable-based, low-VOC inks and acid-free papers that are
recycled, totally chlorine-free, or partly composed of nonwood fibers. For further
information, visit our website at www.cornellpress.cornell.edu.

Cloth printing   10 9 8 7 6 5 4 3 2 1
Paperback printing   10 9 8 7 6 5 4 3 2 1

For Margaret Matthews Cowart,
Genealogist, Publisher, Life-Giver

Amerika, du hast es besser

Als unser Kontinent, der alte,

Hast keine verfallenen Schlösser

Und keine Basalte.

Dich stört nicht im Innern

Zu lebendiger Zeit

Unnützes Erinnern

Und vergeblicher Streit.

—Goethe, from *Zahme Xenien*

≋ Contents

≋ Acknowledgments

The young are often told to count their blessings. Those who learn the lesson continue to do so as adults. Certainly the precept commends itself when one pauses to acknowledge the institutions and friends that help in the shepherding of one's work into print. Steven Lynn, who chairs the University of South Carolina Department of English, has an extraordinary ability to facilitate the work of his colleagues. A model of good humor, generosity, and good judgment, he inspires us all with his vision of departmental becoming. I am also grateful to our College of Liberal Arts (now the College of Arts and Sciences) for a generous grant that allowed me to spend the summer of 2001 working on this project. In 2002–3 the college supplemented a National Endowment for the Humanities fellowship with funds that allowed me two full semesters of release time. I am also, of course, deeply grateful to the National Endowment itself; to Ezra Greenspan (now at Southern Methodist University), who offered immensely helpful advice on writing the grant application; and to Brian McHale, Kathryn Hume, and Ellen Pifer, who wrote reference letters on my behalf.

I learn more and more from those I teach, and not least from those with whom I have read immigrant fiction—undergraduates in a special topics course and graduate students in seminars. All raised questions that will continue to resound in my mind long after the present project is, as journalists say, put to bed. Special thanks to Brittany Dasher, who read and meticulously annotated my chapter on *How the García Girls Lost Their Accents*. My graduate assistants, Rebecca Stelzer, Jessica Wissel, Helen Yitah, Walt Bosse, and especially Jessica Labbé (who introduced me to Achy Obejas), provided invaluable help with notes and works cited.

Mark Shackleton, at the University of Helsinki, gave an early version of my introductory chapter a wonderfully thorough vetting for inclusion in the volume he co-edited with Maarika Toivonen, *Roots and Renewal: Writings by Bicentennial Fulbright Professors* (Helsinki: Hakapaino, 2001). He gets particular thanks for catching my misspelling of "enthymematic."

Thanks, too, to Chase Crossingham, who first nudged my mental telescope toward Chang-rae Lee, and to Gwang-jin Lee, who urged me to read Theresa Hak Kyung Cha and Nora Okja Keller. My friend Sue Mi Powell brought Joe Porcelli's *The Photograph* to my attention and answered my questions about the language and customs of Korea. I first read Eva Hoffman at the instigation of Maria Antonietta Saracino of the University of Rome. John Paul Russo, at the University of Miami, was an invaluable sounding board, and even sent me his extra copy of Helen Barolini's *Umbertina*.

Christian Moraru's invitation to speak on recent immigrant writers at a symposium at the University of North Carolina–Greensboro stimulated me to focus my thinking, as did the responses from his colleagues and students. On a similar occasion at the Charles University in Prague, Martin Procházka, Hana Ulmanova, Erik Roraback, and their students helped me shape ideas; my thanks, too, to Marketa Kolarova and Michael Hahn, of the American embassy there, for making my visit possible. In the summer of 2005 a Fulbright grant enabled me to visit various universities in Japan. I very much appreciated my discussions of American immigrant writers with the students and colleagues of Nobuo Kamioka at Gakushuin University in Tokyo and those of Akitoshi Nagahata at Nagoya University.

I was also honored to present plenary addresses on this subject at the April 2004 conference on (Dis)Locating Identity in the Twentieth Century at the University of South Carolina and the 2005 April X Conference at the Jagiellonian University in Kraków.

As always, I remain deeply grateful for the love and support of my daughter, Rachel, my son, Chase, and my parents.

≋ TRAILING CLOUDS

≋ Introduction

The New Immigrant Writing

All around me I see the face of America changing. So do you, if you live in cities, teach in universities, ride public transport. But where, in fiction, do you read of it? Who, in other words, speaks for us, the new Americans from nontraditional immigrant countries? Which is another way of saying, in this altered America, who speaks for you?
    —Bharati Mukherjee, "Immigrant Writing: Give Us Your Maximalists!"

These rhetorical questions, posed by an immigrant from India shortly after her own 1988 naturalization as an American citizen, imply an enthymematic argument: "we" are (or will soon be) "you." Accepting her implicit challenge, I propose to examine selected major fictions published by immigrants to the United States in the period since 1970. Because they operate in a distinctive, transformative social and cultural climate, these writers differ from such earlier arrivals as Anzia Yezierska (1901), Henry Roth (1907), Ayn Rand (1926), Carlos Bulosan (1930), and W. H. Auden (1939). But in every generation literary transplants restage the very creation of our national literature. The first writing Americans, after all, were themselves immigrants. In our earliest written literature the new world became what various sets of European eyes and various European pens said it was. Many of those enshrined in the opening pages of American school anthologies—notably John Winthrop, John Smith, William Bradford, Anne Bradstreet, and Edward Taylor—were not born on these shores.

This book concerns the contemporary immigrant imagination and its witness. I argue that readers learn much about the durability of or changes in the American way of life from writers who in recent years have come to this country, embraced its culture, and penned substantial literary work in English. Indeed, so robust is the phenomenon of immigrant writing that one may begin to argue for discrimination, to separate out those fictions that, transcending trend, do much more than capitalize on what may prove an unsustainable popularity. Although they show their readers how assimilation—or resistance to assimilation—must be negotiated and renegotiated in every generation, the fictions discussed in depth here recommend themselves on largely aesthetic grounds. Whatever their value as sociological documents, these books stand out as fully accomplished examples of contemporary literary art. They range from the well known to the relatively unfamiliar: *Jasmine* and *Lucy* on the one hand, Mylène Dressler's *The Deadwood Beetle* and the stories of Junot Díaz on the other.

Before proceeding, I should like to clarify a point of usage that often leads to confusion. It concerns the term "first generation," which can mean (according to the *Random House College Dictionary*) either the American-born children of immigrants or the naturalized immigrants themselves. This book, however, requires a distinction between the actual immigrant and that immigrant's offspring. For clarity's sake, then, I reserve the term "first generation" for those born in the United States to immigrant parents. I mean, however, to emphasize *immigrant* writers here, to determine whether their vision differs from that of their already canonized "first-generation" cousins. At the risk of sounding facetious, I see the distinction between these two groups as something like the difference perceived by a Nabokov character between eighteenth- and seventeenth-century pastoral: in the seventeenth century, the sheep were a little whiter and fluffier. Perhaps, by the same token, we shall find the perceptions of immigrant writers ever so slightly more pristine than those of writers always already American.

Readers have heard a good deal in recent decades from the first-generation writers, the David Henry Hwangs and Paule Marshalls whose childhood encounters with the dominant culture and its language often figure as primal scenes in books on the price of assimilation. If at times these writers seek to represent the old country, they must do so at second hand: they must construct pre-diasporic settings through the myth-making memories of their immigrant parents. The American reading public has had good experiences with such material in the texts of a Maxine Hong Kingston or an Amy Tan, but in lesser hands one encounters what

Bharati Mukherjee characterizes, devastatingly, as "hokey concoctions composed of family memory and brief visits to ancestral villages."[1] These first-generation writers have received much attention from critics whose response tends to be modeled on ethnic and postcolonial theory, which emphasizes the conflicts that come with having to live on the margins and write in a non-native language. Considerable academic research has gone into the attempt to articulate the qualities of being an American of African, Asian, Hispanic, or other ethnicity. Often tendentious, these theories of sub-national identity foreground issues of separateness, diversity, political disenfranchisement, and cultural alienation.

Such criticism fails properly to gauge the value and meaning of the growing body of important work by recent immigrants, and one may wish for less relentlessly nuanced discussions of literary ethnicity, discussions more resistant to the cultural balkanizing deplored by Robert Hughes ("the Culture of Complaint") or Harold Bloom ("the School of Resentment"). Though not necessarily inclined to sacrifice separateness and difference on the altar of cultural osmosis, these writers seldom dwell on a perceived marginalization. Rather, they transform some American theme (as Chang-rae Lee, in *Native Speaker*, rewrites *All the King's Men* with a Korean American politician in the role of Willie Stark), reinvent some nominally Western form (as Theresa Hak Kyung Cha, in DICTEE, reimagines both epic and Menippean satire), or marry American characters and landscape to some archetype brought over from the old country (reading *The Vision of Emma Blau*, one suspects that Ursula Hegi has asked herself: How would the author of *Buddenbrooks* tell an *American* story?).

Such writers, whose fictions represent an especially fertile field of transmuted desire, might well benefit from a criticism more answerable to real-world politics and American history, a criticism that will, incidentally, continue the process of making more inclusive the body of work regarded as important and representative of the nation's many-cultured culture. In bringing new immigrant writing under the microscope, moreover, the desiderated *post*-postcolonial criticism will make visible the seismic rapidity with which American culture is moving away from its historically Eurocentric bias. It will foster appreciation of the literary character of the people we are, as Mukherjee observes, becoming.

Availing themselves of the American's right to reflect positively or negatively on the nation, the new immigrant writers contrast to some degree with peers who, defining themselves as expatriates (Salman Rushdie,

Janette Turner Hospital) or exiles (Solzhenitsyn or, until recently, Aleksandar Hemon), seldom write fiction about the country in which they are guests. But why do some writers retain their expatriate status while others naturalize? Nabokov, always a transcender of categories, remains the poster child for both the exilic and the immigrant paradigms. Chastened by Europe's violence, bloodshed, terror, and genocide (his wife was Jewish), Janus-faced Nabokov contemplates America's foibles with wry tolerance. Yes, these people are vulgar, but look how robust and generous their civilization is! At the same time that he pines for and reconfigures his native Russia in one fictive conceit after another, he is an especially sharp observer of cisatlantic mores. In *Lolita*, for example, he records the mid-century American reality as incisively as any social realist, and readers in his adoptive country continue to marvel at the familiarity-stripping accuracy of his snapshots from the highways of the nation. In other works—notably *Ada*—he mixes such observation with candid yearning for the lost homeland. In *Pnin* and *Pale Fire*, similarly, the witty yet humane picture of campus politics in New England academic villages is balanced by, on the one hand, the straightforward nostalgia of Timofey Pnin and, on the other, the hybrid fantasies of Charles Kinbote.

Although his career as English-language writer largely precedes the post-1970 period emphasized in this book, Nabokov represents a kind of ideal prototype of the literary immigrant. Having come to the United States in 1940, he invites brief comment here as a transitional figure, linking the expatriate literati of the early twentieth century to their more settled successors. I should like, therefore, to devote a page or two to *Pnin*, the Nabokov novel that engages the immigrant experience most directly. Because certain features of this text prove highly representative of the travail of the displaced, I have chosen it to introduce—and presently to illustrate—a tentative anatomy of immigrant narrative. By invoking Nabokov (and, in the next chapter, Saul Bellow), I mean to suggest at least some continuity between literary immigrant generations. I mean also to signal the kind of literary standard that figures in my selection of post-1970 exemplars of exilic fiction.

"When I was a child," says Saint Paul, "I spake as a child, I understood as a child, I thought as a child: but when I became a man, I put away childish things." These lines commend themselves to memory because, with eloquent simplicity, they characterize a natural progression, familiar to every adult. But insofar as everything experienced in the formative years falls at least nominally into the category of "childish things," immigrants—those of a certain age, at least—may come to associate the homeland itself with puerility. According to Pauline metaphor, the difference between this world and the next resembles the difference between childhood, with its childish seeing and thinking, and adulthood, with its direct, experiential knowledge of reality: "For now we see through a glass, darkly; but then face to face: now I know in part; but then shall I know even as also I am known"(1 Cor. 13:11–12).

As will be seen, immigrant writers avail themselves of this metaphor as well: at times, that is, they characterize changing countries as death and afterlife. Nabokov cannot resist making fun of psychotherapy, but his passing jab, in *Pnin*, at "Dr. Halp's theory of birth being an act of suicide on the part of the infant" should be read against his more carefully developed, quasi-Wordsworthian idea that immigrants also undergo a painful parturition as the more or less amusingly infantilized citizens of a new country.[2] Remembering the better life from which revolution or Fortune's turning wheel has dislodged them, they arrive, like Wordsworth's infant, "trailing clouds of glory." (Sometimes, of course, fleeing some crime or dereliction, or complicit with a corrupt regime at last forced from power, they arrive *under* the cloud, with blood on their hands.) *Pnin* represents an especially elaborate development of the conceit that the immigrant enters a second infancy or childhood. On the very first page, the narrator remarks that the title character "began rather impressively." Although these words introduce a top-down inspection (from "ideally bald . . . dome" and "strong-man torso" to "spindly legs . . . and frail-looking, almost feminine feet" [7]), one can also understand that he began his life and career impressively, for he grew up in a comfortable St. Petersburg home with good prospects for education and professional success. His betrothal to the lovely Mira Belochkin marked the high point of these years. But in life as in physiognomy, poor Pnin has "ended," as the narrator sighs, "somewhat disappointingly." Not confined to advancing age and debility, Pnin's diminution announces itself as an infantilism not surprising to readers of immigrant fiction. Hence the rotund torso, the useless legs, the "curiously small foot" (131), the "infantile absence of eyebrows" (7) and "infantine eyed" (179) visage. In a moment of intense nostalgia, he weeps tears of "infantine, uncontrollable fluid" (82). Dental surgery renders him toothless as a newborn. His command of English resembles that of a two-year-old. In the course of his life as American, he occupies a series of children's rooms, notably in the Clements home, where he sits in a "rather juvenile rocker" (55) to receive a visit from his ex-wife, and in the house on Todd Road, where his bedroom features "a pennant-shaped red cardboard with the enigmatic word 'Cardinals' daubed on it in white" and "a tiny rocker for a three-year-old Pnin, painted pink" (146). Expelled from the womb of Mother Russia, Pnin must grow up all over again, arrive at shabby middle age, and remember the homeland as other immigrants do: as "a country that could be little more to them than a sad stylized toy, a bauble found in the attic" (45).

Immigrant stories tend to share certain features. To say so need not invite charges of a failure to invent or to imagine or to "make it new" on the part of the storytellers. Reading any novel, one spots traditional or archetypal features that frame, one hopes, fresh perceptions. All art (but especially literary art) observes some conventions, violates others. The balance, however, is of great importance: one should be pleasantly oriented and disoriented at the same time. Too much familiarity and one is reading formula fiction; too little and one loses patience. If modernism skewed this balance toward formal and thematic iconoclasm or novelty, postmodernism recuperates popular forms and themes to serious art. In studying immigrant fiction, in any event, one recognizes certain recurrent motifs, elements of a classic story, something like a grand pattern that these narratives tend often to brush up against if not recapitulate. Some authors—Lan Cao in *Monkey Bridge*, Edwidge Danticat in *Breath, Eyes, Memory*—manage to marshal all or nearly all of these features. Most function more selectively, incorporating elements of particular importance to authorial memory or thematic calculation. To some degree one can chart an author's originality by the way she or he treats the standard mythemes—or configures them in ways that transcend formula. From Lord Raglan's distillation of hero narratives to Vladimir Propp's *Morphology of the Folktale* (1928) and the six volumes of the extraordinary catalogue that Stith Thompson produced, the *Motif-Index of Folk-Literature* (1955–58), formalist and structuralist critics have shown the usefulness of typologies, and it may be helpful briefly to sketch a modest schematic of immigrant fictions as well. To that end, I offer a list of the elements that strike me as especially characteristic of these narratives, accompanied by illustrations from prototypical *Pnin*, in which certain of the generic constituents are foregrounded, others submerged or understated or inverted.

GENERAL FEATURES OF IMMIGRANT FICTION	EXEMPLIFICATION IN *PNIN*
1. Narration often fragmented.	1. If not highly fragmented, *Pnin* is nonetheless episodic, its chapters having been published in the *New Yorker* as freestanding stories. But all of the narrative units concern the same set of characters and experiences, and unity overtakes fragmentation.
2. Old-country folktales or other material interpolated.	2. Pnin is researching a *Petite Histoire* of Russian culture, e.g., observance of "Green Week" in "the woodlands of the Upper Volga" (76, 77).
3. Travail in school, especially in connection with learning English.	3. Pnin's "dzeefeecooltsee" (66) with the English language comes in for considerable notice. In a witty reversal of the way this motif usually figures, it is the pedagogue who has trouble with English, not his students.
4. Narrators make wry, quasi-anthropological observations regarding immigrant diffidence vis-à-vis the self-assurance of native-born Americans.	4. The narrator, a fellow immigrant who has made a relatively smooth transition to the new world, dryly observes cisatlantic manners and Pnin's hapless attempts to fit in.
5. Views of what makes the homeland unlivable.	5. Pnin must sit through propaganda films showing contented Bolsheviks in the homeland to which he can never return.
6. Immigrants struggle with a sense of psychological and cultural doubleness (point of view often shifts: the same character can be both narrator and object of third-person narration, teller and told).	6. In elaborate images of superimposition, Nabokov conflates Pnin's past and present: the protagonist is simultaneously a maladroit immigrant and a child or young man in the motherland. The author introduces an irresolvable paradox in that Pnin's memories diverge from those ascribed to him by the narrator (see 8).
7. In fictions written by women: eating disorders (examples in novels by Alvarez, Danticat, Hegi, Garcia).	7. Not applicable.
8. Immigrants exploit immigrants.	8. Pnin angrily resists the narrator's appropriation of his life, his story, his job.
9. The immigrant must deal with prejudice and homesickness but eventually becomes empowered by a new American identity.	9. Nabokov characterizes Pnin's new dentures as "a firm mouthful of efficient, alabastrine, humane America" (38), but only the smug narrator achieves real assimilation.

10. Cultural contrasts often repre-
    sented as generational conflict
    (older immigrants at odds with
    their more easily Americanized
    children).

    —old world sex prohibitions
    versus new world freedom,
    virginity a trope for ethnic
    integrity (exotic puberty and
    nuptial customs remembered:
    clitoridectomy, postnuptial
    exhibition of blood-spotted sheet).

    —One parent often missing,
    sometimes associated sym-
    bolically with the homeland.

    —the mature immigrant reenters
    childhood.

10. " 'Jazz, jazz, they must always have their
    jazz, those youngsters,' muttered Pnin to
    himself" (133), speaking of the teenaged
    offspring of his fellow émigrés. Nabokov's
    character never finds a permanent home—
    at least not in the novel that bears his name
    (in *Pale Fire* readers learn that he at least
    achieves stable academic employment). On
    more than one occasion the protagonist oc-
    cupies temporary lodgings recently va-
    cated by a child—and decorated and fur-
    nished accordingly. Physically, too, there is
    much of the child about "infantine eyed"
    Pnin, from his hairless cranium and spindly
    legs to his difficulties with language (the
    English language, that is). Presently tooth-
    less as a result of dental surgery, he com-
    pletes the symbolic regression to infancy.
    All of these details drive home the peren-
    nial paradox of immigrant existence: to
    emigrate is to enter a state that resembles
    childhood.

Nabokov helps us to recognize the special freshness with which true literary immigrants write about the land to which they have come—as well as the authority with which they write about the lands they have left. Yet whatever their competence in English and whatever the literary heights they eventually scale, such immigrant literati inevitably experience something of the travail described by their less privileged fellows, whether impoverished newcomers or their first-generation offspring. Amid fictions about the immigrant's country of origin and fictions about the new land, autobiographical narratives of isolation, assimilation, and scrambled ethnicity still figure, still qualify perceptions of the American surround.

But even here, I would argue, the emotions and experiences of new immigrants constitute a bracing corrective to narrowly politicized theories of ethnic identity and literary production. The old theoretical paradigms, at any rate, do little justice to the literary practice of writers with a personal belief and investment in the otherwise embattled vision of America as sanctuary and refuge, a land that can accommodate all ethnicities and allow them to flourish socially, politically, economically, and—yes—literarily. Postcolonial criticism must, then, vie with the perennial renewal of the melting pot (or salad bowl or mosaic) metaphor among those currently encountering and testing the American myth of promise.

Whatever the figure congenial to one's identity politics, the language question remains politically charged. But a number of immigrant writers arrive already speaking English, others as young children who pick it up with relatively little trauma. Julia Alvarez, author of *How the García Girls Lost Their Accents* (1991), came to the United States at the age of ten, having begun to learn English before her departure from the Dominican Republic. (By a curious train of circumstances, she had actually—like Frank McCourt—been born in the States and taken back to her parents' native country as a newborn.) When she was a child in the old country, English *CLASS* was the language of parental secrets, "the sound of being left out."[3] Of her childhood in the States, she recalls less the travail of really mastering English than the liberation it came to embody from the old ways that still prevailed within her family: "Our growing distance from Spanish was a way in which we were setting ourselves free from the old world where, as girls, we didn't have much say about what we could do with our lives. . . . We could go places in English we never could in Spanish."[4] She recalls with great affection the nun in an American classroom who fostered her understanding of idiomatic minutiae, which "became a charged, fluid mass that carried me in its great fluent waves, rolling and moving onward, to deposit me on the shores of my new homeland. I was no longer a foreigner with no ground to stand on. I had landed in the English language."[5]

Though the American-born Richard Rodriguez nominally falls outside the present discussion, his position on language is highly relevant to any attempt to define the space occupied by the immigrant writer. In *Hunger of Memory* (1981) Rodriguez notes that the bilingual schooling movement originated in the 1970s, "that decade when middle-class ethnics began to resist the process of assimilation—the American melting pot."[6] These reformers and their allies failed, however, to differentiate the "middle-class victim of social oppression from the lower-class victim."[7] Both bilingual education and affirmative action, he argues, hurt lower-class immigrants and their children by perpetuating their ghetto. Rodriguez argues the controversial position that English empowers even as it undermines ethnicity. Rodriguez's account of tongue-tied travail in the American elementary classroom (he arrived in first grade with a fifty-word English vocabulary) actually revises a trope common—from Kingston to Chang-rae Lee—to autobiographical and quasi-autobiographical writing by immigrants and their children. Declining to embrace what has come to be the expected position, Rodriguez answers yes to two tough questions: Is English the only route to empowerment, and does one's writing in English constitute an automatic estrangement from the authentic language/culture/self? Rodriguez traces his own success as writer and public intellectual to what he sees as his good fortune in being somewhat painfully obliged to master the language of cultural dominance in America. He suggests that one must view the tradeoff not as some violation of ethnic integrity but as a local instance of the life passage from childhood innocence to adult awareness of the world's unsparing complexity.

In this he echoes another first-generation writer, Don DeLillo. Although DeLillo does not wear his ethnicity on his sleeve, his most ambitious novel, *Underworld*, incorporates personal memories of growing up, the child of Italian immigrants, in the Bronx's tangled linguistic bank. In an interview DeLillo describes the writer's struggle for literary mastery as a struggle, like that of the immigrant, with language: "It occurs to me that this is what a writer does to transcend the limitations of his background. He does it through language, obviously. He writes himself into the larger world. He opens himself to the entire culture. He becomes, in short, an American—the writer equivalent of his immigrant parents and grandparents."[8]

Twinned with the language question in ethnic studies is the issue of a perceived doubleness in outlook—something resembling the African American's much-discussed double consciousness, as described by W. E. B. Du Bois. Rey Chow, one of the more astute critics of literary ethnicity, has written extensively on the Chinese diaspora, with particular attention to the experience of Chinese Americans. She avoids definitions of either Chinese or American cultural essence; nor does she assume "absolute difference." Rather, she seeks to negotiate what in *Women and Chinese Modernity* she calls the "dialectic on which 'Chinese' and 'Western' is played."[9] Thus Chow embraces Michel de Certeau's distinction between "strategy" (for "those who are committed to the building, growth, and fortification of a 'field'") and "tactic" (for those who embrace "a calculated action determined by an absence of a proper locus").[10] Although they may seem to embrace cultural difference and the politics of change, "strategic" thinkers reinforce received ideologies. In her "dialectic" approach, Chow reveals that she understands the impossibility of any attempt at "translating" the discourse of the other (the subaltern) into the discourse of empire.[11] As tactician, however, she contrives to make the subaltern (the "native") the ground or focus or center of her thinking. A version of this tactical dialectic must inform any exploration of writers whose newly American cultural identity ranges from overdetermined to deeply conflicted. At the same time, however, America often represents to the immigrant a myth anchored in a metanarrative; thus tactical negotiation of fresh cultural possibilities proves always tempered by an overarching vision that constantly strives toward some hybrid reconstitution of the strategic.

Shirley Geok-Lin Lim also emphasizes the "double perspective" of "immigrant writers, the ones straight off the boat or the Boeing 747," whose "creative position" she characterizes as "paradoxical, difficult, contradictory, anxious, suspicious, [and] struggling." Lim sees as positive, however, the "self that escapes assimilation," for it "renews American culture, making it ready for the future." She looks forward to the emergence, along with the shift "from a white majority nation to a multiethnic nation of minorities," of a less conflicted model: perhaps "the paradigm of conflict and ambivalence" of "early Asian American texts, which finds expression in internalized alienations and in external racial discrimination and violence, will be transformed into a productive multivalence. 'Valences' speak for the abilities to integrate, combine, fuse, and synthesize different elements. Conflict is almost always a product of dualities."[12]

Though not on the same political page with Lim, Bharati Mukherjee makes similar observations. In her powerful 1989 novel *Jasmine*, Mukherjee depicts the Americanization of her eponymous heroine. In her native India, Jasmine (as she comes to be called) experiences both political violence and the oppression of women. Raped upon her (illegal) arrival in the States, she manages nonetheless to insert herself gradually into the mainstream. She moves in with, becomes pregnant by, and eventually abandons an Iowa corn farmer and banker as part of her immersion in what Pynchon, in *Mason & Dixon*, calls the American mobility. At once Jyoti, Jasmine, Jazz, Jassy, Jase, Jane, and even, at one point, the Hindu goddess Kali, this character exemplifies an *enabling* fluidity of the self: "I shuttled between identities."[13] In an essay published the year before *Jasmine*, Mukherjee argues that for writers like herself, the fluid character of nationality, properly understood, constitutes an advantage to anyone professionally involved with the imagination. The "legacy of the colonial writer" that ought to be "cashed in on," she observes,

> is his or her duality. From childhood we learned how to be two things simultaneously; to be the dispossessed as well as the dispossessor. In textbooks we read of "our" great empire and triumphs (meaning British), "our" great achievements in the arts (meaning the Moslem Moguls) and "our" treachery in the Sepoy Mutiny (meaning "native" troops). History forced us to see ourselves as both the "we" and the "other," and our language reflected our

simultaneity. . . . Perhaps it is this history-mandated training in seeing myself as "the other" that now heaps on me a fluid set of identities denied to
most of my mainstream American counterparts. That training, in our
ethnic- and gender-fractured world of contemporary American fiction, allows me without difficulty to "enter" lives, fictionally, that are manifestly not
my own. Chameleon-skinned, I discover my material over and across the
country, and up and down the social ladder.[14]

To study Mukherjee or other such "chameleon-skinned" writers, then,
one may embrace Chow's "dialectic," Lim's "multivalence," and Mukherjee's vision of fluid identity—as well as views one has perhaps been conditioned to think naïve or idealistic. But for immigrants, who have nearly always chosen this country over others, the American myth or metanarrative
remains valid. They think having to learn English, or work at menial jobs,
or deal with petty discrimination and prejudice a small price to pay for deliverance from poverty, tyranny, bloodshed, and political or religious coercion. To fault the immigrant for her or his embrace of the dream would be
to patronize precisely where one ought, perhaps, to learn anew how to
value what is special about the great cultural experiment that is America.
Indeed, a valuing of America's promise and ideals, imperiled by the ex-
tremes of identity politics, can be recuperated through the writings of
those who have most recently, like so many before them, crossed oceans to
find a haven.

A final word or two about the plan and rationale of this book. T. S. Eliot
remarks "that art never improves," that today's masterpiece "does not su-
perannuate either Shakespeare, or Homer, or the rock drawing of the
Magdalenian draughtsmen."[15] By the same token, I would not argue for
some kind of "progress" in the fictions adduced here. I have not sought to
develop an overall thesis, unless it be the implicit one that these fictions
represent the country of immigrants as, indeed, the country of immigrants. Let me be explicit, though, about my disinclination to group these
authors by ethnicity or national origin: they have seen enough of ghettos.
Thus my juxtapositions of texts are intended to mirror the often uneasy
contiguity of immigrant populations within the larger American social
order. In my pages as in the nation itself, immigrant entities resist the old
sociological amalgamation; they retain their separateness.

Readers may appreciate some further orientation to what follows. The
first chapter, which introduces the large subject of writing and publishing
by émigrés (with a glance at the explosion, in recent decades, of immigrant

memoirs), chiefly concerns a couple of transitional texts by Jerzy Kosinski and Saul Bellow. Chapter 2, which concerns formal and temporal elements of immigrant storytelling, centers on Alvarez's *How the García Girls Lost Their Accents*. In chapter 3, with Hegi's *The Vision of Emma Blau* and Mukherjee's *Jasmine* as specimen texts, I consider the ways in which the struggle to succeed in the new world fosters a crippling monomania. Chapter 4 focuses on Garcia's *Dreaming in Cuban*, which resists certain of the conventions of immigrant fictions even as it recapitulates them. Several important Korean American fictions (notably Chang-rae Lee's *Native Speaker*) figure in chapter 5, which concerns the exilic self as its own tangled web. The sixth chapter, with Danticat's *Breath, Eyes, Memory* as centerpiece, concerns the cultural shift by which the immigrant author becomes fully licensed to tell stories of the old country, rather than stories of ideally American experience. Chapter 7 offers, in Jamaica Kincaid's Lucy Potter and Lan Cao's Mai Nguyen, contrasting pictures of the immigrant as adolescent. Another side of immigrant experience—the dark past that threatens to subvert or poison the new world self—is taken up in chapter 8, which foregrounds a reading of Mylène Dressler's *The Deadwood Beetle*. Again in chapter 9, which chiefly deals with Wendy-Law Yone's *The Coffin Tree*, an immigrant author helps to define the conventions of the sub-genre in which she works: the double consciousness, the eating disorder, the parent or parents left behind, the strangely resilient old world myths. In chapter 10, finally, the stories in Junot Díaz's *Drown* prove instructively resistant to the reader's desire to make them cohere as some such modernist exercise as Joyce's *Dubliners*. In a brief concluding chapter, I consider again the qualities that differentiate these immigrant literati from the exiles and expatriates of their own day and the past. I note, too, the marketplace popularity of this body of work, along with the swiftness with which a remarkable number of immigrant writers have moved into contemporary American literature's front ranks.

1 〰〰 Slavs of New York

Being There, Mr. Sammler's Planet

I am trying to be an American writer and claim only the same rights that other American writers enjoy.

–Vladimir Nabokov, "On a Book Entitled Lolita"

Whatever their focus, the fictions of immigrant writers alternately provide windows on cultures perceived as foreign by non-immigrant readers—or they teach such readers to see the United States in new and different ways. That immigrant authors write for the most part in English has come to seem natural, but foreign-language writing in America—journalism, tracts, fiction in German, French, Yiddish, and other languages—has flourished, historically, in cities with concentrations of the newly arrived. Yiddish-language newspapers, notably Abraham Cahan's *Jewish Daily Forward*, began to appear in New York in the early 1870s, featuring fiction and poetry by the likes of Leon Kobrin, Jacob Gordin, David Pinski, and Z. Libin (pseudonym of Israel Hurowitz), as well as political and devotional writing (Saul Bellow remembers hesitating, as a child in Montreal, to make hygienic use of the Yiddish newspapers in the privy "because of those sacred characters").[1] French writing, meanwhile, flourished in New Orleans long after the Louisiana Purchase; and after the revolutions of 1848, a number of German authors—among them Reinhold Solger, author of the satirical novel *Anton in Amerika* (published in New York in 1872)—emigrated to the United States and continued to write in their native language. Later the author-émigré Robert Reitzel (1849–1898) lived in Detroit and published a German-language literary journal, *Der arme Teufel*.[2]

In modern times, too, a handful of literati have declined, naturalization notwithstanding, to make the professional transition to English. The best known include Thomas Mann, Erich Maria Remarque, Marguerite Yourcenar, and Isaac Bashevis Singer. They remain anomalies, however, addressing homeland readers first, American readers only through translation. Although various communities have at various times supported foreign-language newspapers, no American city has attempted to vie with Berlin, Paris, Zurich, and (more recently) Prague in the hosting of complete literary cultures in exile. London and Paris accommodated virtually all of America's modernists for a couple of decades, and a Russian-language literary scene flourished in the French capital and in Berlin in the years after the 1917 revolution. (Readers of Nabokov, whose exilic pseudonym was Sirin, find this phase of his career especially fascinating.) One might have expected something similar in Miami after the Cuban revolution, but gestures in that direction proved abortive. Though they may lament the loss of their native idiom, Gustavo Pérez Firmat, Cristina Garcia, Achy Obejas, Ernesto Mestre-Reed, and Joaquin Fraxedas all write in English (nor do they live in any Little Havana or other exilic enclave). Indeed, for a variety of reasons—including, ironically, the current marketplace cachet of ethnicity in all its forms—the norm among contemporary literary immigrants, from Nabokov to Eva Hoffman, from Le Ly Hayslip to Edwidge Danticat, is to transform themselves into American authors, writing in English.

With varying degrees of sympathy, each of these writers makes literature out of the experience of otherness in America. Though not an immigrant herself, Lorraine Adams describes the lives of illegals in her novel *Harbor*. Of her protagonist, Aziz Arkoun, she writes, "Days—no, weeks—went by without a person speaking to him, and longer still, without someone's eyes meeting his own."[3] Immigrants, especially those cut off from ordinary social intercourse by language or other circumstance, must often live a kind of false introspection. Frequently inarticulate, their self-communing can resemble that of prisoners in solitary confinement. But immigrant writers, at once introspective and fully capable of representing and moralizing their cultural transplantation, offer valuable perspectives on experience too often perceived as the exclusive province of poor illiterates fresh from steerage. Such perspectives emerge most readily in the numerous autobiographies and memoirs that appeared at the end of the last century: Le Ly Hayslip's *When Heaven and Earth Changed Places* (1989), Kyoko Mori's *The Dream of Water* (1994), Jade Ngoc Quang Huỳnh's *South Wind Changing* (1994), Li-Young Lee's *The Winged Seed* (1995), Gustavo Pérez Firmat's *Next Year in Cuba: A Cubano's Coming-of-Age in America* (1995), Shirley Geok-lin Lim's *Among the White Moon Faces* (1996), Julia Alvarez's *Something to Declare* (1998), Adeline Yen Mah's *Falling Leaves: The Memoir of an Unwanted Chinese Daughter* (1998), Tara Bahrampour's *To See and See Again: A Life in Iran and America* (1999), Edward Said's *Out of Place: A Memoir* (1999), and Marie Arana's *American Chica* (2001).

The best of these, Eva Hoffman's *Lost in Translation* (1989), might well serve as the criterion for all narratives of immigrant experience. Hoffman reflects with great sensitivity on her Polish childhood and her American education and adulthood, and one finds this extraordinarily nuanced memoir especially useful in examining the stories of the author's Polish American landsleit: the real-life Jerzy Kosinski and the fictional Artur Sammler. Such real and imagined immigrants—they include Nabokov and his Timofey Pnin and Mylène Dressler and her Tristan Martens—represent an interesting sub-category within the literature under review here: the displaced person as intellectual. In fictions such as *Pnin* (1957) and *Mr. Sammler's Planet* (1970), the reader encounters immigrant characters of considerable sensitivity, intelligence, intellect, and education. Kosinski's *The Hermit of 69th Street* (1988) also recommends itself, for its protagonist, a literate Holocaust survivor isolated in a New York apartment, displays obvious affinities with Bellow's Mr. Sammler.[4] But Kosinski's last, bloated novel (over five hundred pages long) seems to announce the creative incoherence that would presently lead to the author's suicide. Not well received, it went swiftly out of print. Consequently I have chosen Kosinski's still popular *Being There* (1971) for discussion here; it is contemporaneous with *Mr. Sammler's Planet*, and its simpleton protagonist offers an interesting contrast to Bellow's intellectual hero. One recognizes in Sammler, as Charles Berryman points out, "the first Bellow protagonist not born in the New World"; in *Being There*, as Barbara Tepa Lupack observes, Kosinski presents his "first truly American protagonist in an American setting."[5]

In addition to representing a sharp contrast to the intellectual Slavs that readers encounter in Nabokov, Bellow, and Hoffman, Kosinski's Chance the gardener becomes the vehicle of caustic authorial views on class and politics in America. In *Being There*, a narrator with the sensibility of an observant outsider (rather inclined, like the Polish American author himself,

to old world irony) gives readers an iconoclastic parable of American innocence, along with a decidedly dyslogistic picture of the media that, in their
pernicious ubiquity, constantly shape—and warp—public perception. Almost witless, Chance the gardener becomes Chauncey Gardiner, the perfect tabula rasa on which American experience writes itself, the perfect
mirror of American epistemological limitation. If it does not foreground
the immigrant experience per se (as will be seen, the author deploys the
figure of banishment from an Edenic garden to other ends), *Being There*
nonetheless invites certain recognitions, not least with regard to the
strange experience of a real-life immigrant, Kosinski himself.

An Image Made in the Image and Likeness of Images

From the vantage of "thirty-five years of homelessness," Nabokov's *Pnin*
contemplates new world contradictions and vulgarity with considerable
forbearance: "America, my new country, wonderful America which sometimes surprises me but always provokes respect."[6] One may, just under the
surface, discern reservations in this remark, but the very fact that they figure only as nuance bears out Eva Hoffman's observation that "Nabokov
repaid America's generosity with *Pnin* and *Lolita*, with amusement never
soured by anger. Of all the responses to the condition of exile, his is surely
the most triumphant, the least marred by rage, or inferiority, or aspiration."[7] That last word, however, gives one pause. Suggesting that "aspiration" might *mar* immigrant narrative, might preclude the kind of detachment that enables and fosters literary art, Hoffman also resists the
assumption that it somehow defines Americanness. Doubting its legitimacy as the vehicle of American self-realization, she critiques a national
shibboleth.

For a better idea of what Hoffman might mean by the distortions of
"rage, inferiority, or aspiration" in "responses to the conditions of exile,"
one turns to Jerzy Kosinski, an immigrant author who parlayed the success
of his early novels, notably *The Painted Bird* and *Being There*, into a place
among the nation's rich and famous. Living a crass version of the American
Dream, he married a rich widow and became a jet-setter, the darling of
both the intelligentsia and the entertainment elite. He was friend to a variety of media and Hollywood celebrities, played polo with them, often appeared on the *Tonight Show*, even had a fairly important part in Warren
Beatty's 1981 film *Reds*. Only a baggage mix-up prevented his being at the

home of Sharon Tate and Roman Polanski on the August evening in 1969 when the murderous followers of Charles Manson came to play helter-skelter.

Meanwhile, Kosinski's books were translated into thirty or so languages. But in 1982 the many rumors about the author and his opportunism came to a head in a *Village Voice* article alleging, among other things, his heavy reliance on underpaid ghostwriters to render his poor English readable. The authors of this exposé, Geoffrey Stokes and Eliot Fremont-Smith, also noted the remoteness of Kosinski's own childhood experiences from those depicted in *The Painted Bird* (the author had always encouraged the notion that the book was highly autobiographical). In addition, there were nasty stories about Kosinski's sadomasochism, sex club–hopping (he, too, "liked to watch"), and other general kinkiness. Though a few friends sprang to his defense, Kosinski's reputation never recovered from this exposure.[8]

But the discovery of moral failings seldom does permanent damage to the purely literary part of an author's reputation. One has seen Hemingway, Frost, Philip Larkin, and others exposed as variously unsavory or detestable. Their work, however, has a life of its own—and so it has been since Chaucer's Pardoner, the pilgrim who, though steeped in vice, tells one of the finest of the Canterbury tales. The Pardoner's Prologue and Tale are, among other things, a bizarre act of confession, and *Being There* may be something similar. The intellectual gulf between author and character notwithstanding, one cannot help reading Chance's story as some kind of morality tale, a disguised version of Kosinski's strange experiences as immigrant. How poignant, for example, that a writer much troubled by his own uncertain English should include the detail about Chance's having no discernible trace of region or ethnicity in his speech. As Paul R. Lilly Jr. points out, Chance alone, among Kosinski's protagonists, is not linguistically handicapped in some way: "His language is not a mark of identity, vulnerability, or victimization."[9] By the same token, the readiness of America to fawn on Chance, which suggests a pathological susceptibility to certain kinds of projection, resembles its readiness to fawn on the similarly dubious Kosinski. One may turn from the author in disgust, or one may thoughtfully regret his suicide (in 1991), but one remains unable to declare a novel such as *The Painted Bird* any less powerful for being ungrounded in suffering experienced personally by the author. Few would claim to find all of Kosinski readable (and perhaps his name should appear on title pages in ironic quotation marks), but *Being There* remains a brilliant meditation on the American susceptibility to televisual media, whether in matters political or erotic.

Hence the irony of Chance as object of sexual desire. Early and late, Chance's inability to respond to erotic stimuli—"his organ refused to stiffen out"—is a meaningful detail, for it hints at the essential impotence and sterility of the simulacrum, the copy without an original.[10] Yet its sterility paradoxically proves no bar to endless self-replication. Like the media that foster it, the simulacrum reproduces itself as narcissistic clone, never as real offspring: "The figure on the TV screen looked like his own reflection in a mirror" (6). In its staggering proliferation, in fact, the simu- lacrum burlesques both the biblical injunction to "be fruitful and multiply" (Gen. 9:1) and the liturgical salute to Abraham *et semini eius*.

The vision of world-filling fertility begins, however, with Adam, the biblical figure perennially reinvented in America. Thus Kosinski artfully subverts, from the vantage of his immigrant skepticism, the Adamic arche- type of American innocence. Expelled from no ordinary garden, Kosinski's insipid protagonist reenacts the mythic events described in Genesis, com- plete with hebdomadal frame: the story begins on a Sunday and concludes, presumably after midnight of the Friday soiree Chance attends, on the seventh day. The author hints that the garden tended by the pre-expulsion Chance belongs to his own father. If not made "in the image" of this re- mote, godlike figure, Chance certainly fits nicely into his suits. But Kosin- ski revises and subverts even as he recapitulates the familiar story. The death of the Old Man, for example, thrusts an innocent, ignorant Adam out into a meaningless post-theistic universe. This Adam encounters his Eve (Elizabeth Eve Rand) only after he leaves the garden behind. He exits Eden, moreover, with his innocence intact. The prelapsarian Chance looks at pornographic pictures without recognition or arousal; by the same token, expulsion from the garden confers on him neither libido, shame, nor sexual potency. Thus the original biblical myth plays itself out as exis- tential vaudeville: as the New Adam transfigures and redeems the Old Adam, so does Chauncey Gardiner, national political messiah, redeem the postlapsarian moocher that was Chance the gardener. Indeed, one recalls that the movie version of Kosinski's novel concludes with a shot of Chance seeming to walk on water.[11]

Hal Ashby's film—better known to many than the novel—merits a word or two. Kosinski adapted *Being There* for the movies almost a decade after the novel's publication. By the time the film went into production (it would be released in 1979), the author was more and more a creature of

Hollywood. The film had a fine cast, which included Peter Sellers as Chance, Shirley MacLaine as Elizabeth Eve, Melvyn Douglas as Ben Rand, and Richard Dysart as Dr. Allenby. Sellers and Douglas received major acting awards, and Kosinski himself received the British Academy of Film and Television's "best screenwriter" award, as well as the Writers Guild of America award for "best comedy adapted from another medium." Today, however, the film seems overpraised. One admits that its conclusion, with Chance walking over that samite-sheeted, lakelike glimmer, nicely rounds out the symbolism that makes him, at the outset, an Adamic exile from a *hortus conclusus* of timeless perfection. But the film has worn less well than, say, Sidney Lumet's more accomplished 1976 *Network*, written by the sophisticated Paddy Chayevsky. In his *Film & Video Guide*, Leonard Maltin disparages *Being There* as "fatally overlong" (he gives it two and a half stars to *Network*'s four). Overly earnest withal, the movie version of Chance's little odyssey miscarries in the failure of its satire to become more than what Orson Welles might call dollar-book Voltaire. When Chance, in the novel, says, "I like to watch," Kosinski ingeniously allows the phrase to subsume a world of passivity and voyeurism. But only the kinkier element in this passivity makes its way into the movie: Shirley MacLaine's Elizabeth Eve cheerfully gratifies what she takes to be "Chauncey's" desire to watch her in an act of self-stimulation. The movie strikes one as much less light on its feet than the novel, whose satire, however trenchant, remains subtle. Unsparing as Juvenal or Swift, the book parodies the archetypal story of innocence and experience with an economy that is indeed nothing short of biblical. Brilliant in the novel, the critique of America's embrace of the image, especially the media image, comes off in the movie as unoriginal, even clichéd (perhaps because the studio film, even in the late seventies, was still too much invested in its own image-making, still relatively clumsy at recursive meditations on itself as a medium, itself as part of the cultural problem of shadow and substance). In other words, the viewer is never invited to associate cinema with television (Chance's favored medium) in the culture of the image that is so easy to deplore and despise.

Only the novel, then, fosters an awareness of its own reflexivity, an awareness of other levels of discursive superficiality—including a kind of confession on the part of the author himself (very much the dishonest broker) and a recognition that even the print media, in the latter part of the twentieth century, participate uncritically in the economy of simulacra. Kosinski's working title for the novel was "Blank Page," and a blank page (the phrase appears repeatedly at pp. 127 and 129) seems to ask to be written on.[12] In the scene with "Ronald Stiegler, of Eidolon Books" (103), Chance is almost too obviously—at least in retrospect—the stand-in for an author unable to write coherent English yet courted by publishers and offered lucrative deals, of which he availed himself by hiring ghostwriters. The word *eidolon* ("image," "phantom," "ghost") suggests that even publishing, even books, can subscribe to an ontology of surfaces. This particular editor blithely asserts that the books he publishes require little in the way of actual reading and writing. "Books," he explains, "aren't selling anymore" (105). Clearly, what does sell—he offers Chance "a six-figure advance against royalties and a very agreeable royalty and reprint clause" (104)—is celebrity created by media exposure, and no doubt shaped and buttressed by massive advertising. As commercial considerations elbow aside the once dominant trade in ideas, authorship suffers its own fall. Small wonder that "publishing isn't exactly a flowering garden these days" (105).

All the more miraculous, then, the occasional literary blossom, such as *Being There* itself. Occasionally disparaged as a one-joke book, *Being There* might better be described as the book of an author with, on this occasion at least, a sure instinct for economy. This less captious view discovers in the one joke—the "blank page" on which a nation writes its fantasies of erotic and political empowerment—a rich metaphor with more than one level of meaning and suggestion. Those writing on that blank page, for example, include academics who must negotiate a parable of reading and interpretation. To what extent does the *reader* participate in projection? After all, in "interpreting" Chance, one does what everyone in Kosinski's fictive universe does, and in the pursuit of hermeneutic insight, one risks joining those in the story who construct "Chauncey Gardiner" as the embodiment of their own desire. At the very moment of the novel's publication in 1971, Roland Barthes was suggesting, in *S/Z* (1970), a distinction between the "readerly" (*lisible*) and the "writerly" (*scriptible*) text, the one straightforward in its content, the other requiring the reader's active, collaborative involvement in the production of meaning. In its pellucid simplicity, Kosinski's text masquerades as *lisible*. Yet it seems actually to include among its satirical targets some such concept as *scriptibilité*, construed as mirror for the hermeneutically gullible. Ideally, the reader recognizes this snare and approaches the text's discouragement of passivity with due caution. In any event, such a reader or critic engages Kosinksi's story with an epistemological sophistication never encouraged in watchers of television.

The relevance of Barthes to this text is no doubt fortuitous, but in his merciless dissection of the televisual dynamic, the author of *Being There* may be more directly indebted to the media theorist who held court throughout the decade that preceded publication of the novel. Marshall McLuhan introduced the American public to ideas that would mature, in the works of Baudrillard, into an awareness of the ways in which media were transforming American culture. Insofar as he recognized television and advertising as vastly powerful exercises in manipulation, his ideas were part of the tide that brought an armada of critics and theorists, from Barthes and Foucault to Eco and Žižek, all discovering ways to read cultures in popular tastes, pursuits, pastimes: wrestling, beauty pageants, comic books, advertising, television. But after the iconoclasm of *Understanding Media* (1964), McLuhan became less adversarial. *The Medium Is the Massage* (1967) seems memorable now only for its breathless heralding of the global village and the endless extension, by media, of the human nervous system. One discerns McLuhan's rhapsodic influence in a pronouncement of Bellow's Dr. Lal, the moonstruck biophysicist in *Mr. Sammler's Planet:* "The discovery of America had raised hopes in the sinful Old World of a New Eden. 'A shared consciousness,' Lal had written, 'may well be the new America. Access to central data mechanisms may foster a new Adam.'"[13]

If, like Foucault, McLuhan taught us to look in odd, out-of-the-way places for the dislocations and transformations effected by power, it fell to Baudrillard to parse fully the epistemology of media. What is remarkable is how much closer Kosinski is to the later theorist than to McLuhan. Kosinski, that is, anticipates by a decade Baudrillard's most celebrated insight: that the image, which reigns supreme in the contemporary world, "*plays at being* an appearance" of some "basic reality." The French theorist describes the "successive phases" of the image as a four-step declension:

—it is the reflection of a basic reality
—it masks and perverts a basic reality
—it masks the *absence* of a basic reality
—it bears no relation to any reality whatever: it is its own pure simulacrum.[14]

Baudrillard reframes Plato's parable of the cave, which depicts the possibility of freeing oneself from epistemological bondage to a play of shadows and moving from illusion to reality. Like Baudrillard, Kosinski depicts an alarming, culture-wide movement in the other direction.

Byron L. Sherwin calls Chance "a reflection of the reflections of images he has seen on a television screen. When Chance himself appears on television, the ultimate voyeur becomes his own subject of observation."[15] In *Being There*, public life and American identity become a hall of mirrors, a cultural exercise in recursivity:

> Chance was astonished that television could portray itself; cameras watched themselves and, as they watched, they televised a program. This self-portrait was telecast on TV screens facing the stage and watched by the studio audience. Of all the manifold things there were in all the world— trees, grass, flowers, telephones, radios, elevators—only TV constantly held up a mirror to its own neither solid nor fluid face. (62–63)

Here the author presents television as endlessly self-referring, a version of the signifying chain, its signifieds retreating into infinity, its gaps never to be closed, meaning itself irretrievable.

The televisual image has so conditioned Americans that they will collaborate in the construction, out of whole cloth, of a public personality congenial to unexamined expectation. Kosinski hints that in politics and entertainment Americans embrace individuals very much like Chance— media creations that batten on popular suggestibility and gullibility. On his way to running for high office when last seen, "Chauncey Gardiner" in fact resembles any number of American politicians. Yet Kosinski's political satire remains, if one may make the distinction, more prophetic than topical. When *Being There* came out, the failings of both the sitting American president and his predecessor called for and received satiric exposure of a truly Juvenalian harshness—in *MacBird!*, for example (aimed at Lyndon Johnson), and *Our Gang* (Philip Roth's cruel picture of a pathetic Richard Nixon was exactly contemporaneous with and much more topical than *Being There*). But insofar as his satiric vision seems more true with every passing decade, Kosinski bears out Ezra Pound's observation that artists function as "the antennae of the race." Thus when a Russian diplomat remarks "that Gardiner appears to be emotionally one of the most well-adjusted American public figures to have emerged in recent years" (127), one suddenly realizes how perfectly Kosinski's hero anticipates certain handsome, genial, "well-adjusted" American presidents and would-be presidents, figures who inspire, once again, satire less circumspect and nuanced than Kosinski's. Though advancing much the same satirical premise as *Being There*, Gary Trudeau's *Doonesbury* compilation, *In Search of Reagan's Brain* (1981), actually names its target. Molly Ivins collects her trenchant columns about the politician she calls "Shrub," and others collect "Bushisms" and "Quayle-ludes," in the vain hope of shaming the American electorate out of its choices. Even so, however inarticulate or even stupid, every successful American politician understands the power of the image and the relative inconsequence of actual identity, character, or intellect. As the Russian ambassador Skrapinov says, "People like Gardiner decide the fate of millions every day!" (125). Bellow's Mr. Sammler makes this point more gloomily: "In Russia, in China, and here, very mediocre people have the power to end life altogether. These representatives . . . will decide for us all whether we live or die"(220).

Kosinski draws attention to his skirting of topicality in the allusions to Ivan Andreyevich Krylov (1768–1844), a writer of fables better known in eastern Europe than in the new world. That the Russian ambassador presents Chance with a volume of Krylov confiscated from a Jew affords a glimpse of anti-Semitism at once older and newer than that of the Nazis (Bellow's Polish émigré, Mr. Sammler, has encountered the same disheartening phenomenon). The inscription about not provoking the geese is obviously enough Skrapinov's attempt to ingratiate himself and create a bond of superiority with the man he takes to be, at the very least, a political kingmaker. "To provoke the geese" (from Krylov's fable "The Geese") has entered the lexicon of Russian proverbial expressions (one hears it in Chekhov's *Three Sisters*, for example). The Russian ambassador invokes the phrase to intimate that he and Chance must, in their intellectual and political sophistication and mutual recognition as men of the world, avoid alarming either the bourgeois masses or the Soviet apparatchiks.

For the nonce, in any event, Kosinski invites recognition as another Krylov, writing what James Park Sloan calls "an extended fable."[16] Typological or symbolic, his action and his central character, like his initial setting, constantly resist the circumstantial. Here, as in Orwell's *Animal Farm* and its classical antecedents (the fables of Aesop, Marie de France, and La Fontaine), the actions and character function as thinly disguised illustrations of human nature, especially in its less attractive qualities. Nonrealistic, spare, and pitched toward a moral point or lesson, such works often aim at revealing some broad, often dyslogistic truth about community, nation, or humanity in general.

But however broad its satire, however determined its resistance to topicality, Kosinki's little fable benefits from a reader's keeping in mind or recovering certain of the specific cultural texts with which it shared its initial moment in the literary sun. Having previously noted the affinities—and contemporaneity—of Kosinki's novel with Roth's *Our Gang*, Barthes's *S/Z*, and McLuhan's popularizations of media theory, I conclude with two last instances of what seems a kind of synergistic confluence at the end of the 1960s. One must not forget that the stars at that convergence included Don DeLillo and Andy Warhol. All of these contexts will, I hope, serve not only to illuminate *Being There* but also to introduce *Mr. Sammler's Planet*, which I propose to examine presently.

DeLillo, who can seem a much more recent or current literary phenomenon, actually published his first novel the same year—1971—that *Being There* appeared. Narrated by a rogue television executive, DeLillo's *Americana* is, like Kosinski's novel, a reproach to media culture and its mindless subservience to political and economic power. "All the impulses of the media were fed into the circuitry of my dreams," remarks DeLillo's narrator. "One thinks of echoes. One thinks of an image made in the image and likeness of images."[17] Like other cinematically conceived novels (*Rabbit, Run, Gravity's Rainbow*), DeLillo's *Americana* is its own movie, for the story, centered on the making of a film, is itself ostensibly spoken into a camera.

A communications major in college, DeLillo recurs often in his work to the role of media in American life. In his 1973 novel *Great Jones Street* he anticipates the caustic anatomy of the rock ethos that would figure in Kosinski's 1982 novel *Pinball*. But mostly DeLillo scrutinizes the visual media available night and day in every American living room. In *Libra* and *Underworld*, especially, he contemplates the endlessly screened and rescreened film or video clip that has come to be such a feature of television's coverage of sensational events (one thinks of the footage documenting the *Challenger* disaster, the Rodney King beating, the horrors of 9/11). In *Libra* he examines the first such exercise in endless-loop television journalism, the clip of Jack Ruby shooting Lee Harvey Oswald, as well as the Zapruder film of President Kennedy's motorcade, which was not, for some years, widely seen. The Zapruder footage also figures in *Underworld*, along with another, factitious example: a highway murder accidentally captured on videotape. Here and in a powerful *New York Times Magazine* article, DeLillo dissects the raw televisual documentation, by security cameras and camcorders, of beatings, homicides, and other horrible events. In his 1999 play *Valparaiso*, he comes closest, thematically, to Kosinski, for here an everyman named Michael Majesky, flying to Valparaiso, Indiana, finds himself, by accident, en route to the town of that name in Florida—and then on to Valparaiso, Chile. His bizarre adventure gets noticed by the media, which turn him into an instant celebrity. But unlike Chance the gardener, Michael Majesky is soon destroyed by the same media powers that bring him before the eyes of America. "The fame-making apparatus," DeLillo remarks in his *Times Magazine* article, "confers celebrity on an individual so intense that he or she can't possibly survive. The quick and pitiless end of such a person's career is inherent in the first gathering glimmers of fame."[18]

This sentiment echoes the famous aperçu that first appeared in the catalogue of a 1968 exhibition of Andy Warhol's work: "In the future everyone will be world-famous for fifteen minutes."[19] DeLillo contemplates real events, real history, and real sociologies. Indeed, strange as it may seem, Warhol also refers, in his celebrated remark, to such real-world conditions. Both recognize a corollary: that vast numbers of perfect nonentities continually vie for their fifteen minutes of bogus, media-stoked prominence—or have it thrust upon them.

Yet it may be that Kosinski means to rebut, at least in part, sentiments such as those of Warhol and DeLillo—to wit, their claim (implicit on the one hand, explicit on the other) that the quarter hour marks some *terminus ad quem*. Bound to neither DeLillo's logic nor Warhol's, Kosinski finds himself unable to embrace the comforting thought that the American public must endure *only* fifteen minutes of Tiny Tim, Lorena Bobbitt, Monica Lewinsky, Scott Peterson, and so on ad nauseam. If, after all, the "quick and pitiless end" of his own meteoric career bears out those pronouncements about the brevity and fickleness of fame, Kosinski would nonetheless insist, and with no small legitimacy, that Chauncey Gardiner seems destined to remain "onscreen" indefinitely.

Old World Death, New World Resurrection

Some will object that Saul Bellow does not belong in a book about post-1970 immigrant writers. Some will ask if relocation from one part of North America to another really makes one an immigrant. But Canadians—especially French Canadians—would bridle at the implicit denial of their separate national identity. Surely, too, a nine-year-old Yiddish- and French-speaking Jew might be expected to experience some difficulties in his passage from one America to another. In any event, because immigrant literature (indeed, all literature) needs more than ever these days to be contextualized, oriented to antecedent as well as contemporaneous expression, I should like to devote a few pages to the 1970 novel *Mr. Sammler's Planet*. As with my earlier observations on Nabokov's *Pnin* and similar passing comparisons to a variety of familiar contemporary novels, I seek to provide a broader historical framework for understanding what is occurring in immigrant writing as the twentieth century gives way to the twenty-first.

Certainly in the twice-told immigrant travail of Saul Bellow's parents one sees the precariousness and difficulty of diasporic existence. "At the turn of the century," notes James Atlas in his superb biography of Bellow, "it was illegal for Jews in Russia to live outside the Pale of Settlement . . . without a permit. But Abraham Belo bribed the authorities" and got himself and his family into a comfortable life in St. Petersburg—only to be exposed, some years later, and threatened with deportation to Siberia. With "forged papers," the family went to Canada instead. Their fourth child, Shloime (sometimes Shloimke), was born in Lachine, Quebec, two years later, in 1915. When he was nine, the family emigrated again, this time to the United States. The surname, Belo, had become Bellow in Canada; now first names became Anglicized as well: Shloime became Solomon, Sol, or Solly—and only much later Saul, who would one day confer some of his Slavic and Jewish background on the Polish émigré who gives his name to *Mr. Sammler's Planet*.[20]

In a sense every Jew is always already an immigrant. One of the great ironies of history is that this should be so even in Palestine and even in America, which Richard Powers calls "the country of the universally displaced."[21] Another is that a contested "right of return" for Palestinians should figure among the obstacles to peace between today's Israel and its neighbors. Many populations have experienced dispersal and cultural dissolution, but only one has retained its identity through repetitions of diaspora. The original state of Israel came about only after four hundred years of bondage in Egypt (Gen. 15:13) and lengthy exile in the Sinai wilderness. After another generations-long "captivity" in Babylon, the Jews again returned. The most terrible diaspora followed destruction of the temple in the year 70 CE. For centuries after that climacteric, the Jews resisted (or were refused) absorption into any of the cultures that tolerated their pres-

ence. "Assimilationist" remained, among Jews, a powerful term of reproach. Almost two thousand years after the Great Diaspora, the Jews effected yet another return, this time to found the modern Jewish state.

Bellow's Sammler, survivor of both the Holocaust and the mopping-up
operation undertaken by his own anti-Semitic countrymen, was not part of
that return, that "Diaspora running backwards," in Thomas Pynchon's
kabbalistic figure, those "seeds of exile flying inward in a modest
preview . . . of the Messiah gathering in the fallen sparks."[22] Once, ironically, Sammler had embraced expatriation, and he would have liked to remain "British" (19), the "Englishman" (6) he had become in the years before 1939. History intervened, however, and now, long after the war, the
displaced person finds himself in America. "You are Polish?" someone asks
Sammler. One mentally italicizes the verb in his answer: "I was Polish"
(209). During his twenty-two years in America he visits Israel twice but evidently feels no desire to live there. Still, when his daughter suggests that
he might have been killed while reporting the 1967 war, he calls such a fate
"the finest death I could imagine" (201). This from a man with firsthand
experience of death at its least fine.

In lesser and greater ways, one can compare *Mr. Sammler's Planet* with
Wendy Law-Yone's *The Coffin Tree*, subject of a later chapter of the present
study. Although Sammler twice calls himself "an Oriental" (184, 221) and
reflects that "a Jew, no matter how Britannicized or Americanized, was also
an Asian" (116), it would be too fanciful to say that both fictions center on
the Asian American experience. But both authors orient their actions to
the 1969 moon landing, and both develop the metaphor of emigration as a
death that leads to rebirth or reincarnation as an American. Bellow, whose
book came out in 1970, sets his tale on the eve of the *Apollo 11* mission (in
the spring of 1969, that is) and introduces a thematically prominent "moon
problem." Law-Yone's two main characters arrive in the United States at
the actual time of the lunar landing in June, and the narrator ruefully notes
their astronaut-like sense of disorientation. Both books allow the reader to
reflect that human beings' arrival for the first time on another world may
one day eventuate in a rich new chapter in the history of emigration.
"How long," asks Dr. Lal in the Bellow novel, "will this earth remain the
only home of Man?" (51). The books diverge somewhat in the symbolic
death that leads to resurrection. For Bellow it takes place in the old world;
for Law-Yone, the new. Law-Yone's protagonist comes to terms with her
new national identity only after she attempts suicide, and quotations from
The Tibetan Book of the Dead prompt recognition of her symbolic reincar-

nation—as American. Bellow's Sammler, who "underwent murder" (92) in a Nazi massacre, crawls from a death pit in his native Poland and later hides out—as if to deny the apparent symbolism of resurrection—in a mausoleum. In the Polish resistance and, subsequently, in a displaced persons camp in Austria, his rebirth, like that of Sophie and Nathan in William Styron's famous novel, remains in doubt. Indeed, as "a man of seventy-plus" (3) in the novel's present, he has passed the allotted threescore and ten and is, so to speak, a walking dead man twice over.

But as Henry Adams says, "Even dead men allow themselves a few narrow prejudices."[23] Problematically resurrected in the new world, Sammler contemplates instances of brutality and evidence of cultural dissolution that call into question the popular notion of America as a robust, crescive civilization. "America! (he was speaking to himself). Advertised throughout the universe as *the* most desirable, most exemplary of all nations" (14). Meanwhile, his preterition (as Pynchon would call the enigma of his being "passed over" in Europe's greatest pogrom) continues to trouble his mind and, inevitably, his conscience. As the primal scene in his consciousness and moral life, the mass execution that Sammler survives distills the Holocaust, itself the primal scene of the twentieth century. Alfred Kazin characterizes the story of Sammler's survival, his moving forward through life "past so many bodies," as "the fable that haunts Jewish writers" and fosters their already highly developed "passion for ideological moralism."[24]

Bellow's Artur Sammler is everything Chance the gardener is not. The author depicts in Sammler an immigrant whose intellectualism and intense inner life give new force to the introspection, the mental and social isolation, that is perforce the lot of the displaced. As quintessential Bellow character, Sammler is a man thinking all the time, much concerned with moral and ethical questions that extend outward from his own experience to the spiritual—and material—life of the America in which, like Dressler's Tristan Martens or Chang-rae Lee's Franklin Hata, he finds himself spending his old age. Like those characters, too, he knows something about fascism.

Immigrants tend to see themselves as anthropologists, and certainly their scrutiny of strange customs and practices bears no small resemblance to what the professionals call "fieldwork." Saul Bellow literalizes this conceit, for he actually studied anthropology—as an undergraduate at Northwestern and as a graduate student at Chicago—before entering that less specialized branch of social science called novel writing. Bellow makes of Sammler a kind of Northern Hemisphere Lévi-Strauss (another European

Jew obliged to flee the Nazi juggernaut). Supposedly "disinterested" (118, 160, 236), Sammler scrutinizes American kinship structures, relations with and treatment of the elderly, and mating rituals. "One species," he marvels, "but the sexes like two different savage tribes. In full paint. Surprising and shocking each other in the bush" (208). As immigrant and amateur social scientist, Sammler resembles the Eva Hoffman who recognizes in herself "an anthropologist of the highly detached nonparticipant variety," a field observer seeking to resolve problems of perspective. How to get under the skin of the culture being observed? How to be one of them? "How does one stop reading the exterior signs of a foreign tribe and step into the inwardness, the viscera of their meanings? Every anthropologist understands the difficulty of such a feat; and so does every immigrant" (Hoffman 131, 209).

In a sense, Hoffman contains both the fictional Sammler and the real-life Bellow. Like Bellow, she became an American only after her family's sojourn in Canada. Like Sammler, she is an intellectual, a Polish Jew who struggles to come to terms with a new homeland perceived now as "the land of progress" (51), now as "this goddamn place" (169). Indeed, like the soldier in Joseph Heller's *Catch-22*, the immigrant "sees everything twice." Worse, the twinned components of "everything" tend somehow to be at odds, as in Philip Larkin's image of self-contradictory perceptions or insights, "each one double-yolked with meaning and meaning's rebuttal."[25] The fledglings hatched from Larkin's implied egg are unlikely to fly in the same direction—or pull together, for the pun in "yolked" conjures a pair of oxen, yoked at the neck but facing, absurdly, in opposite directions. Yolked or yoked, the ill-matched twins figure the essential bifurcation of immigrant identity. Thus Hoffman describes her own geminate selves engaged in a strange dialectic regarding the immigrant's inescapable burden: "how to live with a double vision" (132)—not just the overlay of old world outlook and new but the now doubled view of Poland (which one sees, simultaneously, as Pole and as American) and of the United States (seen through another such pair of mismatched lenses). At one point, then, Hoffman laments, "It seems that when I write (or, for that matter, think) in English, I am unable to use the word 'I.' I do not go as far as the schizophrenic 'she'—but I am driven, as by a compulsion, to the double, the Siamese-twin 'you' (121). That she makes this observation in confident first person, however, assures the reader that Hoffman eventually achieves an identity unimpaired by its inevitably twinned perspectives.

Not so the heroine of Hoffman's novel *The Secret* (2002), the premise of which involves an ingenious reconfiguration of the doppelgänger theme once pronounced "a frightful bore" by Nabokov (probably, as I have argued elsewhere, to disguise his own reliance on it).[26] But in that it perfectly captures the uncanny, disjunctive sense of self that perpetually troubles exilic consciousness, the theme of the double naturally lends itself to immigrant storytelling. Hoffman's heroine, Iris Surrey, struggles with unaccountable feelings of "weirdness" that seem something more than ordinary neurasthenia. She also suffers a lifelong ambivalence toward her mother. Eventually she learns that her strange symptoms derive from a single, stunning cause: the product of a cloning experiment, Iris Surrey *is*, quite literally, her mother. *The Secret* is not, alas, altogether successful as fiction, but it is certainly striking as the literary fantasy of an immigrant. Dogged by a sense of duality, of a self that one is yet is not (or a self one once was but is no more), Iris Surrey emerges as a powerful symbol. No doubt she serves primarily to caution readers against certain forms of irresponsible science, but she and her mother happen also to be the perfect reification of self and ghost-self in immigrant consciousness.

Beyond its psychological significance, Hoffman's directly or indirectly autobiographical work frames questions of politics, culture, and history. Like Sammler, Hoffman argues with herself the positive and negative elements of the society in which, for better or worse, her future lies: "I'm ready to dismiss all of American Culture as a misconceived experiment. . . . [T]here's too much reinventing of the wheel going on around here" (207). In other words, America thinks it has invented the ideas it embraces, but the European looks on with weary cynicism and observes, rather like Marlowe's Mephistopheles listening to Doctor Faustus rationalize hell itself out of existence, "Ay, think so still, till experience change thy mind." But no sooner does Hoffman congratulate herself on her tough-mindedness than she begins to see certain cogent elements in the mythology of the new world. She experiences the dawning of "a second unconscious, an American one" (221) that displaces both her "Polish political unconscious" (66) and the inchoate "cultural unconscious" (108) of her season in Canada. "The perennial American experiment . . . consists precisely of reinventing the wheel, of taking nothing for granted and beholding human nature with a primeval curiosity, as though nothing has ever been observed or thought before. This is the spirit that invented the cotton gin and Whitman's free verse, and the open marriage." Perhaps, as the bathos of that last item suggests, she cannot divest herself of skepticism and irony altogether, but she concedes that, as often as not, Americans actually make a better wheel. Americans' "explorations are a road to a new, instead of an ancestral wisdom—a wisdom that may be awkward and ungainly, as youthful wisdom is, but that is required in a world whose social, if not physical, frontiers are still fluid and open and incompletely charted" (209).

Consciously or unconsciously, every immigrant—and especially every immigrant writer—must grapple with the powerful yet intrinsically dubious idea of American exceptionalism. Whether buoyed with extravagant expectation or laden with the heavy baggage of old world fatalism, newcomers struggle to discover the mythic America behind the nation's rude actuality. Bellow's Mr. Sammler, however, finds himself whelmed by that actuality. Scrutinizing the exuberant vapidity of student radicalism on the one hand, the implicit argument of the black pickpocket's penis on the other, he seems persuaded, in 1969, that political and spiritual entropy has set in: "You could smell decay. You could see the suicidal impulses of civilization pushing strongly" (33).

Aldous Huxley observes that "every civilization is, among other things, an arrangement for domesticating the passions and setting them to do useful work."[27] In this remark Huxley distills the argument of *Civilization and Its Discontents*, in which Freud declares it "impossible to overlook the extent to which civilization is built upon a renunciation of instinct."[28] Bellow's Mr. Sammler worries that America has lost its way, that its freedom merely illustrates a kind of negative corollary to Freud's thesis. If renunciation anchors culture (which waxes through the sublimation of desire), then widespread gratification of sensual appetite must reverse the very course of civilization. Sammler "had an idea even that the very special development of the significance of prisons since the eighteenth century had some relation to this shrinking ability to endure restraint" (162). Indeed, the insight is biblical before it is Freudian: "New York makes one think about the collapse of civilization, about Sodom and Gomorrah, the end of the world. . . . [I]t is in the air now that things are falling apart" (304).

No naïve salutes to the Statue of Liberty for Sammler, then (we will encounter the salute ironic in Cristina Garcia's *Dreaming in Cuban*). Europe's Jews, like previous, larger waves of immigrants, may feel thankful for deliverance, but the tragic view of history thrust upon them (even before the Holocaust) precludes their ever resting easy in any American Goshen. This skepticism is of course something that nearly all literary immigrants engage; it has to do with the legitimacy of America's claim to special dispensation. Must they, as the price of assimilation, embrace the myth—or do they allow their old world experience to give that myth the lie? Bellow emphasizes Mr. Sammler's fears that American civilization has slipped into degeneracy. "Like many people who had seen the world collapse once, Mr. Sammler entertained the possibility it might collapse twice" (33). This dread, along with his knowledge of history, prompts his ceaseless, skeptical scrutiny of such late-sixties American phenomena as student radicalism, the worrisome pugnacity of "negroes," and the sexual revolution. "We have fallen," he concludes, "into much ugliness" (228).

Critics have discussed Sammler's pessimistic view of 1960s America at great length—and been a little too quick to equate Bellow with his character. Kazin, for example, sees Sammler as "openly Bellow's mind now." Looking more broadly at the oeuvre, Kazin deplores "the austere, dismissive jeremiads, the open contempt for . . . women," and the "moral haughtiness" that "becomes as audible to the reader as sniffing, and is indeed that."[29] Some readers, of course, were simply too invested in the counterculture to accept the old immigrant's crotchety indictment. Though the response generated by Sammler's fulminations suggests a pervasive fear that they reflect some real pathology, some real rottenness in the culture, many readers deplored what they saw as Bellow's refusal to embrace the energies that, emerging all around him in the sixties, promised to transform a nation mired in ancient racism, a dangerous cold war, and a disastrous conflict in Asia. Sammler, however, has seen this kind of "historical omelet" (214) made before. Toppled from barricades, a lot of innocent Humpty-Dumptys perish in that revolutionary kitchen. Sammler asseverates, with De Maistre and Dr. Lal, that "revolutions . . . end up in the hands of madmen" (218). He observes that the dismantling of the old order tends, historically, to put humanity back in the Zamosht forest, back in a "state of nature" (7).

Few septuagenarians in 1969 thought revolution for the hell of it a good idea. Bellow himself, in his mid-fifties, may have sensed that, for all their anarchic energy, the sixties would in fact be looked back on in mild embarrassment by the Laodicean seventies, which would give way to a perfect orgy of materialism in the *fin-de-millénaire* decades. As a cynical character in Pynchon's *Vineland* keeps asking old hippies, dopers, and radicals, "Who was saved?"[30] Sammler may be premature in sitting shivah over American civilization, but he is hardly wrong to reject the chiliastic pretensions of the Age of Aquarius.

From our more privileged vantage some decades after the time of the novel's setting, we are perhaps better able to gauge the extent to which Sammler is a true or false Jeremiah—and also to discern the extent to which his status as survivor of one of history's harshest lessons confers authority on his judgments. One expects Sammler, as sensitive and educated outsider, to contemplate new world social and political transformations with a modicum of instructive perspicacity. The reader who considers the duality of Mr. Sammler's sociocultural role—as both immigrant and intellectual—may grant Bellow's character more latitude for philosophical reflection and, as necessary, invidious discrimination. Conversely, the reader may discover that Bellow distances himself from and critiques his character.

Much depends on how one reads the symbolism of Sammler's cocked eye: "The damaged left eye seemed to turn in another direction, to be preoccupied separately with different matters" (31). To see Sammler as an immigrant and the literary creation of an immigrant is to recognize a highly discriminating drama of thwarted stereoscopy, and the disparity in Sammler's visual organs—one eye functioning, the other blind—suggests that for depth perception the reader must look elsewhere, seek some authorial prosthesis for the one-eyed Sammler. Most critics take the impaired eye as emblem of a different kind of seeing. "Old, androgynous, half-blind, Sammler is a Tiresias of the Upper West Side. His moral judgments carry the weight of objectivity, his prophecy the integrity of disinterestedness. He has come back to tell us all."[31] The reader may, then, understand Sammler's mismatched eyes as the symbolic reminder of a double focus: whether intellectual or seer, he looks inward as much as outward. Ellen Pifer argues that the mismatched optics suggest "two modes or processes of reflection, the analytic and the intuitive," which "draw Sammler's mind in opposing directions." She sees the book's moral drama as culminating in the protagonist's transcending the detachment, the pose of tolerant, social-scientific objectivity he has evidently embraced since emerging from the mass grave three decades previously in his native Poland. "The best, I have found, is to be disinterested. Not as misanthropes dissociate themselves, by judging, but by not judging" (236). But such disinterestedness only makes him "aloof," as his grandnephew Wallace Gruner observes. "Sort of distant from life" (102). On this score, Pifer maintains, Sammler proves somewhat misguided, for in the end, chastened by his last, distressing encounter with the pickpocket and by the death of decent, altruistic Elya Gruner, he seems to understand that being answerable to other human beings must always preclude the perfect detachment he so desires (and he *does* judge Gruner's irresponsible and selfish children). According to Pifer, then, "the knowledge Sammler has sought in detachment he discovers, instead, through his love for others and his acknowledged participation in the conditions of mortality."[32]

One can, up to a point, accept these arguments for Sammler's recovery of humanity, but they leave unresolved the questions about his identity (no longer Polish, he may still think of himself, after twenty-two years, as "refugee" rather than "American"), his historical pessimism (with regard to the path on which America has set out), and his tergiversation between libidinal apathy and overdetermined revulsion at the elevation of lubricity to cultural shibboleth. Saul Bellow may well identify with the Sammler who makes the turn toward human connection at Elya Gruner's bedside, but where does the reader locate authorial sympathy vis-à-vis the Sammler who so vociferously doubts the validity of the counterculture and so vehemently rails against its general licentiousness—especially as embraced by women like his grandniece, Angela Gruner?

One finds Sammler's loathing of the flesh—in particular female flesh—especially difficult to understand or excuse. His running philippic ranges from mild to wild, from the philosophical to the scortatory and scatological. Mr. Sammler pauses, for example, over Schopenhauer's idea of "the cosmic force, the Will, which drives all things" and sets up local headquarters in "the organs of sex" (209). Exposing himself, the virile "thief in the lobby" had merely displayed "the instrument of the Will . . . his metaphysical warrant" (209–10). Sammler seems also to have considered, with Freud and "other powerful minds," whether "each trifle" of our human frailties might not be "the symptom of a deep disease in a creature whose whole fate was disease" (247). But these examples are rare in their temperateness. Counting casually, I note some thirty-six invidious passages about "the sex business" (58), the culture-wide goal of "sexual niggerhood for everyone" (162). No doubt some of these fulminations reflect the legitimate skepticism of one thankful to be spared the powerful lash of desire, one happily delivered from the tyranny of the sex drive, one who can say, with Sophocles, "I feel as if I had escaped from the hands of a mad and furious master" (71). Yet the reader hardly feels that the disruptive student pays Sophoclean homage to Sammler when he declares: "His balls are dry. He's dead. He can't come" (42, 279). Before and after the disastrous lecture, Sammler reflects on the priapic energy of H. G. Wells, who even in old age "appeared to need a great amount of copulation" (28, 71); nor can Sammler be as "sexually enterprising" (76) as his own father (sixty at Sammler's birth) or for that matter Saul Bellow himself (who sired a child in his eighties).

If "Sammler's own sex impulses" are "perhaps even now not altogether gone" (161), they manifest themselves in odd ways—notably in strange and even morbid speculations about the gross physicality of his female relatives. Not that he limits himself to family; in a pinch, any target will do, for example, the "female generative slime" (82) to which Dr. Gruner owes his prosperity or the "female bum drunkenly sleeping like a dugong, a sea cow's belly rising, legs swollen purple" (106). Sammler has no patience with the intellectual earnestness of the remarkably efficient Margotte, the niece by marriage who has given him a home. Gender makes her ridiculous: "Females! The drafts must blow between their legs" (133–34). In the same way, Sammler's perceptions and mental characterizations of his daughter, Shula, disturb the reader in their cruelty, their vast lack of charity. "Below the neck," he coldly observes, "there was a mature dorsal hump" (200). Walking in on her when she is bathing at the Gruner house, Sammler sees "the black female triangle, and the white swellings with large rings of purplish brown. The veins. Yes, yes, she belonged to the . . . gender club" (194). Subsequently, his mental review of her body, "especially beneath the waist, where a thing was to make a lover gasp" (197), makes one's flesh crawl.

But he reserves full revulsion for his grandniece, Angela, who inspires him to Jacobean paroxysms of disgust. Sammler waits for Shula to get dressed in the room Angela occupied when, as "a young girl," she was only "an apprentice whore" (194). The old man cannot have a conversation with Angela without becoming aware of "the pink material of her undergarment" (303), inadequately screened by her "sexual kindergarten dress" (300). He wishes not to hear more about her carryings-on in Mexico with Wharton Horricker and another couple, yet he harps mentally on and eventually confronts her with a detail—fellatio (247, 306, 307)—that is in fact not part of what Wallace or Elya or Angela herself has told him ("his imagination," as Sarah Blacher Cohen observes, "supplies any lurid omissions").[33] Now "diffusing woman-odors" (305), now "smearing all with her female fluids" (278), Angela becomes an extended, sick fantasy, "her female effluence . . . very strong, a salt odor, similar to tears of tidewater, something from within the woman" (296): "As she detached herself from the plastic seat . . . an odor was released" (164).

One discerns elements of psychoneurosis in Sammler's seemingly trenchant view of the "sexual madness . . . overwhelming the Western world" (63). Sammler considers American culture's obsession with sex outrageous, but he comes close to something like hysteria over the sexuality of women. His vehemence on this score hints at some deep pathology in his mental and emotional makeup. Though not entirely free of misogyny himself, Bellow invites considerable doubts about the attitudes toward women espoused by Sammler, not to mention the validity of his observations regarding the age's rampant "sex-ideology" (16, 55), whether manifested in the literal exhibitionism of the black pickpocket or the moral exhibitionism of Angela Gruner, who confesses to sexual practices so shocking as to cause her saintly father, Elya, on his deathbed, to call her a "dirty cunt" (177) with "fucked-out eyes" (178, 272).

Sammler shakes his head over what a character in *Ulysses* calls "an age of exhausted whoredom groping for its god."[34] Bellow's protagonist has reflected on the historical phenomenon of Puritanism and at one point half-seriously accuses himself (mocking a certain kind of sixties rhetoric) of the "bad puritanical attitudes from the sick past which have damaged civilization so much" (300). More seriously he reflects on Max Weber's *The Protestant Ethic and the Spirit of Capitalism* and even quotes its antepenultimate paragraph from memory. Puritanism, he reflects, "had . . . given all power to material processes" and thereby, ironically, "translated and exhausted religious feeling . . . Or, in the crushing summary of Max Weber, known by heart to Sammler, 'Specialists without spirit, sensualists without heart, this nullity [the "modern economic order"] imagines that it has attained a level of civilization never before achieved'" (54). But Sammler has learned from his reading of Weber only to doubt the spiritual pretensions of American capitalism. He evidently refuses to recognize as aberrant the sex-hating joylessness that led H. L. Mencken to define a Puritan as "someone who is desperately afraid that, somewhere, someone might be having a good time." Perhaps, then, rather than Weber or Schopenhauer or the numerous historians of civilization he reads before he turns more or less exclusively to the Bible and Meister Eckhart, Sammler should have dipped into Hawthorne, who uncovers the reptiles bred in the Puritan unconscious, or Blake, who teaches that "he who desires but acts not, breeds pestilence," or Henry Adams, who concerns himself chiefly with the failure, on the part of Puritan America, to comprehend sex as natural dynamo: "In America neither Venus nor Virgin ever had value as force. . . . No American had ever been truly afraid of either."[35] Adams puts his finger on Puritanism's refusal to see fertility—sex itself—as a spiritual principle, whether embodied in the Venus of the ancients or in the Virgin of the papists. In short, Sammler might have considered that, far from undoing the mechanism at the heart of civilization-building, the sexual revolution that acquired category-five force in the 1960s—to Sammler's bewilderment and disgust—represents only a long-postponed remedy for the repression endemic to Puritan America.

Yet one makes allowances for Sammler's unregenerate views. Recognizing the disagreeable perceptions and remarks as symptomatic of some deep-seated and malign pathology of the spirit, one senses behind such violent opinionation a kind of tragic, Shakespearean energy. Indeed, several angry or embittered or sex-nauseated Shakespeare characters seem to "ghost" the sharp rhetoric of Bellow's hero. "We have seen better days," says a character in *Timon of Athens* (4.2.27), and like Timon himself, Sammler might speak of "life's uncertain voyage" (5.1.207). As modernist Wandering Jew (if one can liberate this conceit from tendentious gentile fantasy), the Sammler who seems condemned to death-in-life would nod in sympathy at Timon's bitter remark: "My long sickness / Of health and living now begins to mend" (5.1.191).[36] Victim of some vast usurpation, Sammler also resembles the Hamlet who declares, "Man delights not me: no, nor woman neither" (2.2.296–97). Echoing Shakespeare's most famous tragic protagonists, Sammler embodies the pessimism that resists the age's endless, smug self-congratulation. More specifically, he recoils in disgust and horror from the idea that easier, more abundant sex might deliver Western civilization from its demons. Of course, some Shakespeare characters—Hamlet, Othello—have at least nominal justifications for their *Weltschmerz* and fevered expressions of disgust at the sorry spectacle of human beings—especially any pair of them making the beast with two backs. Others—King Lear, Angelo in *Measure for Measure*—deny the flesh with less obvious rationale. But as an old man unhappily immersed in revolution and ill served by the younger set, raging impotently and appalled at the universal lust of nature, Sammler most resembles King Lear. That neither sees very well only underscores the affinity.

"See better, Lear," says Kent (1.1.150), but clear seeing comes about only after much symbolic and literal blindness. In the play, this visual problematic culminates in the blinding of Gloucester, whose unsanctioned venery produced the monstrous bastard, Edmund. "The dark and vicious place where thee he got," Edgar tells his brother, "Cost him his eyes" (5.3.200–201). Whether or not Edgar's moralizing just here contains something of the "Precisian," as the English Renaissance styled its Puritans, one can link this trace detail to the sex nausea of old Lear, whose fevered imagination, like that of Artur Sammler, runs to what lies "beneath the waist":

The wren goes to 't, and the small gilded fly
Does lecher in my sight.
Let copulation thrive; for Gloucester's bastard son
Was kinder to his father than my daughters
Got 'tween the lawful sheets. To 't luxury, pell–mell!
For I lack soldiers. Behold yond simpering dame,
Whose face between her forks presageth snow;
That minces virtue, and does shake the head
To hear of pleasure's name;
The fitchew nor the soilèd horse goes to 't
With a more riotous appetite.
Down from the waist they are Centaurs,
Though women all above.
But to the girdle do the gods inherit,
Beneath is all the fiends': there's hell, there's darkness,
There's the sulphurous pit, burning, scalding,
Stench, consumption! Fie, fie, fie! pah, pah!

(4.6.111–27)

Charles S. Berryman, sketching the extensive parallels between Lear and Sammler, notes that Bellow spares his character the comprehensive, tragic devastation visited on Shakespeare's old king. I think, however, that Berryman overstates the argument for Bellow's hero as, finally, a daft and "endearing" comedic figure.[37] Such an argument tends to deny Sammler's stature and to forestall the possibility of importing Lear's tragic lessons into a fiction that, although written in an age no longer capable of tragic elevation, nonetheless does some justice to the anguish with which some individuals must face history. Borrowing some of its seriousness from Lear, *Mr. Sammler's Planet* manages to become—if one may use the term in a non-pejorative sense—a kind of tragic simulacrum. Invoking the tragic pathos of Lear, Bellow draws upon one's assent to the old king's self-characterization as "a man / More sinn'd against than sinning" (3.2.62–63). For all his crankiness and misogyny, Sammler inspires some comparable sympathy in the reader. At the same time, his fears for American civilization may take on some of the dignity and cogency of the terrible anagnorisis at the heart of *King Lear:* that civilized and civilizing institutions—kingship, statecraft, private property, clothing, shelter, marriage, family, and the laws of legitimacy and inheritance—shield humanity from the violence and cruelty of nature. When Lear relinquishes his crown, divides his kingdom, and disowns his child, he sets in motion the unraveling of a whole civilization, so that chaos, as another of Shakespeare's tragic heroes says, is come again.

The intertextual presence of Shakespeare's archetypal misanthropes and crazed vilifiers of the flesh precludes a reader's simply dismissing Sammler as just another New York loon, shuffling along muttering imprecations to himself. Sammler's single eye hints at the monocular vision imposed on him by history itself. Literally without stereoscopy and depth perception, he figuratively struggles, a belated Bloomsbury Laocoön, with the serpents of historical *force majeure*, serpents that augur, here at the end of the decade that has seen the Kennedy assassination (1963) and the Johns Hopkins conference on "The Languages of Criticism and the Sciences of Man" (1966), the final razing of the modernist citadel whose last champion, H. G. Wells, had long since left the literary and philosophical field to the cruel shock troops of a new aesthetic, a new model of culture. How fitting that 1939, the year of Sammler's botched execution and interment, the year history with a flaming brand barred any return to the Bloomsbury of Lytton Strachey, John Maynard Keynes, and, yes, H. G. Wells, was also the year in which, according to Thomas Docherty, Arnold Toynbee first introduced students of history and culture to the word "post-modern."[38]

2 ≋ Immigration and Primal Scene

Alvarez's *How the García Girls Lost Their Accents*

"Displaced Persons," he said. "Well now. I declare. What do that mean?"
"It means they ain't where they were born at and there's nowhere for them to go—
like if you was run out of here and wouldn't nobody have you."
—Flannery O'Connor, "The Displaced Person"

Every artist must discover or devise the form that will contain or embody or convey her vision. One thinks of the overdetermined intertextuality of a Kathy Acker, the artful symmetries of plot in Jane Austen. Joyce begins his famous *Künstlerroman* with the near-inchoate sensory impressions of infancy, ends it with a shift into the first-person journal from which the text just read will grow. The second act of *Waiting for Godot* meaningfully recapitulates the first. The literary art of immigrants similarly demands distinctive structures, and the more resourceful the individual artist, the more likely she or he will transcend the merely subjective and achieve work that will compete for readers long after the current vogue of ethnicity has been displaced by newer cultural trends. In *How the García Girls Lost Their Accents*, Julia Alvarez marshals a number of formal and thematic elements to represent one family's troubled passage to America. In addition to the reversal of temporal sequence, her techniques include a constantly shifting perspective (even for the same character) that captures the fragmentation of subjectivity itself. Periodically her story arrives at what might be called cryptic epiphanies that tease with the prospect of experience finally given meaning as well as form. The substance of these epiphanies varies from chapter to chapter, but collectively they expand a basic diegesis—we came to this country, struggled, survived—into the fresh thematic possibilities that emerge from original questions about language, sexuality, madness, art, and exile.

Like Charles Baxter's *First Light* (1987) and Martin Amis's *Time's Arrow* (1991), or films such as *Memento* (2000) and *Irreversible* (2003), *How the García Girls Lost Their Accents* unfolds backwards through progressive flashbacks, each succeeding chapter taking the reader further into the past. Even within chapters, the author favors a retrograde temporal movement, what Joan Hoffman calls a "topsy-turvy wandering into remembrance."[1] At both levels, the narrative technique complements the fundamental reversal in immigrant experience. In life, birth and childhood normally give way to and shape the adult achievement of autonomy and, often, self-knowledge. But for immigrants, this maturational sequence breaks down: suddenly powerless, without language, and stripped of autonomy, they become, in effect, children again. "The immigrant's arrival in his new home," declares Abraham Cahan, "is like a second birth to him. Imagine a new-born babe in possession of a fully developed intellect."[2] Such intellectual development, however, merely exacerbates the helplessness. After the second birth of immigrant dislocation, the secure sense of self that most adults can take for granted seems located exclusively and paradoxically in the past, in the first, literal childhood and in whatever maturity preceded the fatal embarkation. In later years the immigrant remembers—or constructs—that past as a time in which identity, at least, was stable.

In addition to the reversal of time's arrow, Alvarez breaks her narrative into discrete segments, so that first-time readers may think the book a series of linked stories rather than a novel. "Due to the shifting, unstable terrain they inhabit," remarks Jacqueline Stefanko, "Latin American (migrant) women writers question and reject the assumption that a unitary, synthesizing narrator is capable of telling the stories they have to disclose, instead opting for a narrative stance that includes multiple voicings."[3] Thus Alvarez's story moves from the present into the past, from objective to subjective, from sustained third-person narration (the first four chapters) to sustained first-person narration (the last four chapters and the concluding sections of the chapter that precedes them). An outline of these intriguing shifts of perspective will illustrate the overdetermined quality of this feature:

In part 1, the first four chapters are narrated in third person, from a variety of points of view: Yolanda, Sofía, "the daughters," "the mother." Point of view shifts to first person for the first time in the fifth chapter, in which Yolanda speaks in her own voice of the verbally uncouth suitor Rudy Elmenhurst.

Part 2 begins with a chapter in first-person *plural* (not an individual saying "we" but an imagined collective, a familial voice rather like the one that addresses the reader in the extraordinary prolusion to Naylor's *Mama Day*); next, a third-person account, from the mother's point of view, of Yolanda's travail with writing a school address; then a third-person description of Carla's experiences at school and on the street, where she encounters an exhibitionist; then another first-person narration by Yolanda; and finally a third-person account, from Sandra's point of view, of an unpleasant dinner and floor show (on which occasion Mrs. Fanning either makes a pass at or indiscreetly reveals an ongoing dalliance with the García paterfamilias).

Part 3 begins with a long chapter detailing the family's last day in the Dominican Republic. Point of view is especially fluid, shifting from that of the father, hiding from the *guardia* in the closet, to that of the girls and their terrified mother, to that of the thuggish Checo and Pupo, to that of Doña Tatica (a madam), to that of Victor Hubbard, the CIA agent of deliverance. This chapter culminates in two first-person sections, as Sofía (Fifi) speaks from the vantage of the present, followed by Chucha, who, though left behind, speaks a kind of valedictory on behalf of the departing family. Of the last four chapters (all in first person), Yolanda narrates two, Sandra and Carla one each.

In the fifteen chapters that compose her story, Alvarez seeks to represent numerous discontinuous perspectives that capture something of the logic—or illogic—of immigrant experience. Indeed, extra perspectives at times invade, as it were, narration ostensibly from one character's point of view; often one viewpoint is twinned with or cocooned within another. When Yolanda performs at a poetry reading, the scene is momentarily narrated from the double perspective of her postmarital lover Clive (to whom she has dedicated a presumably erotic poem, "Bedroom Sestina") and the woman seated next to him in the audience—the poet's mother.

Unaware of his intimate connection with Yolanda, Mami strikes up a conversation with the stranger, telling him about his lover's prior relationship with the "guy who wrote that poem about a blackbird"—that is, Edgar Allan Poe, whose raven had once reified Yolanda's neurasthenia[4]. But Clive's initial thought—that his talkative seatmate must be referring to Wallace Stevens—may be another clue to this book's meanings and form (especially when the reader subsequently learns that Yolanda had "misquoted Stevens," among others, during her breakdown [79]). As in Garcia's *Dreaming in Cuban*, Stevens figures as a shadowy presence here, for Alvarez at times favors the kind of obscure intimations characteristic of this poet's verse. In fact, the multiple points of view in the Alvarez novel may owe something to Stevens's "Thirteen Ways of Looking at a Blackbird" (the poem Clive seems to have called to mind), which one critic explains as an exercise in "thoroughgoing perspectivism" that "finds its ideal expression in aphorism. Aphorism's resistance to definitive meaning, its emphasis on the sense of things, on interpretation—all these in turn depend on a form that dictates the notion of a plurality of views that assume no larger context. . . . In order to give this sense of the multiplicity of seeing, the poem must isolate each perspective while indicating that they are all directed toward the same general subject."[5] These observations help one read both Stevens and Alvarez—though the inaccuracy of the term "aphorism" is distracting. One recognizes an aphorism by its economy and clarity, its being "what oft was thought, but ne'er so well expressed." Stevens's verse statements display the economy but not the transparency of aphorisms. Leaving true aphoristic expression to poets such as Horace and Pope, Stevens favors koan-like intimations that chasten the intellect, challenge it to more subtle perception.

Alvarez, who invokes "Zen masters" more than once in *Something to Declare* (her memoir),[6] poses similar challenges to perception and subtlety in the arresting or puzzling images, the cryptic epiphanies, with which she punctuates or ends the various sections and chapters of this novel. The "Rudy Elmenhurst" chapter, for example, which concerns Yolanda's resistance to unnuanced seduction in college, concludes with an explosively uncorked bottle that suggests the intertextual presence of a certain aphoristic poet after all. In *The Rape of the Lock*, his great poem about legitimate and illegitimate modes of sexual pursuit and sexual surrender, Pope speaks of "maids turned bottles" that "call aloud for corks" (canto 4, l. 54). Another example is more suggestive and more disturbing: recovering in a private clinic after her breakdown, Yolanda at one point hallucinates a "huge, black bird," a "raven" (83) that mysteriously objectifies her loss, her anger, her desire, and her "personality disorder" (84). If this troubled artist is the true central character here, then her raven hypostatizes the obscure affliction that lies at the heart of the novel, whose chapters might be described as fifteen ways of looking at that black bird.

But eventually the sufferer recovers a more primal image: in its earliest embodiment, the raven of neurasthenia was a helpless kitten—Poe's black cat manqué, as it were. By a kind of sympathetic magic, Yolanda becomes the little animal that she has traumatized. The novel concludes with the story of this maltreated creature, which Yolanda takes from its mother (as she herself will be taken from the motherland). An infinitely gentle, infinitely suffering thing, the kitten is an emblem of the psychic wound that disables yet also compels creation. Thus cathected, the kitten proves older, more disturbing, and if anything more pathological than the raven that replaces it (earlier in the narrative but later in time). Its grieving mother becomes the "black furred thing lurking in the corners of my life, her magenta mouth opening, wailing over some violation that lies at the center of my art" (290). Like a Hemingway hero, or Sterne's Uncle Toby, or, indeed, a Fisher King, Yolanda claims the primal wound that is always, as her own term "violation" implies, sexual. Expatriation, then, takes on a negative erotic cathexis, and the author, that other Yolanda, weaves relentless figures of sexual menace into a story about her loss of homeland and her problematic assimilation as *norteamericana*.

Other epiphanies are equally suggestive, especially the one embodied in "a yellowing poster for Palmolive soap" (14) that incongruously graces a rustic cantina in the Dominican heartland. In 1989, when Yolanda visits the country from which she had emigrated twenty-nine years previously (11), the conversation turns to an odd Spanish word, *antojo*, defined (and redefined) as "like a craving for something you have to eat" or like being "taken over by *un santo* who wants something" (8). Yolanda experiences such a craving for guavas (apparently no longer growing in an orchard adjoining the compound), but this *antojo* hints at another, larger yearning of the kind characterized in philosophy and psychoanalysis as *Begierde*, *Wunsch*, *désir*. The trouble the heroine experiences in her pursuit of guavas suggests the larger difficulties attendant on the more substantial desire she does not speak of to her relatives. "Yolanda is not so sure she'll be going back. But that is a secret" (7). Hers is the universal immigrant *antojo*: the yearning for a return to the natal shore, an end to the furcation of identity. Miryam Criado suggests that "in the return to her country of origin,"

Yolanda "begins the road to recovering her own identity as woman and, therefore, as human being."[7] But I would argue that these destinations have long since been reached. As authorial surrogate, Yolanda is nearly forty, and the identity problems that continue to occupy her are not so easily described, nor is there a simple road that will lead to their resolution. However "susceptible"—in Gilbert H. Muller's phrase—"to an ideology of return or reverse migration,"[8] she discovers (or rediscovers) the social and psychological barriers to any such wish fulfillment. As Ibis Gómez-Vega remarks, "She has become an 'other,' an outsider who has learned to see Dominicans and, by extension, herself through the distorting lens of her foreign upbringing."[9] Although the author does not state explicitly whether Yolanda acts on her desire for repatriation, the conclusion of this introductory sequence suggests that she will not. As noted previously, the chapters here usually culminate in some evocative tableau or image, a teasing intimation of meaning that resists a reader's desire to understand fully. In "Ten of My Writing Commandments," Alvarez quotes an eleventh-century Chinese master, Wei T'ai:

> Poetry presents the thing in order to convey the feeling.
> It should be precise about the thing
> and reticent about the feeling.
> (*Something to Declare* 260)

Thus the novel's first chapter ends with an image—the Palmolive poster introduced earlier—that makes no obvious statement. It does, however, suggest that Yolanda will never fit in again, that to stay in the Dominican Republic would be to stick out like that outlandish emblem of North American consumer desire posted in a backwater cafe.

But perhaps one errs to construe return or repatriation too literally. Contemplating "the phenomenon of exile" in this novel and Cristina Garcia's *Dreaming in Cuban*, Ludmila Kapschutschenko-Schmitt points readers to "its effect on the creative process."[10] "What I needed," says Alvarez in her memoir, "was to put together my Dominican and American selves" (*Something to Declare* 167). This need, this desire for reintegration, lies at the thematic heart of her first novel, published shortly after her forty-first birthday—only a couple of years, that is, after her alter ego, at the beginning of that novel, celebrates a birthday back in the Dominican Republic and struggles with *antojos* that may include the kind of craving experienced in pregnancy (Maribel Ortiz-Márquez notes that the word can have this connotation).[11] This teasing hint resembles a similar intimation in Pynchon's *The Crying of Lot 49*. Oedipa Maas, that novel's neurotic heroine, thinks herself pregnant at one point, but what she struggles to deliver is not a baby but an ineffable epiphany: "Your gynecologist has no test for what she was pregnant with."[12] By the same token, the only offspring Yolanda is likely to bring to parturition is a literary one, a book of the kind delivered by the author, herself childless, of *How the García Girls Lost Their Accents*.

Yolanda has recently declared herself "not a poet anymore" (46). Whether or not she now becomes a novelist in the literal sense, she goes on, here, to achieve her heart's wish, to satisfy her immigrant's *antojo*, through narrative. But the desired return to the Dominican Republic, a place of Edenic perfection for Yolanda and her family, is fully effected only in the last part of the novel, the part, paradoxically, in which the author must represent the primal scene of expulsion itself. The pathos of that expulsion is expressed not by the articulate Yolanda but by Chucha, the family's old Haitian retainer, in one of the novel's judiciously doled-out moments of first-person narration (221–24). A longtime voodoo practitioner, Chucha resembles Herminia Delgado, the *santería* communicant in Garcia's *Dreaming in Cuban*—or Christophine, the devoted servant, surrogate mother, and obeah priestess in Jean Rhys's *Wide Sargasso Sea*. In the Rhys novel, the heroine's catalogue of objects lost to postcolonial dislocation— "the golden ferns and the silver ferns, the orchids, the ginger lilies and the roses, the rocking chairs and the blue sofa, the jasmine and the honeysuckle, and the picture of the Miller's Daughter"[13]—anticipates Chucha's vision of loss: "How the grass will grow tall on the unkempt lawns; how Doña Laura's hanging orchids will burst their wire baskets, their frail blossoms eaten by bugs; how the birdcages will stand empty, the poor having poached the *tórtolas* and *guineas* that Don Carlos took so much trouble to raise; how the swimming pools will fill with trash and leaves and dead things" (222–23). Placing this lament, this proleptic *ubi sunt*, in the mouth of the genuinely sorrowful Chucha, Alvarez softens the effect of having excessively rich Dominicans bewail their losses. (Rhys, from another place called Dominica, invites her readers at least momentarily to despise her heroine, Antoinette, who mourns the loss of a privileged life founded on slavery and colonial exploitation.)

"You are going to a strange land" (220), Chucha tells the García de la Torre girls, echoing a familiar biblical phrase about displacement. Of course, Chucha is herself an exile, and hers is an immigrant narrative within an immigrant narrative—a *mise en abîme*. A Haitian from the wrong side of the island, Chucha is (like the German artist, Doña Charito) a life-long stranger in a strange land. Like Moses, indeed, she is the offspring of a people in bondage, a survivor of genocide, and her presence in the story affords the reader a glimpse (218) of Trujillo's 1937 massacre of some 20,000 Haitians, identified by their mispronunciation of the Spanish word for parsley, *perejil*.[14] Such a word, instrumental in differentiating one group from another, is a "shibboleth," from the Hebrew for an ear of corn or a stream. In ancient Palestine the Ephraimites, unable to make the "sh" sound, pronounced the word *sibboleth*. This trifling distinction enabled their Gileadite enemies to identify and slay an alleged 42,000 of them (Judges 12).

Although taken in by the de la Torre family as a small child, Chucha cannot pronounce the Spanish "j." Her linguistic deficiencies among the Dominicans recall those of the biblical Ephraimites and anticipate those of the García family among the *estadounidenses*. Schoolboys, for example, call Carla a "dirty spic" and mock her pronunciation: " 'Eh-stop!' they mimicked her. 'Plees eh-stop' " (153). That the book's title refers to the losing of accents suggests the centrality of the shibboleth, correct pronunciation, as badge of national belonging.

Biblical or post-biblical, the shibboleth remains a matter of enormous consequence, and the references to this verbal standard here take their place within a larger thematics of language, as Alvarez sketches a sensitivity to words on the part of her chief viewpoint character, the troubled poet whom language at once liberates and imprisons. Finding "the natives . . . unfriendly, and the country inhospitable," Yolanda "took root in the language. By high school, the nuns were reading her stories and compositions out loud in English class" (141). The trace of an accent, however, qualifies such classroom successes. Later, language functions as a kind of *pharmakon*, the site or medium of both psychological collapse and emotional restoration. In pathologies of language, that is, the author represents the failure of Yolanda's marriage and the breakdown that leads to her going, like Sandi, into a private mental hospital. Yet it is language, too, that enables the heroine to put herself back together after the descent into mental chaos. Like T. S. Eliot, who also suffered a nervous breakdown, Yolanda shores fragments—not of the exploded art and culture of a failed civilization but of a life once geographically and psychologically centered.

Of John, her estranged husband, Yolanda declares, "We just didn't speak the same language" (81). Sandi tearfully reproaches her sister, "Miz Poet," for being "so goddamn sensitive to language" (60). Much earlier, opposed conceptions of language had stood between Yolanda and amorous consummation with her collegiate pursuer, "Rudolf Brodermann Elmenhurst, the third" (88, 89). Alvarez represents the struggle for Yolanda's virginity as a kind of literal language game that turns on Rudy's hardheaded but principled refusal to misrepresent the exact nature and extent of his desire. This struggle has both literary and nationalistic dimensions. The virginity in question is again a metaphor for ethnic identity, an identity at the point of becoming fully American. His "odd, ornate name" the legacy of a rich German grandfather (94), Rudy himself seems to have at least one immigrant parent. But he displays the credentials of a thoroughly American undergraduate in his insistence on plain speech, his relegation of fine language to poetry and the poetry classroom. As creative writer, in fact, Rudy is something of an epigone, for his one poem, which features the line "The coming of the spring upon the boughs" (93), seems to recycle Ezra Pound's "A Virginal" ("Green come the shoots, aye April in the branches").[15] Also a modernist in matters erotic, Rudy insists on a stripped-down, unadorned lexicon of sexual desire. But Yolanda, with a real vocation for poetry, wants to be wooed with language that is "romantic" in every sense; rejecting repeated invitations to be "screwed, balled, laid, and fucked" (97), she wants her sex verbally aestheticized. Her notion of a suitable language of seduction may strike some readers as syrupy ("Sweet lady, lay across my big, soft bed and let me touch your dear, exquisite body" [96]), but in retrospect she will prove refreshingly capable of describing this collegiate contest of artistic and erotic wills in language that enacts precisely the grace and wit desiderated: with what Nabokov calls "a bright foreigner's fondness for puns" (*Pnin* 149), she declares that if her suitor had been willing to be poetic, she "might have felt up to being felt up" (96).

In Yolanda's agon with Rudy, Alvarez represents the encounter with eros as potentially liberating. Indeed, this novel seems to incorporate and process a great deal of libidinal energy, to transform it into further symbolic representations of the exilic struggle for autonomy, self-knowledge, and deliverance from identity confusion. But sexually this struggle is Janus-faced, for the stages of Yolanda's emotional and artistic *Bildung* are accompanied by alternating currents of license and inhibition, erotic emancipation and sexual danger. On one side are various gestures of libidinal liberation, led by the youngest (and thus most Americanized) of the García girls, Fifi, the one who, having most openly defied the old world proscription of going "behind the palm trees" (30), outrageously tongues the paternal ear in a wicked parlor game. But her sisters, too, claim considerable sexual experience, even as college girls summering in the Dominican Republic. A cousin titillates these three (and himself, no doubt) by showing them the inside of Los Encantos, a tryst motel and brothel. On the other side of this coin are numerous encounters with perversion or the threat of violation, sex that is by turns menacing or oppressive. Twice an erection is depicted as requiring some kind of bridle, whether the "lasso" (157) of the exhibitionist whom Carla encounters or the "halter" (250) that restrains the demented but sexually potent artist whom Sandi observes. The men who change the tire after Yolanda's guava harvest seem at first to be the very incarnation of sexual menace. The terror engendered by the *guardias* Checo and Pupo has its sexual edge, too: even little Fifi knows better than to let one "sit me on his hard-on and pretend we were playing Ride the Cock Horse to Banbury Cross" (217). On this occasion Fifi and her family are delivered only when Don Victor can be torn briefly from the brothel, El Paraiso, where his activities literalize what some would say the CIA has been doing to the country all along.

Throughout the story, then, the prospect of sexual violence seems to counter possibilities for sexual fulfillment. This ambiguity registers, among other things, the familiar anxiety of women who, brought up in a repressive culture, must make difficult adjustments to life in a famously permissive one: America in the sixties. Compounding the difficulty is the assimilationist imperative of that day. As Alvarez remarks in an interview, "It was a time when the model for the immigrant was that you came and you became an American and you cut off your ties and that was that."[16] Alvarez's fellow immigrant and sometime editor Marie Arana tells much the same story in *American Chica*, her memoir of a Peruvian childhood that ended in emigration to America. She describes her father's "first step toward becoming an American" as the moment when "the future interests him more than the past."[17] The legacy of mixed-message sexuality also figures in Arana's narrative. As a small child Marie adores the family gardener, and once, when she sees him urinating against a wall, he allows her to touch his penis. Not represented as sexual abuse per se, the encounter seems inconsequential until, later, a much less excusable incident proves to have its origin in the first one. By the same token, chronicling her parents' stormy relationship, Arana can never resolve the questions in her mind regarding the erotic depths of her mother's personality. The Alvarez text, however, features a more thorough unfolding of what sexuality's pleated

cunning hides. The frequent references to sexual danger seem to complement and deepen the fundamental dislocation—that of the immigrant's
identity and sense of self—but one must remember that negative depictions of sexuality are not limited to the exilic phase of the life stories narrated here. As will be seen, this evenhandedness corrects for the idealizing
tendency to perceive the family compound—and, indeed, the native country it strives to symbolize—as some perfect Eden, exempt from real-world
afflictions.

María Inés Lagos argues that this novel's "alternation of narrative
voices" contributes to a dismantling of stereotypes and, even within a
single immigrant family, the establishing of a normative diversity. "Although the four sisters have passed through similar experiences, each one
of them is different," she asserts.[18] But other critics make more of the
prominence of Yolanda and the relative inconsequence of her sisters. Het-
eroglossia notwithstanding, the immigrant experience central to the novel
is that of Yolanda, whose sobriquet (Yo) puns on the Spanish for "I" and so
signals a particular affinity with Alvarez herself. The author represents the
extensive splintering of this *cogito* in the many names given to the central
character: Yolanda, Yoyo, Joe, Joey, Josephine, Jolinda, Yosita, Miss America, Miz Poet, Squirrel, Cuquita, and so on. Nor should the reader fail to
notice three more names: Carla, Sandra, Sofía. With their many names,
diminutives, and nicknames, the four siblings come to represent the red-
shifting fragments of a single, once integral identity after the diasporic big
bang. Carla and Sandi, and to a lesser extent Fifi, invite recognition as mirrors of Yolanda, each clarifying some aspect of her emotional and artistic
sensibility. By the same token, when one of the planetary siblings encounters some sexual menace, the reader senses the expansion of a dynamic that
in the end centers on their poet sister. The experience of Carla with the
mechanical Virgin Mary bank or, later, with "a pervert" (107) tells the
reader more about the conflicting libidinal energies of Yolanda than about
those of her older sister. Sandi is even more the Yolanda reflector: as the
central sibling declares her art founded on a mistreated feline, so does the
artistic talent of Sandi first manifest itself in depictions of cats. Both discover art's strange pact with eros—and with lunacy. Both suffer nervous
breakdowns.

Carla, Sandi, and Yolanda all require psychotherapy, which involves
what psychoanalysts call "transference"—the investing of the physician
with parental authority and responsibility. Yolanda and Carla play out a familiar Oedipal drama by falling in love with—and, in the older woman's

case, marrying—their psychotherapists. Sandi may suffer the most debilitating mental problems of all, but we do not hear that she falls for Dr. Tan-
dlemann, who treats her. Her version of the Oedipal fixation, as will be
seen, is played out at a much earlier age. Fifi, the daughter who most firmly
establishes independence from her father (who, indeed, in the chapter ti-
tled "The Kiss," blithely mocks the incest prohibition), is the only one
who seems not to be arrested at the Oedipal stage of libido development.

Chucha observes that the sisters "will be haunted by what they do and
don't remember" (223). In childhood each García daughter commits some
relatively small transgression that, in the hothouse of the unconscious,
provides its own little false justification or rationale for the subsequent suffering that begins as expatriation, as expulsion from the geminate Eden of
childhood and native country, and continues through other afflictions: di-
vorces, breakdowns, sexual neurasthenia, an eating disorder, estrangement
from the father. The author does not make clear the age at which each
child commits her little sin, but its magnitude varies, suggestively, according to the age at which she emigrates. "I'm the youngest," declares Fifi,
"the one who doesn't remember anything from that last day on the island . . . and so the other three are always telling me what happened." Because vicarious recollection—"Fifi, you almost got Papi killed for being so
rude to that gestapo guy" (217)—does little to foster guilt, Fifi remains (on
this score) the least damaged. Yolanda, the next youngest, is sufficiently
troubled to present a screen memory (of pulling her panties down at the
behest of a curious cousin) before admitting to the incident with the un-
weaned kitten. Sandi spies on a demented artist and gets her arm broken
and her artistic talent scared out of her (or perhaps simply displaced onto
another sibling). Carla, the eldest, inadvertently promotes the dismissal of
the hapless servant, Gladys, who covets the mechanical toy bank that, fed a
coin, launches the Mother of God on high.

Carla's little narrative about the bank swells with meanings related to
Yolanda and the larger García chronicle. It also reconstructs—and re-
demolishes—the deplorable accountancy model of Catholic piety so mem-
orably satirized in Joyce's "Grace." The toy conflates the idea of salvation
with that of saving—perhaps, indeed, "saving oneself for marriage," which
none of the girls ends up doing. "They grew up in the late sixties . . . sleeping with their classmates" (28), a narrator declares at one point. Later,
Yolanda iterates, "It was the late sixties, and everyone was sleeping around
as a matter of principle" (87). Broken, the bank becomes yet more suggestive, for in that condition it symbolically invites the rifling of what a good

Catholic girl has so jealously safeguarded. The image hints at violation, at damage to one's most precious possession. Or it hints at some delirious release, as in Philip Larkin's contemporaneous figure for the sexual revolution: the "brilliant breaking of the bank" that came about "between the end of the *Chatterley* ban / And the Beetles' first LP."[19]

Sandi's experiences (and the psychosexual profile they shape) prove similarly suggestive. Like Marie Arana, Sandi observes a parent's disturbing sexuality; indeed, she witnesses a version of the primal scene not once but twice, for the episode in which Mrs. Fanning kisses Dr. Carlos García in front of his daughter recapitulates, diminuendo, the more elaborate incident in which the child sees Don José, the mad artist whose medical education hints at his symbolic identity, between the legs of the Virgin he is "making" in more than just the artistic sense. Sandi notices how carefully the artist has sculpted the feet: "She could have stood on those soles and walked all the way to Bethlehem" (250). This observation echoes a line about sexual appetite from a famous play: shortly before her demise, Shakespeare's Desdemona speaks with her maid, Emilia, about marital unchastity, about women who "abuse their husbands / In such gross kind." Emilia has remarked of a handsome courtier, "I know a lady in Venice would have walked barefoot to Palestine for a touch of his nether lip" (*Othello* 4.3.63–64, 39–40). Like Emilia, Mrs. Fanning is a creature of candid sensuality, a later foil to the guilty little Electra who spies on the symbolic father brandishing his erection between the legs of the ultimate symbolic mother. But achievement of the unconscious wish here proves self-punishing: although the face on the Virgin presently becomes that of the jealous daughter, it is the motherland, not the mother, that Electral ambition displaces.

In addition to its elaboration of an Electral wish, this chapter addresses the imponderable calculus of artistic vocation. When the family first recognizes her artistic talent, Sandi remarks, " 'Gifted' descended upon my hitherto unremarkable shoulders like a coat of many colors" (241). She becomes, in other words, a Joseph—on her way, perhaps, to the mad creativity of that other Joseph, the Don José she will spy on and follow, years later, into extreme mental instability. In the biblical story the fine coat leads to exile for its owner, who nonetheless becomes one of the several Old Testament deliverers who prefigure the Messiah. Sandi telescopes this patristic typology, for the woodworking artisan she spies on is recognizably the saintly carpenter crazy enough (I intend no sacrilege) to marry a pregnant virgin. Looking into his workshop, Sandi becomes, briefly, the child whose relationship to Mary and Joseph constitutes the ultimate family romance.

Psychological maturation normally eventuates in renunciation of Oedipal desires, but Sandi in effect renounces her artistic gift, which passes to a sibling successor who will also put in a brief appearance as Christ figure. When Yolanda disappears one day, her worried parents presently find the precocious tyke reciting Edgar Allan Poe, "surrounded by a crowd like Jesus and the elders" (49). Perhaps the reader, thus prompted, will expect the little girl to follow in the divine footsteps and thereby realize some local or personal version of eschatological expectation—to effect, if not humanity's return to paradise, at least a return to her own personal Eden. But the allegory is inchoate and attenuated; it gutters like a candle without oxygen. The myth of redemption and return, whether for one immigrant or for the entire human race, is precisely what the exile must sooner or later surrender. Having "lost their innocence and accents," as William Luis puts it, the García women must make their solitary, postlapsarian way in a world brimming with fellow exiles.[20] But at least one of them—her nicknames include Joe, Joey, Josephine—can inherit the mantle of creativity, the coat of many colors that makes her a Joseph of such deliverance as art can afford.

3 ≋ Survival on the Tangled Bank

Hegi's *The Vision of Emma Blau* and Mukherjee's *Jasmine*

"I want to get somewhere in the world, that's what I mean. Europe's rotten and stinking. In America a fellow can get ahead. Birth dont matter, education dont matter. It's all getting ahead."

—John Dos Passos, *Manhattan Transfer*

In Aleksandar Hemon's novella "Blind Jozef & Dead Souls" the quasi-autobiographical title character, a Bosnian trapped in the United States when civil war breaks out in his homeland, has a conversation with a couple of Generation X layabouts, who assume he will stay in America. When Pronek expresses concern about his family back in the Balkans, one of the young Americans declares, "Man, I wish I'd never see my fuckin' family again." The other American, a "history student," views both immigration and war as exercises in Darwinian selection. He interrupts his electronic gaming long enough to deliver a painfully funny little homily:

"I mean, fuck, war is good. If we didn't have war, there would be way too many people, man. It's like natural selection, like the free market. The best get on top, the shit sinks. I don't know much about you, Russkie, and I don't like you, but if you got here you must be worth something. It's like those immigrants, man, they were shit at home, they got here, they became fucking millionaires. That's why we're the toughest motherfucking country in the world. Because only the fittest survive here."[1]

Hemon's economy and tonal control are perfect—he need not comment on the difference between wanting to escape one's family and having no choice, nor does he need to draw the reader's attention to the superficiality of the half-baked apologia for the rigors of free enterprise. Pronek's companions are hardly examples of capitalist mojo: they are freeloading on the absent Andrea, who freeloads on her parents. There seems to be latitude for a modicum of parasitism here on the American tangled bank. What especially fascinates one, though, is the acuteness of the immigrant author's vision. Hemon brings what feels like centuries of east European irony to bear on this moment of spurious slacker sagacity.

Part of the comedy of *The Russian Debutante's Guide* (2002) lies in the cheerful willingness of its Russian American author, Gary Shteyngart, to depict immigrants as hustlers, loons, and con artists. An Abraham Cahan for the twenty-first century, this Shteyngart. His protagonist, Vladimir Girshkin, strives to extricate himself from the loser category to which fate seems to have consigned him. An American for roughly half of his twenty-five years (and evidently a schlemiel from birth), Vladimir manages to stay afloat in a sea of troubles just long enough for fresh storms to develop. Eventually this Jewish picaro takes his gift for survival on the road, joining the lively but feckless arts scene in Prava, Stolnaya (a thinly disguised Prague), where he poses as litterateur and helps assorted East Bloc mafiosi take advantage of less cagey American expatriates. In Prava, the playing ground leveled between naturalized and native-born Americans, one immigrant comes very much into his own—at least until his past catches up with him. He ends up married to one of the expatriates, living in the Midwest, and working for his wife's father. The very banality of his fate would seem to constitute the moral of his story, but the spectacle of complacent and privileged Americans as exilic poseurs has been edifying: they merely play at what is for others a wrenching life passage. Real exiles and immigrants seldom enjoy much latitude for affectation; rather, they must somehow wring substance from decidedly un-ludic role-playing and disguise. Before they become Americans, in other words, immigrants must act the part.

Whereas Hemon and Shteyngart satirize the myth of immigrant energy and immigrant success, other authors look more squarely at the less savory newcomer, the figurative as well as literal arriviste, the one who (short of actual criminal activity) stops at nothing to realize a vision of new world achievement. Because they can seem somehow representative, these pictures of immigrant cupidity prove disturbing. Always they embody a critique of the mythology of immigration. Unless she or he is what Shteyngart wryly calls a beta immigrant, every new arrival in this country is to some degree or other propelled by ambition—especially ambition to prosper. Though a few are crushed by an exacting economic system, most immigrants manage, eventually, to make a living. And though they risk a full surrender to deforming appetites, a fair number do much more in their single-minded pursuit of the fulfillment universally expected in America. In this chapter I examine two examples of monomania, one a German whose obsession undermines his considerable achievement, the other an Indian whose energy proves frighteningly elemental. In the achievement of her character Stefan Blau, Ursula Hegi critiques the American Dream; by contrast, in the rootlessness (and ruthlessness) of her character Jasmine, Bharati Mukherjee critiques the American penchant for the peripatetic.

Immigrant Desire: *The Vision of Emma Blau*

For the naming of her fifth work of fiction, German-born Hegi seems to have embraced the practice of Austrian-born Walter Abish, who favors semantic ambiguity in his titles, e.g., *Eclipse Fever* (the first word can function as verb or adjectival noun) or *How German Is It* (unpunctuated, it can be emphatic or interrogative). The title of Hegi's novel works the same way: it can refer to the fateful vision of a child playing in the courtyard of a splendid building (a vision realized when Stefan Blau erects the great apartment complex he calls the Wasserburg), or it can refer to the monomania—the twisted "vision"—that years later will motivate the child herself, Stefan's granddaughter Emma, when she comes into possession of the that obscurely symbolic piece of real estate. Hegi evidently wanted some such element of semantic play, for the book's working title, *The Passion of Emma Blau*, also evinces it. At the same time, the onomastic parallel with Abish inclines one to imagine this novel with a subtitle or, under erasure, a shadow title: *How American Is It*. Though the author orients her characters and action to this side of the Atlantic, the reader is a little unsure whether the literary themes in *Emma Blau* belong to the old world or the new. Indeed, immigrant writers sometimes present problems to the critic who would chart the influences on their art. Do they seek to import, along with themselves, the myths and literary antecedents of their homelands? If they desire—as Aleksandar Hemon claims—to repudiate the stale old stories, do they also repudiate, as only slightly less superannuated, those of the new world? In the case of Ursula Hegi, who in 1964 emigrated from her native Germany at the age of eighteen, one finds little in the way of explicit allusion to or reinscription of storytelling archetypes, regardless of which side of the Atlantic they come from. Yet a story such as the multi-generational saga *The Vision of Emma Blau* may benefit from some contextualization of its artistic strategies, some account of the "vision," so to speak, of the author herself. That vision has both its sociological and its literary underpinnings.

Werner Sollors observes that "works of ethnic literature—written by, about, or for persons who perceived themselves, or were perceived by others, as members of ethnic groups—may . . . be read not only as expressions of mediation between cultures but also as handbooks of socialization into the codes of Americanness."[2] Thus Hegi recurs to the immigrant's never fully exorcised anxiety about fitting in—especially during those years when the new country is literally at war with the old. The distress of the Blaus, however, never rises to the level suffered by the Japanese Americans interned during World War II (as seen, for example, in David Guterson's 1995 novel *Snow Falling on Cedars*), nor even to that experienced in the anti-German persecution of the World War I years, as glimpsed in Steinbeck's *East of Eden*). When a Jewish tenant, Nate Bloom, reproaches the endlessly acquisitive immigrant and his family—"You people want everything that isn't yours"[3]—the reader may feel, with the accused, the imputation of a larger German guilt, though in fact the Blaus are at pains to affirm positive relations with Jewish friends and neighbors in both the old world and the new.[4]

But what of Hegi's literary vision? Artists, like immigrants, hover between the magnetic poles of what Sollors characterizes as "descent" relations (influence, tradition) and "consent" relations (literary self-fashioning)—and one notes, in passing, that "freedom of expression" is as important to the immigrant artist as to any other kind, as examples from Thomas Mann to Mikhail Baryshnikov show. Although this novel harks back to the realist-naturalist tradition, the high-water mark (complete with deterministic undertow) of fiction's willingness to engage reality at its most harsh, the author tempers her grim saga of familial devolution with magical or supernatural touches. Stefan Blau sees a child dancing in the courtyard of the Wasserburg some years before he builds the apartment complex—and some decades before little Emma actually dances. Stefan's daughter Greta, who has the gift of healing, is also more truly psychic. Stefan's third wife, Helene, can experience orgasm through blushing. Eventually this family will give rise to individuals whose storytelling becomes fully magical-realist. Though few would mistake the tonality of this author's work for that of Isabel Allende (a fellow immigrant) or García Márquez, certain details resonate. As Remedios the Beauty, the Buendía woman who inspires such desperate love in all quarters, one day disappears into the heavens among billowing sheets, so does Robert Blau tell his son Caleb a story about a woman who levitates, a woman who "loved with— with such abandon that it made her float in the air" (311). Realizing that this fanciful tale really concerns his father and mother, Caleb learns that "in telling a story through someone else, you could get at it closer. And by letting that changed story pass through you, you arrived at a greater truth" (312). He also goes on to make films (390) in which a fabulous or "magic" element transfigures personal experience: "Whenever Caleb took fragments from his own life and made them magical, he felt magical himself" (350). Indeed, as on the large canvas of García Márquez's *One Hundred Years of Solitude*, Hegi's *Vision* reconfigures history as family chronicle. But where Latin American history of a particular kind has gone tragically unrecorded (necessitating the inspired conceits of magic realism), European and transatlantic history has asserted itself so aggressively as often to obscure the lives of ordinary people. Thus Hegi relegates cataclysmic events—the sinking of the *Titanic* and *Lusitania*, World War I, the stock market crash of 1929, the Great Depression, World War II—to the margins as she looks more and more closely at those citizens, now of Burgdorf, now of Winnipesaukee, whose lives hardly require "history" to reveal themselves in all their human complexity. In sifting the century's great events through the lives of the Blau family, Hegi has undertaken, like the *Annales* historians, to seek the meaningful past not in epiphenomenal events but in the lives of those whom history's dark wing scarcely brushes.

Hegi's novel includes a passage about the men of many nations who work in the restaurant run by the Hungarian who befriends and mentors the protagonist, Stefan Blau. "Not all had come to America as willingly as Stefan: some had fled from religion; others from family or war; but what kept each of them here was hope" (18). The last term resonates, of course: only one out of many will arrive with anything like the "extraordinary gift for hope" observed by Nick Carraway in Jay Gatsby, that archetype of American success.[5] But *The Vision of Emma Blau* is a looser, baggier monster than *Gatsby*, and, knowing, perhaps, that the story of immigrant hope has been told so often before as to become a cliché, Hegi undertakes to re-configure or hybridize it, to darken the diegesis, move it conceptually closer to Dreiser's naturalism than to Fitzgerald's modernism.

As a generational or family chronicle novel, *Emma Blau* has affinities, too, with Helen Barolini's *Umbertina* (1979), or with such recent fictions as Jeffrey Eugenides's *Middlesex* or Updike's *In the Beauty of the Lilies* (which also spans the twentieth century, also culminates in a film career). But given the ethnicity of what Eliot would call the individual talent here, tra-dition surely takes its most concrete form in a novel by that earlier Ger-man American, Thomas Mann, who emigrated in 1938 but continued to write in German and, like the Nabokov who despised him, lived out his final years in Switzerland. Though written long before Mann turned his back on Germany, *Buddenbrooks* exhibits interesting parallels to Hegi's novel. Each work chronicles the decline of a successful bourgeois family; each moves toward engagement with an emergent aesthetic alternative to the materialism of the middle-class, mercantile mind. As the scions of Mann's Buddenbrooks embrace contemporaneous art and philosophy (no-tably Schopenhauer, Wagner, and Nietzsche), the family loses its mercan-tile edge, goes gradually slack. From her later perspective as a more youth-ful immigrant and more fully Americanized writer, however, Hegi reverses this story's premise, arguing that the emergence within a family of individ-uals capable of nuanced sensitivity and artistic expression is precisely what redeems a particular kind of mercantile rapacity over time. This genera-tional development emerges first in the spiritually gifted Greta, who must wait years for Noah Creed, a Catholic priest, then glimmers briefly in To-bias, whose doomed matchstick creations might have led to a real artistic vocation, then nearly gutters out in the shrouded sensitivity of Robert Blau, whose obesity symbolizes that which smothers and chokes off his creative, impressionistic, artistic spirit. Only in Robert's filmmaker son Caleb—the author's surrogate, one suspects—does the redemptive artistic vision flourish. In his own work, in fact, Caleb transmits the music his fa-ther played (308). The first candidate for redemption is Caleb's sister Emma, a second Stefan in her obsessive devotion to the Wasserburg. All turns, in the end, on the degree to which this sister, her initial vision chas-tened, can transform the bitter legacy—the heavy hand of the past on the wincing shoulder of the present—of a grandfather's fixation. Indeed, be-fore they register the emergence of any redemptive artistic vision, readers of this novel may apprehend, as corrective to American insouciance, a pervasive *Mitteleuropäisch* fatalism. As a Nabokov narrator remarks, "Harm is the norm. Doom should not jam."[6]

This fatalism dictates the prominent astronomical imagery in *Emma Blau.* In the heavens, that is, one reads the destiny of Stefan Blau and his family. Hegi's frequent references to moon, stars, and constellations relate the immigrant's painfully fluid condition to familiar perceptions of heavenly fixedness and mutability. The moon, for example, represents the inexorable change to which, no matter how passionately he aspires to permanence, no matter how solidly he builds, a Stefan Blau remains in thrall. For his daughter Greta, the vision of a half-moon reflected in the waters of the lake becomes a kind of psychic annunciation. As Tom Brangwen, in Lawrence's *The Rainbow*, takes his little stepdaughter Anna out to the barn when the sounds of her mother giving birth to another child become too terrifying, so does Stefan Blau take three-year-old Greta for a walk beside the lake on the night her first stepmother, Sara, gives birth to a half-sister, Agnes, doomed to die in infancy. Gifted with second sight, Greta knows, seeing that "moon . . . on the water like a slab of frost" (43), the fate of both mother and child. Thereafter she will experience certain kinds of painful prevision—notably in the period just before her father's death—as "sudden images of a half moon lying cold upon the lake" (279).

Stars, by contrast, traditionally represent order, law, destiny, fate, eternity (one thinks of George Meredith's sonnet "Lucifer in Starlight"). Like "descent" relations among immigrants (those fixed, according to Sollors, by blood, nature, heredity), the "eternal language of the stars" (180) may circumscribe the destiny immigrants aspire to command, the destiny to which, in their marriages, education, and political choices, they "consent." Yet from another perspective, immigrants aspire to patterns of permanence, seek to realize in their new lives something like the fixed and orderly routines of heavenly bodies arcing so predictably across the nocturnal sky. Perhaps, too, the immigrant mind is seeded by the constellations, those archetypal shapes on high, those embodiments of the myths and stories by which humanity defines and sorts recurrent experience. If no Steerage Passenger shares the heavens with Eagle, Swan, Cross, Ship, and the rest of the wheeling constellations, "the true subject of this novel" nonetheless proves to be, as *New York Times* reviewer Diana Postlethwaite points out, "the constellation that is the family."[7] Certain members of this family aspire, indeed, to some approximation of the heroic achievement commemorated and enshrined among the celestial narratives. Thus the star-and-constellation motif receives its most suggestive elaboration when Emma and her son Stefan recapitulate the story of Andromeda and the sea monster (a "whale") that will devour her, absent some heroic deliverance (375–77). In moral chains beside her distant northern sea, Emma becomes another such Andromeda, at the mercy of the all-consuming monolith erected by her grandfather. But as she reviews the story with little Stefan, she evidently fails to see that forces in the world can still require the sacrifice of young women. With the Wasserburg as Poseidon's monster, Emma awaits deliverance by Justin Miles, local doctor and unlikely Perseus.

American Ark

Like Alexander Sukorov's brilliant 2002 film *Russian Ark*, Hegi's *Vision of Emma Blau* concerns a splendid edifice that enshrines history. Sukorov escorts viewers through the dim corridors, echoing ballrooms, and art-glutted galleries of St. Petersburg's Hermitage; Hegi presents a great building, the Wasserburg, that encapsulates the immigrant ethos at the heart of the American experience. One of the most intriguing challenges of this novel is to sort out the meanings implicit in the grand structure that battens, like its builder, on the fresh green breast of the new world. Literature is replete with symbolic houses: one thinks of Gilbert Osmond's palazzo in *Portrait of a Lady*, or Darcy's Pemberley in *Pride and Prejudice* (not to mention Sir Thomas Bertram's Mansfield Park), or the slave-built house the McCaslin twins find themselves unable to live in in *Go Down Moses*, or Thomas Sutpen's house in *Absolom, Absolom!* (doomed to the very flames that Stefan Blau most dreads for the Wasserburg). Each of these houses suggests the moral profile of its owner, whether positive (Fitzwilliam Darcy, the McCaslin twins) or negative (Gilbert Osmond, Thomas Sutpen). But the greatest literary houses—Howards End, for example—embody more than their individual owners. The eponymous house in Forster's novel becomes a problematic legacy, and by the time it has passed from the ethereal Mrs. Wilcox to Margaret Schlegel (who becomes another Mrs. Wilcox), it has evolved into an elaborate symbol of England itself. Hegi's Wasserburg, another contested legacy, may also emerge as an emblem of national identity. Like the first Mrs. Wilcox, moreover, the owner of the Wasserburg resists easy labels. Indeed, Stefan Blau represents an equivocal version of the archetypal architect or builder: guilty of nothing so flagrant as Sutpen's violent racism or Osmond's fortune hunting, he suffers from failings that, not fitting neatly into the major categories of opprobrium, seem almost venial.

Like the great houses of literature, then, the Wasserburg offers itself as a symbol at once multivalent and ambiguous. A microcosm of some kind (a temple, an ark, a vessel in the tradition of the Knarrenschiff, the Ship of Fools), it contains a modest cross-section of human types. Like the passengers of John Ford's *Stagecoach*, or like the Canterbury pilgrims, or like the patients gathered in the doctor's waiting room in Flannery O'Connor's "Revelation," the tenants of the Wasserburg seem to define the classes—from the maids domiciled in the basement to the American gentry presiding in the penthouse. Others include a rail tycoon, a lawyer, a retired factory worker, a dentist, a geologist, an accountant, and—in the building's decline—a mechanic, a hairdresser, and the upwardly mobile great-granddaughter of one of those maids.

The Wasserburg also hypostatizes experience peculiar to the immigrant. The never-squared loan the Flynns make to Stefan and their daughter, an important part of the symbolism, hints at some universal obligation of the newcomer to these shores, a debt the immigrant can never repay. Like the *Titanic*, to which it invites comparison (and whose fate it shares, albeit in slow motion), the Wasserburg seems ultimately to reify a specifically European variety of hubris—as does America itself, the splendid edifice that European "vision," with the help of an unrepaid "loan" (an entire continent), has erected on these shores. For the critic who seeks meanings specific to Hegi's historical moment (a moment in which nothing about the character of old or new Americans can be taken for granted), the house emerges as metaphor for the immigrant family and its social intersections. It also embodies an idea of hybridized identity. After the deaths of her grandfather, grandmother, and father, when Emma Blau imagines "buyers inspecting the house" (her mother, its latest inheritor, may sell it), "she felt *stateless*, homeless" (353, emphasis added). This thought makes of the house nothing less than a little enclave, the immigrant's own personal, miniaturized country, not a nation-state but a *person*-state that a newcomer fills with his family and the finer trappings of old world elegance: "Italian marble and Dutch tiles; stenciled beams and oriental rugs; German carvings and crystal chandeliers; balconies with flower boxes atop the ornate railings; a stone fountain with two tiers like something you might see in picture books of Venice" (52). All of this imitation of European opulence, this bid for cathedral-like permanence, comes about almost without thought, for at the beginning of his life in the new world, Stefan is conscious only of a desire "to be American in every way possible" (18). But the assimilation that eventually comes about undermines the purity of what Stefan builds. Within a generation or two, its original grandeur notwithstanding, the Wasserburg begins to decay. As a legacy, moreover, it becomes a *casus belli* within the family. Stefan tells Helene to "keep everything together" (286), but one doubts that he means for her to disinherit her stepchildren. In any event, single ownership of the Wasserburg only divides, sows discord.

Stefan's disaffected son Tobias observes that "keeping the house together will destroy it and drive this family apart" (411). He should know: as monomaniacal in his way as Stefan and Emma, Tobias reveals his own proclivity for obsession in his boyhood hobby, making pairs of matchstick animals, and in his lifelong rancor over their forced destruction. His capacity for self-blighting behavior replicates that of his father—first on a juvenile scale, then with the settled ferocity of a mature neurosis. Long after Stefan forces Tobias to destroy his little models, the boy continues to think of their loss: when movers carry Mr. Perelli's trophies into an apartment in the Wasserburg, Tobias sees the menagerie he tried to envision and create "coming back into the house" (208). He cannot let go of this conceit, and his bitterness poisons relations with his father for the rest of their lives.

His own obsessions notwithstanding, Tobias instinctively reacts against those of his father, who first harasses a holy figure associated with uneasy paternity (that is, he buries Saint Joseph upside down), later makes—or thinks he makes—a bargain with God. Subsequently thinking that the deity has not kept up his end, Stefan refuses ever again to enter a church. In an act of private sacrilege, he imagines the Wasserburg a rival temple, its owner-occupier (by implication) a rival deity. "The house of God. The house of Stefan. Blasphemy" (116).

Though he cannot really understand the impiety, Tobias seems to have intuited his father's notion of the Wasserburg as temple. At the same time, however, the boy consciously thinks of the enormous construction at water's edge as an ark. Not that ark and temple are unrelated: symbolically and typologically, they are the same thing, as those who have contemplated the depiction of the ark in the stained glass at Chartres know. As the means whereby the creation is preserved, Noah's vessel is, from the vantage of later biblical history, a symbol of the church, the "vessel" that will deliver sinners on the last day from a deluge not of water but of fire (the conflagration proleptically threatened in Tobias's building materials). Ostensibly a juvenile Noah, Tobias must imagine the crafting of matchstick animals as a son's legitimate imitation of the work done by fathers. But the biblical patriarch does not *make* the animals he shepherds aboard his ark, and in fact Tobias attempts to usurp the divine prerogative of creation itself. In other words, he commits all over again the transgression of the father who, not content to be Noah, insists on an ill-advised contest with the being Noah serves.

In the menagerie he creates for the Wasserburg ark, then, Tobias sins against both deity and paternal demiurge. Stefan, always fearful of fire, treats the activities of Tobias as an Oedipal challenge and visits a castration-like punishment on the boy. Appropriating the "raw head and bloody bones" motif from *Ulysses* (another story of problematic paternity), Hegi gives Tobias a recurrent dream or vision of a severed calf's head (151, 189, 195, 294). In this dream he transforms conscious antagonism and unconscious castration anxiety into the desire to become Cronos to his father's Uranus, to reverse the direction of the supreme Oedipal punishment.

Ignorance of his own nascent sexual identity complicates this psychomachia. Among its other meanings, the story of Noah and the ark contains a primitive account of mating dynamics, about which the young Blau is perforce confused. Before becoming aware of his homosexuality, Tobias cannot know that he will never mate as Noah's creatures do. But a dawning awareness of heteroclite sexuality may announce itself to Tobias in his insistent perception of a dead sister, Agnes, who is somehow half of himself. In fact, his crafting of little mated animal pairs finds its ironic complement in constant thoughts of this sibling, who becomes his own female side, his persona, his ideal self. At the same time, mistaking intimations of his sexual identity for the survival of Agnes in his own psyche, Tobias makes of her an inchoate, prepubescent object of desire. She is, in the recurrent, motif-like phrase, the "someone like me" (53, 147, 151, 188–89, 294) that he fantasizes and yearns for. So oft-repeated, the phrase gradually modulates into an intimation of the like-gendered partners—someone *sexually* like him—in Tobias's future.

Unlike Tobias, who eventually achieves a degree of domestic content in the relationship with Danny Wilson, Stefan lives to see desire traduced. In the end, he has erected neither ark nor temple but a graven image, a golden calf that alienates him from God, family, neighbors. The people of the town know "that Stefan loved the *Wasserburg* more than his third wife and his children" (143). "*For him it was always the house,*" thinks Helene (307). Early on, "the one person who cherished his house as much as he did" is the first of this novel's impotent artificers, Miss Garland (184–85), whose apartment will later be occupied by Emma (363), the granddaughter who "knew she was the only person he loved as much as his building" (275). Presently its inheritor, Emma finds her own life stunted by the obsession passed on to her. Her lover says to her at one point: "Your real lover is this house. I'll never be as important to you" (383, echoed 414). In the end she comes to *"knowledge that it can take generations for a curse to come to fruition"* (431).

The reader may, however, be a little baffled about this curse, which costs Stefan Blau two wives and much of the sustained love of a third, estranges him from his eldest son, breeds contempt for the younger, and goes on to blight the one legacy he might leave to the family. The curse becomes increasingly virulent as it proceeds through the generations, until Emma nearly destroys herself in her yet more extreme obsession with the grandfather's handiwork. But what is the curse, and what causes it to fall on Stefan and his life's work? What causes it to eventuate, in later years, in the symbolic "decay that had settled in the cracked plaster of the walls" (363)? Keen, perhaps, to discern the larger meanings that reside in archetype, one seeks to view Stefan's single-minded drive as the hubris of an old world Faust or a new world Gatsby. Similarly, one might look for parallels between the "house of Stefan" and the doomed lineage of, say, the Atreides (or, closer to the American grain, the Kennedy family). But the working-out of the Wasserburg curse, insofar as it falls on heads that never rise to heroic purpose or action, fails to rise to tragic levels.

Readers may also see Stefan Blau as merely the latest American Adam. Having heard that story so many times before, however, they will take particular interest in the ways that Hegi, as American literary hybrid, might depart from or at least freshen the classic diegesis. What, for example, constitutes the primal sin of this Adamic figure? Has the Blau patriarch sinned so terribly in erecting a splendid edifice on the shores of that New Hampshire lake? Emma wonders if the curse began with burying Saint Joseph upside down (411) but also imagines that it originates in the agon between her grandfather and her uncle Tobias. When she begs Tobias to lift whatever anathema he has pronounced, he declares that the Wasserburg "was cursed before I was born" and invites his half-sister Greta to tell the story confided by her grandmother, the story of the loan never repaid. (Old Mrs. Flynn had advised her granddaughter "not to trust him [Stefan] in matters of money" [340]). But does this dereliction really poison the well of Stefan's success? A debt not repaid to one's relatives seems an odd cornerstone for any American doctrine of the Fall (not that the original transgression in Eden was—on the face of it—particularly grave). No, the curse on Stefan Blau and the inexorable decline of what he creates on the shore of Lake Winnipesaukee—a restaurant, a grand apartment house, a family—seem in excess of any particular act of omission or commission. It resists the reader's desire to understand—especially if one expects a more traditional parable of American rising and falling. But perhaps this refusal to comply with coercive myth, this resistance to spurious metanarrative, is deliberate on the part of an author who recognizes that in fact no one story defines a nation. Thus she opts to qualify the authority of what is perhaps America's greatest literary myth by simply subjecting it to deconstructive or postmodern non-closure. However superficially familiar, her tale has a certain freshness: it has not been told and overtold. For whatever reason, Hegi insists here that the weave of betrayal or deceit or moral compromise, the "taint" or "flaw" that leads to corruption down through four generations, begins as something relatively inconsequential. The point, ultimately, is that ordinary human fallibility need not be mythologized as original sin. It is perfectly adequate to build a hell in heaven's despite. Pursuing a "vision" (perhaps, indeed, a Dream), Stefan Blau allows a cancerous obsession to doom his line and the mansion in which that posterity was to dwell. What brings catastrophe in its wake is the failure of humility (to use the Faulknerian word), the assumption that one is not subject to human moral limitation.

Like Bellow's *Henderson the Rain King*, *The Vision of Emma Blau* unfolds as a set of variations on the theme of "wanting." Unaware of the irony, Stefan Blau reproaches his third wife, Helene, for becoming pregnant against his wishes: "You just take what you want" (136). The irony lies in his failure to recognize how aptly the phrase applies to himself and his blood. "Getting what you want," he tells his granddaughter, "has to do with holding it in your mind so strongly that you keep returning to it—without thinking—so that you are always linked to it" (275). The wanting that initially propels Stefan (22) no sooner fades (286) than it is renewed—often in twisted forms—in subsequent generations: we hear of Greta's yearning for Noah Creed, of Robert's appalling appetite (287), of Tobias's "wanting more than you already have" (359), of Emma's having "been born with his [her grandfather's] furious wanting in her blood" (287). Emma troubles Yvonne, her mother, who laments the child's endlessly "wanting more than I can give her" (365). "How God awful it was," thinks Emma at the end, "to only want what wasn't yours" (429). "Why did she always have to want what belonged to others?" (383).

In its insatiability, this wanting figures the "desire" of post-Freudian psychology. Lacan traces it back to the Imaginary, back to the mirror phase, back to the primal encounter with an other, an *objet (petit) a* that betrays us into a lifelong pursuit that can never be successful. It is the very *archê* of division. This division has its particular instantiation in the life of an immigrant—an instantiation that in effect ratifies and compounds that first experience of lack. In other words, the absence upon which Lacan founds his system (of the unconscious, of identity, of desire) figures so strongly in the psychological plinth on which an immigrant, Stefan Blau, erects a new national identity that he must deal with desire that is doubly evanescent, doubly absconded, doubly insubstantial. It may be that the peculiar desire of the immigrant is commonly subsumed under the universal human sense of absence, loss, need for something without a name (just as the loss of the homeland is subsumed under the universal myth of a lost Eden, a proscribed womb), but in the case of a Stefan Blau or other immigrants of his kind (those whose ambition eventually betrays them), it becomes a curse that begets yet more division.

"Had he known how the *Wasserburg* would seduce and corrupt him and his family," the author suggests, Stefan might not have surrendered to his fateful cupidity, "but to detect rot is often impossible in its early stages: it starts beneath lush surfaces, spreading its sweet-nasty pulp, tainting memories and convictions. It entangles. Justifies" (25). At the moment of his death, Stefan "understood that the vision he'd seen from the rowboat that long-ago day had contaminated something within him" (289), and he feels alarm for his granddaughter, who had been part of the vision. Initially Emma exemplifies the curse, having learned too well the "wanting," especially the wanting of what is "not yours"; her "vision" is to be in sole possession of the Wasserburg. But this vision is supplanted by one of the Wasserburg destroyed by a fire that she herself would set, visiting on the venerable structure precisely the fate most dreaded by her grandfather (430–32). Happily turning from this desperate gesture, Emma seems at the end to have opted for relinquishment (again, the Faulknerian word): she will strive, hereafter, to correct some of the abuses to which she has been a party. The Wasserburg will at long last become only an old-fashioned apartment complex—no longer the Moloch to which the patriarch and his granddaughter, in their blasphemous obsession, sacrifice what they ought to hold most dear. On the last page of the novel, the stars are significantly occluded, as if to affirm that an ancient European fatedness has at last given way to American self-fashioning.

Seeing America Steadily and Seeing It Whole: Mukherjee's *Jasmine*

The fragmentation of modernist forms, often thought to represent the breaking up of old certainties (especially as a result of the vast carnage of World War I), also reflects the conditions of exile in which Joyce, Eliot, Pound, Cather, Barnes, Boyle, Fitzgerald, Dos Passos, and so many others of their generation labored. A later literary generation, expatriating itself *to* America, reverses the old pattern, yet recurs to themes and forms of fragmentation, dismemberment, masking, and psychological multiplicity. Whether temporary or permanent, voluntary or involuntary, modern or postmodern, diaspora seems to dictate a thematics of disarticulation. Readers of contemporary American immigrant literature see instantiation of this precept in the dismemberments of *A Gesture Life*; in the touching attempts of Akiko, in *Comfort Woman*, to foster in her infant daughter an awareness of tiny limbs not yet "articulated" in language; in the doubling theme in Danticat's *Breath, Eyes, Memory*; and, in Bharati Mukherjee's 1989 novel *Jasmine*, in the uneasy coexistence of disparate cultural forms, in the multiple identities the title character remarks in herself, and in what she describes as "the war between my fate and my will."[8]

Some—perhaps many—readers of *Jasmine* dislike its heroine, whose early travail and suffering may not extenuate the ruthlessness with which she sweeps tornado-like across America. For a reader such as Kathryn Hume, Mukherjee keeps "a tally of victims" and "makes plain the unrealistic expectation embedded in the American Dream—namely, that everybody can prosper."[9] Other readers, perhaps missing the panorama of the American underclass that might be expected to underscore such a message, wonder if they should discern celebration or critique in the avidity with which Jasmine embraces her new country and what she takes to be its ethos. Does she speak—and act—for her creator, the author who in interviews defends an assimilationist vision and repudiates the hyphen in her own American identity? Or does Mukherjee intend a calculated irony, an elaborate satire on precisely those American traits Jasmine salutes?

These questions contain or subsume others. What do immigrants see when they look at their new country? Do they behold it with more clarity than the native-born, or do they view it only through the lens of their own idealizing—or invidious—constructions? After all, human beings rarely manage to free themselves from myth. However intelligent, however educated, they remain to a greater or lesser degree bound epistemically, given to illusion in its various forms. They misgauge the referentiality of sign systems, they do not recognize the implications of indeterminacy, they fail to correct for subjectivity, they project. A few physicists, psychoanalysts, and literary theorists try to think rigorously about reality, but they, too, remain susceptible to confusion. Many, avoiding *pseudodoxia* of one kind, become oversubtle and embrace fresh error. Sometimes they seem to see no difference between the Japanese Imperial Army's assault on Nanking and the assault, decades later, of American capital. Some think the failings of the West graver than those of other cultures. Thus one discerns some important differences between the intelligent immigrant and the American-born intellectual, for the Western intelligentsia—even when not wedded to precisely those pernicious ideologies that have failed most spectacularly when put into actual practice—often lose proportion when engaged in the otherwise legitimate business of criticizing our flawed institutions. Immigrants, by contrast, usually see the world with remarkable clarity. No doubt they, too, struggle imperfectly with illusion and project their needs onto the phenomenal world. But as the Greek proverb has it, *pathemata, mathemata:* sufferings are lessons. The experience of immigrants, especially insofar as it is painful or arduous, schools them in ways to remain grounded, to look on their new country with something like the keenness of Matthew Arnold's Sophocles, who "saw life steadily and . . . saw it whole." Nor should one lump these newcomers together with the domestic poor and disadvantaged, whose experience, early and late, consists of an immersion in America's great sea of illusion, what George Steiner once called "the tidal mendacity of journalism and the mass media." This victimization, moreover, is seldom attended by hunger, disenfranchisement, and oppression on anything like the scale of such afflictions elsewhere. The American poor do not emigrate.

By the same token, American intellectuals seldom break absolutely with their homeland. For every Henry James or T. S. Eliot or W. E. B. Du Bois who actually becomes a citizen of another country, there are numbers who merely live abroad while remaining Americans (James Baldwin, Russell Hoban, Rachel Ingalls, even Eldridge Cleaver). Often these exiles return to their native shore, like the quondam expatriates of the Lost Generation, or like their less famous peers who parked themselves in Prague for the *fin-de-millénaire* decade. As Mukherjee observed in a 1996 *New York Times* article comparing her own decision to naturalize to her sister's opting to remain an expatriate, "the price that the immigrant willingly pays, and that the exile avoids, is the trauma of self-transformation."[10]

Among the exiles and literary expatriates of other nations who dwell in the United States, one encounters—saving the occasional St. John de Crèvecoeur, Cristina Stead, or Alexander Solzhenitsyn—relatively few who repatriate. Some become permanent, non-naturalized residents, and as ethnicity has become increasingly chic and even remunerative in the literary marketplace, one notices more and more who opt to keep their postcolonial cachet untrammeled by imperial citizenship, or who at least remain coy about the passport they carry. I have found it surprisingly difficult to pin down the current nationality of such figures as Jamaica Kincaid, Vikram Seth, Meena Alexander, even the Salman Rushdie who in 1999 moved from England to the United States. Still, most of these "specular border intellectuals," as Abdul JanMohammed calls them, sooner or later break with their past and become citizens—of the United States or some other Western country.[11] The present study concerns those who, choosing to become naturalized American citizens, take their new homeland as subject.

Bharati Mukherjee is in many ways the ideal example, especially insofar as she has often (and publicly) descanted on the peculiar openness of American society to newcomers. Any American who has long resided in another country knows that, however cordial its people, actual transformation of an outsider into one of them remains highly problematic. Yet in a land of immigrants such transformations are routine. "I've lived everywhere," Mukherjee remarked at the time of *Jasmine*'s publication. "I'm truly touched and moved by the idea of America. It *includes* you and is curious about other people. Includes you, allows you to think of yourself as American. Other countries in Europe, and Canada, deliberately exclude you. You wouldn't dare to think of yourself [as belonging]."[12] Such words, like Mukherjee's other public statements, at once oblige recognition of America's uniqueness and reaffirm the American immigrant myth.

Born in India, educated there and in England, and expatriated to Canada before she became an American citizen in 1988, Mukherjee chose the United States over other prospects because here she felt intellectually free—free, as she has remarked, to define herself, even to resist, as de facto ghettoization, the currently fashionable concept of a "hyphenated" identity. Mukherjee describes herself as an American, not an Indian American. "I maintain," she told Nicholas Basbanes,

> that I am an American writer of Indian origin, not because I'm ashamed of my past, not because I'm betraying or distorting my past, but because my

whole adult life has been lived here, and I write about the people who are immigrants going through the process of making a home here. I write in the tradition of immigrant experience rather than nostalgia and expatriation. That is very important. I am saying that the luxury of being a U.S. citizen for me is that I can define myself in terms of things like my politics, my sexual orientation or my education. My affiliation with readers should be on the basis of what they want to read, not in terms of my ethnicity or my race.[13]

Like author, like character. "I changed because I wanted to," observes Jasmine. "To bunker oneself inside nostalgia, to sheathe the heart in a bulletproof vest, was to be a coward" (185). In her work, then, Mukherjee probes—subverts, even—certain pieties of the multicultural ethos. In interviews and in "Immigrant Writing: Give Us Your Maximalists!," the 1988 *New York Times Book Review* article on her own naturalization, she hints that hyphenated Americans, even as they lay claim to victimhood, smugly exploit the basic difference between themselves (prosperous, complacent) and their uncouth immigrant forebears—not to mention the old world cousins whose parents never emigrated. All too often, secure in their Americanness, their native ease with vernacular English, the American-born children and descendants of immigrants make a great deal of their hyphenated identity, undertake sentimental pilgrimages to the old country (there to parade the trappings of their expatriation), display decals, bumper stickers, and license plates proclaiming their roots, and so on. The point, however, is that these actions and gestures amount to little more than middle-class attitudinizing, consciously or unconsciously aimed at romanticizing socially problematic origins. As such, they resemble nothing so much as the affectation that offends Jamaica Kincaid's Lucy when her WASP employer, Mariah, declares herself proud to have Native American blood: "How do you get to be the sort of victor who can claim to be the vanquished also?"[14]

Refusing such romantic mythology, Mukherjee separates herself from the many immigrant writers—indeed, the many Indian expatriates—who work an exclusively retrospective vein. These are the Kamala Markandayas and Anita Desais—the writers who, in the many nations of the Indian diaspora, trade on exotic tales set in the homeland and on the very "nostalgia and expatriation" that Mukherjee repudiates: Vikram Seth, Rohinton Mistry, Suril Mani, Arundhati Roy, Amitav Ghosh, Manju Kapur, and one or two more, it seems, in every issue of the *New York Times Book Review*. Though Mukherjee set some of her early work in India (e.g., *The Tiger's*

Daughter), and though she has always integrated Indian characters and scenes into her novels, her emphasis swiftly came to be on the experience of the Indian immigrant in America. At the same time, however, she has "refused to commodify ethnicity," as she explained to an interviewer. She has "refused to write about the ghettoes" or, generally, "to commodify things into uniform victim-status for all minorities." Professionally, this has required a good deal of courage, because publishers demanded that she write about "little India," not Iowa, not Florida. By "not doing the . . . hyphenated American thing," Mukherjee fails to do "what's expected of Asian American writers."[15]

The Immigrant as Mutagen

Critics expecting to encounter truculence at or resentment of the treatment of immigrants must go to considerable lengths to recuperate Mukherjee's vision to the dominant theoretical paradigms.[16] In *Jasmine*, Mukherjee sets out to champion an idea of immigrant adaptation somewhat at odds with the usual politics of ethnicity. The author presents America as experienced by the newcomer who finds that, in adjusting her old world perceptions, she effects an inner transformation as compelling as the surface-level changes in dress, speech, behavior, personality. Meanwhile, that complex thing identity undergoes its own sea change as Mukherjee stages the artful interpenetration of Indian and American mythologies of character and fate. Mukherjee by no means views the immigrant as a tabula rasa, nor does she endorse a vision of passive conformity or cookie-cutter Americanizing. The eponymous heroine cannot simply discard the old self, and her ways of seeing and judging remain deeply affected by her Indian past. Through her heroine Mukherjee at once scrutinizes American mores and social institutions and gauges the often parochial outlook of those who take them for granted. At the same time, she seeks to refurbish terms long banned from the multicultural lexicon. If in the end the author affirms Jasmine's "assimilation," the term must be understood with reference to its Latin root (*assimilare*), which means simply "to make like," without hierarchical specificity. As immigrants become Americans, in other words, America itself is made over in the immigrants' likeness. The same goes for the much-maligned figure of the "melting pot," from which must issue not sameness but perennially new and different alloys of national identity.

Samir Dayal sees the story of Jasmine, especially the "syntax of her self-articulation," as "a parable for the social transformation of the Indian postcolonial." More specifically, Jasmine engages in "the struggle of post-colonial subject-formation"—a struggle exacerbated by "migrancy, a perpetual subtext of Mukherjee's fiction" that "is figurally repeated as displacement and deferral of unitary selfhood."[17] In other words, before this immigrant can claim an American identity, she must negotiate a series of selves. Now "Jasmine the reliable caregiver," now "Jase the prowling adventurer" (176), she goes through multiple faces, multiple names, among them Jyoti, Jasmine, Jazz, Jassy, Jase, Jane. Even in India, with its seemingly changeless society, the nominal self was fluid: born Jyoti, she becomes Jasmine to her progressive young husband, Prakash Vijh. "Jyoti, Jasmine: I shuttled between identities" (77). Presently, however, the shuttling gives way to something more linear, each self canceling its predecessor in a serial progression, a negative catalog: "Jyoti of Hasnapur was not Jasmine, Duff's day mummy and Taylor and Wylie's au pair in Manhattan; that Jasmine isn't this Jane Ripplemeyer having lunch with Mary Webb at the University Club" (127). And these are only the nonce identities of a woman still seeking a definitive self, a definitive name, at story's end. Thus Deepika Bahri, in one of the best essays on Mukherjee's novel, characterizes its heroine as "always in the process of dodging the stasis demanded of her through her assigned subjectivity as Third World underclass woman/victim and migrant."[18]

Upon arrival in America, her sense of self at its most tentative, Jasmine must struggle with a person she refers to only as "Half-Face," a name that hints at obtunded or distorted identity. Indeed, if by "face" one often invokes the exterior and superficial, the mere mask of some inner reality of character, then how much more impaired is the self figured as only half of such a mask. The ghastly facial bifurcation of this piratical figure originated in Southeast Asia, but every half-faced Westerner who stumbled out of Vietnam left behind hundreds of the similarly mutilated. Like Mrs. Nguyen of *Monkey Bridge*, with her napalm-scarred visage, these victims bear witness to the same dark equation implied in the rapist's face and the cognomen that describes it. The twisted features of Half-Face also reify less visible mutilations, e.g., those visited on innocents such as Du, the orphaned Vietnamese refugee whom Jasmine and her common-law husband later adopt. For Jasmine, the face of the rapist exemplifies the evil of inhumanity (116), evil that seeks to replicate itself in those who, like herself and Du, have had to kill to survive.

In an interview Mukherjee calls this novel a fable.[19] But what, then, is its moral? I suspect it has to do with what Jasmine calls "the war between my fate and my will" (12) as viewed from perspectives—old world, new world—that prove surprisingly complementary. The "ceaseless, flexible dialogue between cultures," remarks John K. Hoppe, lies "at the center of Mukherjee's work, and represents, in her view, the polar opposite of multi-culturalism's aim to stabilize difference."[20] "The star on my forehead throbs," says Jasmine, to signal "pain and hope, hope and pain" (225), and so does her life resolve itself into balance between the poles of suffering and triumphant (some would say ruthless) self-realization. This balancing of opposites figures with particular clarity in the Half-Face episode, for in her violent struggle with the rapist, Jasmine may be said to encounter a symbolic reification of the problematic identity on which, as (illegal) im-migrant, she must as it were put a face. In the rapist's visage (as much doubled as halved), Jasmine encounters, as in a proleptic mirror, a hyper-trophied form of the two-facedness that, as immigrant, will be her lot.[21]

But the whole point of this fable is that Jasmine's two-facedness—unlike that of other, more problematically assimilated immigrants—will prove temporary. In time she will repudiate the kind of double life led by the pa-thetic Professor Vadhera, whom she calls "Professorji." Creating and seal-ing himself into a bizarre little Punjabi enclave in alien New York, Vadhera cannot allow his own family to know how he makes a living in the new world. Reflecting on the choice made by her whilom host, the heroine ob-serves that "his real life was in an unlivable land across oceans" (153). Os-tensibly a rueful, almost Nabokovian comment on the lost homeland that every exile mourns, this remark has a kind of allegorical, self-deconstructive valence, for it not only characterizes Professorji as a person unable to let go of the old country but also hints at some absolute psychological inter-diction. That is, the irretrievable "real life" suggests an exilic sublime; the "unlivable land," by the same token, resembles the Lacanian Imaginary in its ability at once to generate and frustrate desire. The authentic life one might lead there remains inaccessible to all who enter exile's Symbolic order.

The trope of facial duality takes another form in the unstable "hyph-enization" (225) that Jasmine observes in Du. When her foster son decides to abandon the Ripplemeyer home to live with his sister in a Vietnamese enclave in California, he becomes momentarily an Asian American Huck Finn, evading the Ripplemeyers' attempts to "sivilize" him. But his arche-typally American gesture serves a vision of hyphenated identity that

Mukherjee interrogates, as if to remind her readers just how recently that model of American ethnicity became the cultural norm. Richard Rodriguez, whose parents emigrated from Mexico, hints at a context for what Du does when he turns his back on one family for another: "Americans like to talk about the importance of family values. But America isn't a country of family values; Mexico is a country of family values. This is a country of people who leave home."[22] Perhaps familial cohesion in Vietnam and in the Vietnamese diaspora resembles that of Rodriguez's Mexico. Du's "family values," however, dictate that he leave a home and hearth in Iowa to join his sister in another alien city, another place that remains only home's simulacrum.

Jasmine does not seem to resent Du's choice—some go one way into their American experience, some another. Treating him always with sympathy and respect, neither Jasmine nor the author despises Du. But Jasmine describes herself as "afraid to test the delicate thread of his hyphenization. Vietnamese-American: don't question either half too hard" (225). Of immigrants like herself and Du Jasmine remarks, "We murder who we were so we can rebirth ourselves in the images of dreams" (29). She knows that "once upon a time, like me," Du "was someone else. We've been many selves" (214). Still, her "transformation has been genetic; Du's was hyphenated" (222).

What is the distinction that the heroine articulates here? At best a suspicious category for the author, hyphenated identity resembles metaphysical wit, as famously defined by Dr. Johnson: it represents a *discordia concors*, a yoking together by violence—sometimes literal violence—of heterogeneous elements. Thus the hyphenated fall short, even, of hybridity. Genetic transformation, by contrast, involves change at the level of what the dictionary calls "germ plasm." Genetic change fosters evolution, and Jasmine, claiming it, recognizes herself (and many an immigrant before her) as mutagen. As America changes the immigrant, the immigrant changes America.

To gauge the mutational effects, one must learn just how this novel's now subtle, now overdetermined pairing of Eastern and Western perspectives, mythologies, and frames of reference amounts to something more than formal and thematic hyphenization. After all, her endorsement of assimilation notwithstanding, the author takes fully into account the Indian heritage of her protagonist. On this score, incidentally, Mukherjee undertakes an act of authorial impersonation only slightly less daring than that of, say, Pearl S. Buck, impersonating Chinese peasants, or William Styron speaking for Nat Turner. As a Calcutta-born, Bengali-speaking, highly educated Brahmin, Mukherjee must, after all, make a considerable imaginative leap to represent or speak for Jasmine, who grows up in an impoverished village in the Punjab. In other words, the Indian chapters of this novel are not grounded in the India that gave birth to Bharati Mukherjee. Indeed, the naturalized author may speak with more authority about Jasmine's America than Jasmine's India, in connection with which, according to some critics, Mukherjee traffics in stereotypes.[23] But in writing a fable, Mukherjee may in fact deploy stereotype to advantage. She does not, in any event, aim at the social realism that would give her readers some distillate of authentic Punjabi folkways. Nor does Jasmine seem less legitimate than, say, *Wife*'s protagonist, Dimple, who shares the author's Bengali background. Such cavils aside, Mukherjee treats Jasmine's pre-American life in considerable detail, then allows credibly Indian perspectives and Indian perceptions to permeate the rest of the narrative, coloring and qualifying the account of how the American panorama comes to dominate the imagination of the heroine. Though swift to embrace American possibility, Jasmine cannot simply elide Asian memory.

One is struck, in fact, by the extent to which Eastern perceptions prove congruent with experience in the West. The novel's vision of American social mutability has its complement in Eastern philosophies emphasizing cycles of death and reincarnation. Jasmine shows, over and over again, an Indian and specifically Hindu awareness of creation's fluidity, its endless rebirth out of violent dissolution (hence her repeated identification as tornado [205, 215, 241]). But Mukherjee's heroine comes from a culture of fixed social forms and so finds it difficult, at first, to believe that in America the cosmic fluidity finds its mirror in or simply subsumes society and self. She must learn the lesson articulated by a famous cultural historian, Frederick Jackson Turner: "American social development has been continually beginning over again on the frontier. This perennial rebirth, this fluidity of American life, this expansion westward with its new opportunities, its continuous touch with the simplicity of primitive society, furnish the forces dominating American character."[24] Brought up on the Eastern vision of perpetual creation-dissolution-renewal, Jasmine should not be surprised at its instantiation in the new world. Yet how shocking, nonetheless, for one also brought up on the myth of America's social and political steadiness, to discover this dynamic in America, perhaps thought somehow to have exempted itself from the flux. "In America, nothing lasts. I can say that now and it doesn't shock me, but I think it was the hardest lesson of all for me to learn" (181, cf. 138).

Thus the embedding of different cultural material cuts both ways: Western allusions figure in the Indian chapters, Indian references in the American chapters. The references to Western culture in the Indian chapters, however, are explicit and tend less to subversion than to mild irony—unlike the Indian perspectives that manifest themselves with considerable subtlety in the American chapters. Thus in India, Jasmine has been exposed to an American movie, *Seven Village Girls Find Seven Boys to Marry* (45, 83)—presumably *Seven Brides for Seven Brothers* after translation into Punjabi and back into English. She also reads (or attempts to read) some American and English fiction: books like *Shane, Alice's Adventures in Wonderland, Jane Eyre*, and *Great Expectations* (40–41)—all of which offer comment on the course her life takes. Shrinking and expanding, she will eventually find herself in the American Wonderland, where she will wrestle with the extravagance of great expectations and decide against marriage to her Rochester before, like Shane, moving on. Stymied in her initial plan to die *sati* amid the flames of Prakash's clothes, Jasmine in the end rejects the Western version of this dread custom: to remain, like the Jane Eyre whose story she never finished reading, caretaker of the impaired man who fathers her child. Implicitly she declares, "Reader, I did *not* marry him."

More than one critic has noted that Mukherjee's story ironically replicates a whole Indian mythology that offers terms by which a reader can understand the experience of its heroine. Perhaps it is significant that Mukherjee's native city, Calcutta, takes its name from the Kali-ghat, the temple of the goddess Kali. In one of the more important moments at which this mythology surfaces, Jasmine turns on her rapist, Half-Face, and becomes the goddess, the very incarnation of female destructiveness and rage, the temptress and terrible mother traditionally depicted, according to the succinct account in *Brewer's Dictionary of Phrase and Fable*, with "red eyes, four arms, matted hair, huge fang-like teeth, and a protruding tongue that drips with blood."[25] In Jasmine's native culture, as Carmen Wickramagamage observes, "Kali . . . haunts the interstices of the dominant patriarchal narrative of normative femininity and contests that norm."[26] Indeed, many who consort with the goddess risk the fate of Half-Face—or so Jasmine hints when she remarks that in "not marrying" Bud Ripplemeyer, she "saved his life" (12). Already he has been crippled by an assassin's bullet; surely, as spouse, he would share the fate of Half-Face and, before him,

Prakash. One husband or companion after another meets violence. Like Pynchon's V. (herself a lifelong exile), Jasmine can seem, from one perspective, a kind of mythic incarnation of some terrible principle of carnage. This element in the story sharply qualifies the sense—as Jasmine, Taylor, and Duff reunite in the closing pages—of a happy ending. Taylor may yet find that he has rescued a particularly baleful avatar from Iowa. As will be seen, however, his half-joking theory of "weak gravity" suggests that he at least understands the precariousness of contentment.

Jasmine also becomes successively all the members of the *trimurti* or "Indian trinity": Brahma (Creator), Vishnu (Preserver), and Shiva (Destroyer). Under her various aspects, indeed, Kali exhibits characteristics of all three—especially, according to Joseph Campbell, with regard to the universal mutability: "As change, the river of time, the fluidity of life, the goddess at once creates, preserves, and destroys."[27] After the violent interlude with Half-Face, Jasmine calls herself "walking death. Death incarnate" (119), echoing Vishnu's line in the Bhagavad Gita: "I am become Death, destroyer of worlds." Yet under a different aspect she embodies the reproductive principle. The same Jasmine who mimes Kali at her most horrific, extruding her blood-dripping tongue at the moment she butchers Half-Face, will presently, in Iowa, become "so potent, a goddess" (12) of fertility for whom "it wasn't hard to get pregnant" (35). In this condition she becomes the local avatar of Vishnu, the Preserver. Back in India, her grandmother had "told stories Of Vishnu . . . containing our world inside his potbellied stomach" (223–24). In Iowa, a "whole new universe floats inside me" (235). In the remarks with which she takes her leave of Karin Ripplemeyer, to whom she is returning a husband, Jasmine conflates the Vishnu myth with a conceit that seems to derive from the reading she did as a child in India (40): "Like creatures in fairy tales" (like Alice-in-Wonderland, in fact), "we've shrunk and we've swollen and we've swallowed the cosmos whole" (240).

Thus India and Iowa parallel each other in curious ways. Like Jasmine, Bud Ripplemeyer has eight siblings. The size of the Ripplemeyer property (three hundred acres) bears a certain resemblance (allowing for scale) to the thirty acres of Jasmine's family in India. "The farmers around here," declares Jasmine, "are like the farmers I grew up with" (11). Pitaji's goring resembles Bud's shooting. Each country has its lunatic fringe, dreaming of—and committing—political violence.

This specular element may help the reader understand the folk saying to which the narrator refers on three different occasions: "The villagers say when a clay pitcher breaks, you see that the air inside it is the same as outside" (15). The pitcher breaks for Vimla (a woman in Hasnapur) when her husband dies; for Jasmine's father when he must leave his beloved Lahore forever (43); and for Jasmine herself when rape brings personal dishonor and deflects her from an intended self-immolation (120). Also depicted on the novel's original dust jacket, the pitcher is one's life, one's little world. However catastrophic the breaking of this vessel, the great world goes on, and the once-contained air returns to or remixes with the cosmic whole. In Hindu terms, individual *atman* rejoins collective *Atman*. Like the Western *pneuma* or *spiritus*, the Sanscrit word for the spiritual self has the literal meaning "breath," "air." But as Mukherjee's examples show, not every breaking of the pitcher is mortal; indeed, a pitcher breaks with any terrible accident or dislocation. By the same token, the contained air can be merely one's comfortable daily existence. After the rupture, one continues to exist, to breathe air that is in fact no different from what one breathed before. But when the act of emigration shatters, seemingly, the very foundations of the self, the sameness of the air in, say, India and Iowa provides little reassurance. The identical air is not what matters to the person whose sense of national identity—that frail vessel—is destroyed.

But Jasmine presents a special case, for her residual Indianness does not subvert her determined embrace of a new country; rather, specifically Indian habits of perception arm and enable her keen observations of American idiosyncrasy. The point seems to be the extraordinary cast American experience takes on as old world perspectives, however vestigial, give distinctive color to immigrant perceptions. Chief among these—for the immigrant from a Hindu culture—might be conflicted conceptions of mutability and permanence. Americans fully invested in the national myths embrace a paradoxical vision of cultural permanence only slightly qualified by the conviction that the future will always be better. But the newest Americans—especially those from ancient cultures such as India—do not so easily shake off their centuries-old fatalism. When Duff's mother decamps, when Harlan Kroener shoots and cripples Bud Ripplemeyer, when Jasmine herself runs out on Bud, when Darrel Lutz sinks beneath the weight of expectation and commits suicide, the author suggests that even the most materially well-to-do Americans are subject to a tide that can sweep them and all they own away. Ironically, moreover, such tidal change was always already part of the American vision.

The illusion of permanence breeds a dangerous complacency, an inability to imagine and respond to change, whether the kind of catastrophe visited on Bud Ripplemeyer or the perceived slippage that so exercises the paranoid "white Christian survivalists" (232) and other extremists who lurk in the narrative's Iowa periphery (195, 218). On this score, by the way, Mukherjee shows herself ahead of the cultural curve that would shortly bring the disasters of Ruby Ridge (1992), Waco (1993), and the Oklahoma City bombing (1995). Such people understand neither their fate nor its peculiar American character. They can*not* survive, they can*not* arrest the flux. America reprehends such rootedness. Those who refuse change must perish in the misguided attempt to ignore, defy, or freeze the national mutability. Having witnessed, in India, the "final phase of a social order that had gone on untouched for thousands of years," Jasmine evinces little sympathy for the dissolution of rural Iowa's relatively short-lived culture, its "baseball loyalties, farming, small-town innocence," its naïve enthusiasm for "the Hawkeyes—football or basketball." With eyes much older and wiser than those of the Shakespearean heroine she quotes, Jasmine notes change that only the old order finds incongruous: "In the brave new world of Elsa County, Karin Ripplemeyer runs a suicide hot line. Bud Ripplemeyer has adopted a Vietnamese and is shacked up with a Punjabi girl. There's a Vietnamese network. There are Hmong, with a church of their own, turning out quilts for Lutheran relief" (229). Mukherjee anticipates Jane Smiley's *A Thousand Acres* (1991), in which the Iowa scene is relentlessly dissected for its subsurface breakdowns, the hidden, emblematic horrors eventually revealed as incest and child abuse. Mukherjee, too, depicts the Iowa heartland as profoundly troubled—though more by drought and bad bank loans than specific human dereliction. Indeed, the land's afflictions suggest a familiar myth of natural and societal collapse: in this Iowa a "wounded god" (215) can do nothing to restore fertility. As this "secular god of Baden" (196), Bud Ripplemeyer is the local Fisher King, his neighbor Darrel the hanged man whose sacrifice does not fructify. Jasmine's fertility promises redemption for the Waste Land, but it must be realized in truly American terms: through dissolution, movement, perpetual alteration. The archetypal Iowa vision fades, giving way to a cultural checkerboard of Hmong and Vietnamese and Punjabi immigrants, all hungry to realize themselves in the endlessly vital America of tomorrow.

In the end, how does one read Jasmine's abandonment of Bud, her departure for California with Taylor and Duff? Has she learned America's least attractive lesson: that nothing lasts, that roots preclude mobility, that one should stay on the move? Or does she understand and embrace an authentic myth of possibility or promise? Sufficiently American to love her adopted country even as she holds the mirror up to its often disturbing reality, she at once laments and salutes the "fluidity of American character and the American landscape" (138). But come what come may, she will enter into this fluidity, embrace the myth of infinite possibilities for remaking the self.

No doubt the author intends certain ironic qualifications—some of them at the expense of her heroine, who can seem at times, as one's students occasionally argue, excessively dependent on the men in her life: father, brothers, Masterji, Prakash, Professorji, Bud Ripplemeyer, Taylor Hayes. She seems to need the approbation of even Darrel and Du. One must not miss, however, the series of resistant gestures this initially helpless (and illegal) immigrant makes: she withdraws over and over again from these men—walking out on Professorji's cozy little ghetto and abandoning Bud, the father of her unborn child. Half-Face, of course, she leaves in a pool of blood. Meanwhile, as character and as narrator, she treats women with considerable sympathy, forbearing to denounce the maternal dereliction of Wylie Hayes and empathizing with the unhappy Karin Ripplemeyer. At the same time, she salutes the strongest women in her purview: "Lillian Gordon, Mother Ripplemeyer: one day I want to belong to that tribe" (197). To pause over that last word, by the way, is to discover an interesting nuance—not so much the distant echo of Leigh Hunt ("Abou ben Adhem, may his tribe increase") as the denotative *archê*. Many Americans, associating the word with the "Indians" of the new world, may think briefly of the ways in which women and immigrants share their place at the cultural periphery with a generalized other, safely marginalized as primitive, "tribal." But Jasmine actually invokes a classical concept of community in her momentary vision of a venerable female "tribe": the word properly describes the familial and social groupings of ancient Rome. Words, too, make their way across oceans, and they prove as Janiform as human immigrants.

"Language," Mukherjee observes in *Days and Nights in Calcutta*, "transforms our ways of apprehending the world."[28] Thus her character Jasmine, paying close attention to the ways in which language shapes culture, characterizes Iowa as "a place where the language you speak is what you are" (11). This remark glances at the essential distinction between the native-born American monoglot and the immigrant who must learn one or more new tongues—each, presumably, the vehicle of a fresh identity. But if language speaks its speakers, as Heidegger and his followers asseverate, those spoken by more than one language receive lessons—perhaps disabling—in the tenuousness of the world around them. This thought, or something like it, leads Henry Park, the Korean American narrator of Chang-rae Lee's *Native Speaker*, to resist the idea that his American-born, half-white, English-speaking son should learn Korean; Park had hoped that the boy "would grow up with a singular sense of his world, a life univocal, which might have offered him the authority and confidence that his broad half-yellow face could not. Of course, this is assimilist sentiment, part of my own ugly and half-blind romance with the land."[29] But Mukherjee, however friendly to assimilation, knows that the linguistic and cultural unidimensionality of the increasingly neurasthenic Darrel and his Iowa kin betrays them into thinking of identity in naïve terms: they subscribe to a mistaken idea of the self and become the victims of a world in which failure to understand and accept the principle of universal fluidity precludes adaptation—even (indeed, especially) in the Darwinian sense.

This fluidity, along with the impermanence that is its corollary, seems to figure in the "weak gravity" that Taylor Hayes converts into a droll yet suggestive metaphor. Taylor jokingly characterizes weak gravity as "what keeps your dreams inside your head so they don't go flying about." It also "keeps Jase and Duff together . . . so they don't fly off the bed at night." Taylor's locutions encourage his listeners (and, momentarily, the reader) to imagine a discrete physical force, "weak gravity," with its own properties. As a physicist, however, Taylor knows perfectly well that there is no such separate force and that gravity, though relatively strong or weak depending on the mass of attracting objects, is by definition a weak force. But his conceit discovers an unexpected gravitas: "When you look around, weak gravity is everywhere" (178). Always already weak, gravity is unlikely to retard the catastrophe famously lamented by Yeats: the center cannot hold. Indeed, the purely gravitational attraction between individual human beings is nugatory, as Taylor himself will discover when Wylie, his wife, achieves escape velocity from the gravitational pull of home, hearth, husband. Soon Jasmine, too, will go spinning off from the familial orbit, having already learned that only weak gravity binds a person to her native country. Learning now to see America, also, as "fluid and built on flimsy, invisible lines of weak gravity," Jasmine comes to realize that she errs to think herself enough of "a dense object" to become "rooted" (179).

Even as Mukherjee quietly critiques American values, then, even as she concedes that the American ethos can become a juggernaut (to use an Indian figure) under whose wheels the weak must perish, she nonetheless registers the enormously creative vitality of a nation founded on the repudiation of every kind of fatalism. Thus she endorses her character's increasingly bold appropriation or forging of an American identity: out of the melting pot, so unsparing of old pieties, come newer, stronger alloys. *Pace* the apologists of multiculturalism, Mukherjee and her character mean to be assimilated, mean to shed their foreignness in that refining fire. Mukherjee's defense of assimilation does not, one must emphasize, mean erasure of the immigrant's original ethnicity. But in an interview with Runar Vignisson the author characterized "letting go of the old culture" as

> in some ways very healthy. The traditional attitude of white American sociologists as well as immigrants, European or non-European, is to say to lose one's original culture is sad, it's a loss, net loss. And I am saying No! In the case of Jasmine and in the case of me it's, again, we sometimes want to change. I'll always know who I am, the Indian is what shaped me as a child and as a very basic person. But there are many aspects of it that I want to throw out, many aspects of it that have fallen away whether I wanted them to crumble or not and that I think of myself as very much a new world citizen and that that's exhilarating. That energy that comes from being a pioneer is enormously invigorating.[30]

Jasmine, then, offers fresh and often startling views of America, its landscape, people, customs, and mores. Mukherjee deftly captures the viewpoint of heartlanders who view Jasmine and, by extension, all "foreigners" as wholly exotic. Although she ultimately embraces America and its fluidity, she registers the pain of Americans whose mobility is impaired. Both Bud and Darrel, the one paralyzed literally, the other figuratively, must deal with symbolic afflictions. Such characters (and others trapped by debt, drought, and bad crops) suffer from something almost as bad as what afflicts peasants in still feudal Punjab. They must, in the American scheme of things, be ground to pieces while others—first Du, then Jasmine—do the truly American thing: recognize that nothing lasts and light out for the territory.

In the end, seeing America steadily and seeing it whole, Mukherjee achieves her Sophoclean view. If she stops short of affirming that her adopted country is the *summum bonum* among nations, neither does she reproach it as the colonial or postcolonial imperium that some readers expect to see represented. As she remarked in another of the interviews contemporaneous with *Jasmine*'s publication, "Mine is a clear-eyed but definite love of America. I'm aware of the brutalities, the violences here, but in the long run my characters are survivors; they've been helped, as I have, by good, strong people of conviction. Like Jasmine, I feel there are people born to be Americans. By American I mean an intensity of spirit and equality of desire."[31]

4 ≋ Language, Dreams, and Art in Cristina Garcia's *Dreaming in Cuban*

"Find your roots, son. It's what everybody is doing these days."

—Salar Abdoh, *The Poet Game*

Immigrant writers display a proclivity for narrative fragmentation. In Achy Obejas's 1996 novel *Memory Mambo* the Cuban American narrator speaks of "creating a new syntax from the pieces of our displaced lives."[1] From Julia Alvarez to Sandra Cisneros, from Junot Díaz to Cristina Garcia, and from Amy Tan and Maxine Hong Kingston to Ty Pak and Theresa Hak Kyung Cha, immigrant and first-generation writers tend to arrange their narratives (especially first books) as linked stories or sketches, from varying points of view. They revisit the technique of modernist fragmentation from the naturally postmodern perspective of the marginalized, the cultural other. At the same time, they simultaneously invoke and deconstruct the modernist myth of a more ordered past, a *cultus quo ante*.

Immigrant writers also favor certain patterns in their subject matter. With the exception of an occasional Asian American writer (rooted in a culture whose Confucian deference to elders proves especially tenacious), the greater freedom that young people enjoy in America is a source of friction with their repressed parents. Alvarez, Danticat, Tan, Kingston, Garcia—all chronicle the generational clash, which marks both the death of the old culture and the definitive transition to Americanness. Often the struggle between a younger generation and its imperfectly Americanized elders concerns limitations to opposite-sex interaction among the young. The younger immigrants record with dismay or disgust their parents' failure to question benighted courtship codes and marriage customs brought over from the old country. Both Carlos Bulosan and Kingston embed cautionary tales about the fate of women who do not come to the marriage bed as virgins. Sophie Caco, the heroine of Edwidge Danticat's *Breath, Eyes, Memory*, speaks of a kind of "virginity cult, our mothers' obsession with keeping us pure and chaste."[2] The custom of displaying bloodstained sheets after the wedding night gets mentioned so often that one begins to resist, to suspect that these writers are not always above improving on more colorless and routine versions of the essential patriarchal imperative, female chastity. The alleged pre-diasporic ubiquity of this custom surely exceeds what Wilde's Lady Bracknell calls "the proper average that statistics have laid down for our guidance."[3]

When they do not bring such benighted customs with them, immigrants stumble into afflictions rooted in their new circumstances. In the fictions written by women, eating disorders figure with some frequency, for the immigrant often suffers from self-doubt as extreme as that which troubles her American-born sister in a culture wholly given over to artificial images of the female form. Danticat's Sophie suffers from bulimia, and one of the title characters of Alvarez's *How the García Girls Lost Their Accents* struggles with anorexia. Lourdes Puente, in Cristina Garcia's *Dreaming in Cuban*, alternately balloons and shrinks by a hundred pounds or so. Lourdes runs her bakery like a sweatshop, exploiting newer, more desperate immigrants, and this unsavory aspect of the immigrant ethos, this exploitation by one's own, also figures in such books as Bulosan's *America Is in the Heart* and Chang-rae Lee's *Native Speaker*.

Cristina Garcia, in her novel *Dreaming in Cuban*, avoids or transforms the clichés of immigrant storytelling. For example, she depicts the older generation, in the person of Lourdes Puente, as the one enjoying a largely untrammeled assimilation, while Pilar, Lourdes's daughter, idealizes the world they left behind in Cuba. This almost Shavian reversal provides an ironic frame for the more familiar features of their story, for, along with her frank acceptance of the new homeland, its language, its ways of making a living, and even its politics, Lourdes expresses a good deal of traditional immigrant dismay at her daughter's independence and perceived looseness. Both the flag-waving and the parental chiding infuriate the rebellious, punk-obsessed, and passionate daughter, a standard-issue American teenager with "enough attitude" to shatter every convention of polite society.[4] One of the most dramatic scenes between this daughter and mother involves the one's artistic representation of Liberty on the back wall of the other's Yankee Doodle Bakery. This episode, as will be seen, evokes contrasting yet ultimately integrated elements of the immigrant experience and immigrant vision. Liberty means different things to each character, yet Lourdes and Pilar experience a moment of solidarity when the picture is unveiled. Both have reflected on language without giving explicit thought to the cherished American freedom of speech. Here that freedom is enacted by Pilar and defended by her mother, who thereby reveals a grasp of American ideals that goes beyond the materialism she espouses and the anticommunism she frequently articulates. As Jamaica Kincaid once remarked, "I'm really glad I did come to America, which is a place that has allowed me to denounce it."[5]

Unlike Kincaid, who frequently denounces her native Antigua as well, Garcia presents a sympathetic—and subversively gendered—picture of the lost homeland. Written by a woman, and with a number of compelling women imagined in its pages, *Dreaming in Cuban* invites recognition of the female soul in what Castro and his revolutionaries insist on calling "the fatherland." As Maribel Ortiz-Márquez observes, "the text establishes a matriarchal succession that problematizes the masculine character of the discourse on Cuban national identity."[6] Thus the author transforms a patriarchy of dictators—Machado, Batista, Castro—into some primal motherland, the fresh green breast first glimpsed by the Spaniards and other Mediterraneans who arrived with Columbus. In time Cuba would come to resemble Yeats's Helen, who ran away with Paris and "later had much trouble from a fool"—that is, her husband.[7] Embracing a paramour from Moscow rather than Ilium, Cuba likewise must suffer tragically, stalked for years by her aggrieved American Menelaus.

Celia del Pino, most important of the characters who continue to live in Cuba, is herself a Helen briefly loved but never carried off. She appears at times the very incarnation of the island in all its seasons, a version of the ancient ceiba tree she visits in the Plaza de Armas at the heart of Havana (a single letter separates her orthographically from this tree, at once a symbol of Cuba and "a saint, female and eternal" [43]). Before the revolution, Celia chafes at religious and political constraints that translate personally to restrictive social codes, a husband disinclined to side with her against abusive in-laws, and physicians who pack her off to an asylum. Increasingly agnostic, increasingly left-leaning, Celia also registers—like the Cuban collectivity she embodies—the country's pervasive destitution, the appalling gulf between rich and poor, "the bare feet, the crooked backs, the bad teeth" (54), "beggar families from the countryside looking for work in the iron-fenced mansions of Vedado," and "smart couples in their convertible roadsters driving by without a glance" (98). Loathing Batista and, before him, Machado, she welcomes and supports El Líder (the never named Fidel Castro) but misses husband, son, daughter, granddaughters, grandson, and all the other exiles and emigrants they represent. In her vigil beside the sea, especially after her husband's departure, she resembles another of Cuba's female avatars, Doña Inés de Bobadilla, who governed the island "after her husband, Hernando de Soto, left to conquer Florida." Like Jorge del Pino, de Soto died abroad, leaving a wife "frequently seen staring out to sea, searching the horizon for her husband" (43).

The sea that surrounds Cuba recurs in this text, but what does it mean to immerse oneself in it, as Celia does early and late? To walk on it—as her dead husband does? To gather shells on a foreshore that, before a tidal wave, extends to the horizon? Many things have been characterized as "oceanic"—passions, religious feelings, the self in its mysterious depths, and maternity (the sea is our great sweet mother says Swinburne, its belly vast, undinal, says Hart Crane). Nearly half a century before she consigns herself to the sea, Celia writes to Gustavo, her Spanish lover, "I wish I could live underwater" (49). She describes heartache with a marine figure: "A fish swims in my lung" (37). Her affinity with the sea finds its definitive expression, however, in the Lorca poem she knows by heart and on one occasion reads aloud to her broken-hearted son Javier:

> Me he perdido muchas veces por el mar
> con el oído lleno de flores recién cortadas,
> con la lengua llena de amor y de agonía.
> Muchas veces me he perdido por el mar,
> como me pierdo en el corazón de algunos niños.
>
> (156–57)

"I have lost myself in the sea many times / with my ear full of freshly cut flowers, / with my tongue full of love and agony. / I have lost myself in the sea many times / as I lose myself in the heart of certain children."[8]

As the quotations from Lorca suggest, a delicate weave of allusion enables Garcia to project the pathos of Celia's defeats against the screen of twentieth-century Cuban American politics. Celia has indeed lost herself repeatedly in the hearts of her children and grandchildren—Lourdes, Felicia, Javier, Pilar, Luz, Milagro, Ivanito, Irinita. But she also loses their hearts. One daughter stumbles from lunacy into death; the other emigrates, bitterly repudiating her native land. Javier, the son, returns to Cuba only to become a drunk. Celia never even meets Irinita, who remains with her Czech mother, Javier's estranged wife. Luz and Milagro remain loyal to their derelict father, and Pilar connives at Ivanito's *huida*, or flight. Celia's failures with children and grandchildren seem to represent a cruelly ironic variation on older, prerevolutionary frustrations. The revolution itself, when it comes, progressively estranges her from those she holds most dear. One must, then, recognize her last swim, with its poignant surrender of the drop pearl earrings nearly always mentioned when she appears in the narrative (a gift from Gustavo, they symbolize her undying passion, her affinity with the "ocean blue"), as an act of despair, for the loss of daughter Felicia to death and grandson Ivanito to emigration saps her final reserves of moral strength. Her death literalizes the (unquoted) conclusion to Lorca's "Gacela de la Huida": "Ignorante del agua, voy buscando / una muerte de luz que me consuma" ("Ignorant of the water I go seeking / a death full of light to consume me" [Lorca 166, 167]). Tragically, neither personal nor political circumstances offer Celia any light in which to seek a transcendent immolation. Immersing herself in the sea, the insular element itself, she shares the "slow extinguishing" (244) of the pearls she consigns to its depths.

Though passionate about poetry and music, Celia may lack the sensitivity to language shared by other major characters. This alone dooms her in the eyes of an author who repeatedly suggests the importance of the medium by which human beings communicate. As Mary S. Vásquez has remarked, "language functions in *Dreaming in Cuban* as a measuring device gauging both affinity and distance."[9] Celia's granddaughter recognizes both the verbal and extraverbal amplitude of this medium. Quizzed by a psychiatrist about her paintings, Pilar declares: "Painting is its own language. . . . Translations just confuse it, dilute it, like words going from Spanish to English" (59). Thus she admires the work of a Dutch artist who "refused to title her paintings. . . . I mean, who needs words when colors and lines conjure up their own language? That's what I want to do with my paintings, find a unique language, obliterate the clichés" (139). Sensitive to verbal nuance, Pilar and a boyfriend "speak Spanish when we make love. English seems an impossible language for intimacy" (180). Her demented Aunt Felicia, by contrast, seeks to become a conduit for divine communication: as if to illustrate the Lorca line about "la lengua"—the tongue, language—"llena de amor y de agonía" (full of love and agony), the *santería* priests "made eight cuts on her tongue with a razor blade so that the god could speak" (187). Slipping into psychosis, Felicia perceives the words of her son Ivanito as "a code she must decipher, a foreign language" (81). Ivanito in turn "will never speak his sisters' language" (86), but Luz and Milagro, who despise "the cheap bead necklaces of words" spoken by their mother, discern in the "sagging eyes" of their father "the language we'd been searching for" (124).

Lourdes, Pilar's mother, embraces English. As she surrounds herself with North American trappings, naming her business the Yankee Doodle Bakery and dressing in red, white, and blue, Lourdes "welcomes her adopted language, its possibilities for reinvention" (73). Later, Pilar will want to tell her mother to give up trying to lecture the Cubans she encounters on their trip back to the island: "I pull my mother from the growing crowd. The language she speaks is lost to them. It's another idiom entirely" (221). Indeed, a considerable part of diasporic pathos inheres in the progressive breakdown of communication between Cuban and Cuban American. The author of *Dreaming in Cuban* knows at first hand the shrinkage or attenuation of any lingua franca between those who emigrate and those who stay home. With or without literal loss of the native language, "translation" becomes increasingly problematic.

But "literary language," as Carlos Fuentes once remarked, "is the language of languages,"[10] and literature has always demanded fluency in this or that sub-language of artistic convention. The novelist must master the language, the semiotic system, of realism or naturalism or symbolism or surrealism or metafiction—or, better, devise a local dialect, as it were, a hybrid idiom such as the magic realism of Gabriel García Márquez and Isabel Allende (the *real maravilloso* first described by a Cuban writer, Alejo Carpentier). Born out of the struggle to articulate, in various Latin American countries, a postcolonial vision, magic realism represents, in part, an imaginative reclamation of the history elided in the master narrative of colonialism. As Pilar laments, "there's only my imagination where our history should be" (138). This recognition lies behind the technique of *Dreaming in Cuban*, especially the occasional supernatural touches—the melting *santera* (160), for example, or the dead Jorge striding across the sea toward his wife and appearing repeatedly to his daughter, or the ability of certain characters (Celia, Pilar) to communicate telepathically or "remember" the future.

Even the three-word title of this novel plunges one into perplexities about competing languages. What is "Cuban," and how does one dream in it? Readers must reflect that the characteristic gestures and mores of any and every distinctive culture may be said to constitute a system of symbolic representation, a language. It is one thing to speak English or Spanish, another to know "American" or "Cuban." If dreams, too, are symbolic systems, as psychoanalysis affirms, the title would seem to announce the co-existence and problematic integration of languages that may share no common grammar or lexicon. There is always the danger that the natural estrangement of words and what they strive to represent will only be compounded when linguistic systems coexist and overlap. But one's sense is that the multiple languages here—the languages of art or literary convention, the dream language, "Cuban," and literal Spanish or English—function mutualistically to discover certain truths to those willing to undertake the mapping of one discourse upon another.

In any event, literal dreams also figure prominently in the signifying weave of Garcia's novel, adding an extra dimension, a glimpse of the Lacanian subject, the self as always already inaccessibly other. Jacqueline Stefanko sees here "a mixture of third person character-specific narrators, first person narrators, and epistolary interjections to convey the rich texture of subject positionalities and the multiple worlds where the subject of consciousness travels."[11] But Garcia takes an equal interest in the discourse of the unconscious, itself structured—as Lacan famously has it—like a language. Even Rubén Florín, the Peruvian student with whom Pilar briefly involves herself, has a "recurring dream" in which his girlfriend appears "in aqua robes threaded with gold, stepping through trapezoidal doors into the sun" (179). The dream proves transparent, an Inca fantasy, a Peruvian complement to the more complex dreaming in Cuban of the novel's viewpoint characters and narrators: Lourdes, Celia, Pilar, Felicia, Ivanito, Herminia Delgado. The dreams reveal affinities between and among characters—often, poignantly, between characters at odds with each other. Lourdes dreams that "the continents strain to unloose themselves" (17), as her mother, Celia, reflects on how "the continents pulled away slowly, painfully after millions of years" (48). Images of "women raped" (82) and otherwise abused out in the violent world (218) trouble the dreams of both Felicia and Celia, neither of whom knows consciously that Fidelistas had raped Lourdes. Lourdes's own dream of "thousands of defectors fleeing Cuba" (238) seems to complement that of Ivanito, who on the eve of joining a mass defection dreams of himself in a stampede on a runaway horse

(228). Pilar dreams of herself borne on an antlered throne (33–34)—much as her Aunt Felicia sits on a throne in the course of her initiation as "novice *santera*" (188). Felicia appears "in her bathing suit with her pail of cowries" (189) in a dream of Herminia Delgado, her playmate and *santería* mentor. For Felicia's mother, a similar "dream recurs. A young girl in her Sunday dress and patent shoes selects shells along the shore, filling her limitless pockets. The sea retreats to the horizon, underlining the sky in a dark band of blue. Voices call out to the girl but she does not listen. Then the seas rush over her and she floats underwater with wide-open eyes" (45). The child in Celia's dream is at once the daughter who collected shells on the beach before the great tidal wave of 1944 (a recurrent motif) and the dreamer herself, who foresees her own surrender to the whelming tide. Pilar, too, will envision Celia's open-eyed immersion. All of this Garcia frames in dreamlike strategies of approximation and intimation. She unfixes the action in time, taking her readers into and out of the past, into and out of her own dream.

Ambiguous, symbolic, and shrouded in indirection, dreams resemble poetry, for both evince what Wallace Stevens famously called the need to "resist the intelligence / Almost successfully."[12] Indeed, Stevens is an important presence here, as is Federico García Lorca (Felicia remembers the poetry of Lorca from her childhood, "recited as if in a dream" [109] by her mother). By turns breathtaking, whimsical, surreal, profoundly suggestive of the ways in which artifice helps one bridge the gulf between appearance and truth, these two poets happen also to represent something of the political and cultural agon that never ceases in Cuba, for the one is a Spaniard, the other an American; the one a martyred leftist, the other a sometime socialist who, like John Dos Passos, drifted far to the right.

Garcia has remarked that verse sets her mental stage: "I read poetry a couple of hours before I write. I wait for the images to appear or language or weird juxtapositions."[13] She has also mentioned that the poems of Stevens remained on her desk throughout the writing of the novel and that she took from him her working title, *Tropic of Resemblances*.[14] Surviving as a kind of pentimento in the epigraph, the phrase derives from the 1947 poem "Someone Puts a Pineapple Together," in which Stevens contemplates a fruit so exotic that it drives his speaker to a frenzy of comparisons. Called "this husk of Cuba," the pineapple sits on its table, resembling "a jar of the shoots of an infant country" or "a venerable urn."[15] Written twelve years before the Cuban revolution would see the birth of an infant country out of the ashes of an old, corrupt one, the poem constantly, magically glosses Garcia's novel and its images. As readers familiar with Stevens might expect, the poet invokes imagination, a "third planet," as license to devise a series of twelve analogies. The "exfoliations" thus introduced (hut, genii emerging from bottle, yesterday's volcano, coconut and cockerel, humped owl, and so forth) are the poem distilled, in miniature, the promised "profusion of metaphor" fully realized. The poet salutes the pineapple in fanciful image after fanciful image—until the scrutinized object seems to embody metaphor itself (as the sphinx, in Hegel's formulation, symbolizes symbolism).

Its epigraph, then, invites readers to understand *Dreaming in Cuban* as a similar series of analogies, metaphors, and resemblances that realize or at least adumbrate the contested island as it figures in the Cuban American imagination. Again, the Stevens poem provides the gloss: "Here the total artifice reveals itself / As the total reality." Garcia further invokes Stevens's third planet as part of the trinity imagination/memory/truth. Felicia represents one facet of imagination: she teaches her son Ivanito that it "can transform lies to truths" (88). Celia wonders "what separates suffering from imagination" (101). Pilar, thinking about the way her mother "rewrites history," eventually concedes that perhaps "in the end the facts are not as important as the underlying truth she wants to convey." This, Pilar recognizes, is what the artist also does: "I'm guilty of a creative transformation or two" (177), she remarks, recalling how she had painted a punk Statue of Liberty within sight of the original.

Joyce called the artist a priest of eternal imagination, and in *Dreaming in Cuban*, Cristina Garcia undertakes, for another land riven by political strife, something very much like the forging of an uncreated conscience contemplated by Stephen Dedalus. Pilar, her sometime narrator and authorial surrogate, proceeds in the course of her story through more than one artistic calling. A painter early on, she later takes up the string bass, and one imagines her eventually turning to the art of writing, mining that register hidden "in the lining of her winter coat," the diary in which she "records everything" (7). On the occasion of Pilar's birth in 1959, her Abuela Celia ends the custom of writing a monthly letter to her long-lost lover Gustavo because this granddaughter "will remember everything" (245). In 1980, the year of Pilar's majority, Celia will give her granddaughter the diary-like collection of unsent letters to Gustavo, and the reader knows that Pilar will soon experience the literary vocation for which she was destined all along. Like *Portrait of the Artist, Dreaming in Cuban* ends with intimations that the viewpoint character closest in age and situation to the author will presently begin to write the novel one has just read. But unlike Joyce, who wrote as an exile, Garcia writes as an emigrant, and the cultural anatomy she essays ultimately concerns her new nation as much as her old.

Along with the letters to Gustavo, Celia gives Pilar a cherished volume of Lorca, whom she had heard and seen at a Havana lecture series in 1930, the year of her own thwarted majority. Indeed, Garcia highlights the already fervid passions of her characters through patterns of allusion, and from epigraph to closing pages, poetry and other arts figure importantly here. Art at once springs from and promotes the imagination, and for this author art fosters the imagining of Cuba and the Cuban diaspora at the same time that it provides a complex and subtle means of spanning the exilic gulf. Allusion functions with great elegance to situate or characterize the taste and passion of characters such as Celia and her granddaughter Pilar. Thus the author places considerable emphasis on Pilar's painting and on what Celia feels for the poetry of Lorca and the music of Debussy (the playing of which husband and physicians forbid, owing to the "rashness" [8] it might unleash in her). She associates the Debussy piece "La Soirée dans Grenade" (from *Estampes*) with her leftist lover Gustavo, a native—like Lorca—of Granada. The repression of her violent feelings never quite succeeds, and even as an old woman with a chance to interrogate Pilar's I Ching, Celia asks, "Should I give myself to passion?" (231)—the passion, that is, to be free of the old, circumscribed life. Always striving to outlast the rigid constraint of an ancient patriarchal order, she dreams of herself (and later asks to be painted) in flamenco costume because the dance is so strongly associated with passion—and with Granada. As passionate, restive, and rebellious as her grandmother, Pilar, too, yearns for the freedom and sensuality flamenco embodies. But Celia never learns the dance, and Pilar will take only one flamenco lesson before her censorious mother (always closer, temperamentally, to her faux-Yankee father than to her restless mother) terminates their classes.

Pilar finds her Debussy in Lou Reed, Iggy Pop, the Ramones, and the rest of the punk rock scene. Whatever one thinks of her taste, the choice of musical fare highlights a rebelliousness that, seeking to transcend commonplace resistance to a seemingly unimaginative parent, strives to engage the larger issues of identity and class dynamics that British culture critic Dick Hebdige has so rigorously dissected. With particular reference to the punk ethos and aesthetic, Hebdige notes the proletarian bias in the "youth subcultures" whose "emergence . . . signaled in a spectacular fashion the breakdown of consensus in the post-war period."[16] The accouterments of punk—the chains, straps, safety pins, even swastikas—all announced a thoroughgoing refusal of everything the middle class holds sacred: "These objects become signs of forbidden identity, sources of value" (3). Further, these "mundane objects"—Hebdige mentions the safety pins a number of times—"take on a symbolic dimension, becoming a form of stigmata, tokens of self-imposed exile" (2). Hebdige's terms seem made to order for any analysis of Pilar, always tempted to think of herself as having a "forbidden identity": more Cuban than American, "exile" rather than immigrant, and star—as Adriana Méndez Rodenas remarks—of her own family romance.[17] Pilar, that is, unconsciously enacts a classic self-ennobling fantasy of fosterage: some day she will reclaim the natal palace and royal parents of a Cuban identity.

Pilar's adolescent truculence finds expression in her cynical commentary on the American immigration myth embodied in that cherished icon the Statue of Liberty. More than the embodiment of America and the freedom that flourishes here, Liberty is supposed to be, in Emma Lazarus's words, the "Mother of Exiles," the emblem of immigrant desire. But whatever their lip service to the famous lines engraved at the base of that monument ("Give me your tired, your poor, / Your huddled masses yearning to breathe free, / The wretched refuse of your teeming shore"), too many Americans seem to agree with the notoriously xenophobic, even racist lines penned in 1895 by Thomas Bailey Aldrich: "O Liberty, white Goddess! is it well / To leave the gates unguarded?"[18] Framed as a piece of quasi-infantile punk disruption, then, Pilar's subversive painting of the Statue of Liberty offers a trenchant critique of the myth reified in the great colossus of New York Harbor:

> That night, I get to work. But I decide to do a painting instead of a mural. I stretch a twelve-by-eight-foot canvas and wash it with an iridescent blue gouache—like the Virgin Mary's robes in gaudy church paintings. I want the background to glow, to look irradiated, nuked out. It takes me a while to get the right effect.
>
> When the paint dries, I start on Liberty herself. I do a perfect replication of her a bit left of center canvas, changing only two details: first, I make Liberty's torch float slightly beyond her grasp, and second, I paint her right hand reaching over to cover her left breast, as if she's reciting the National Anthem or some other slogan.
>
> The next day, the background still looks off to me, so I take a medium-

thick brush and paint black stick figures pulsing in the air around Liberty, thorny scars that look like barbed wire. I want to go all the way with this, to stop mucking around and do what I feel, so at the base of the statue I put my favorite punk rallying cry: I'M A MESS. And then carefully, very carefully, I paint a safety pin through Liberty's nose.

This, I think, sums everything up nicely. *SL-76*. That'll be my title. (141)

Pilar is never more the author's surrogate than in this painting, which functions as *mise en abîme*. As the novel unfolds in narrative fragments, moving backward and forward in time, being told now in third person, now in first, so does the painted image dismantle or disfigure Liberty's familiar features. All the details of the picture invite comment: the blue background, the black stick figures like barbed wire, the pledging gesture, the torch beyond her reach, and—least subtle—the safety pin, by which the artist intimates a world of ironic reservation. Pilar mentions that she has adopted the Virgin's iconographic blue, as if to hint like Henry Adams that in America a secular female archetype occupies the place consecrated, in Catholic countries, to the Virgin. The torch beyond her reach may remind readers and viewers of the Browning line "A man's reach must exceed his grasp, else what's a Heaven for?" In other words, humanity ennobles itself in reaching for, not possessing—in the pursuit, not the having—of happiness. Yet, unable to grasp what she reaches for, this Yankee version of supreme female sanctity seems to fall short of the ideal she supposedly embodies. If in reaching for that torch of freedom or knowledge she ends up giving a fascist salute, that, too, is part of the point about American compromise, the excesses bred by American hubris. Hand over heart, the American Virgin may sing the national anthem or pledge allegiance—or merely cover her breast like a good Puritan. Pilar specifies, incidentally, that her figure makes the pledging gesture with the *right* hand. Unless the painter has the wrong hand reaching for the torch (the *left*), the verbal description contains a perhaps meaningful absurdity, a hint that Liberty is somehow torn between conservative allegiance and the reaching for something finer.

The number in the painting's title, *SL-76*, refers most obviously to the year 1976, when the country was immersed in the endless self-congratulation of its bicentennial observances, but Pilar may also intend (or get credit for) a reference to the 76 Club in Burton-on-Trent, where in that same year the Sex Pistols performed "Anarchy in the U.K." and other songs. In giving Liberty a safety pin through the nose, Pilar anticipates (as she notes with delight) the outrageous Jamie Reid cover of the Sex Pistols' 1977 single "God Save the Queen" (177), with its similarly accoutered Queen Elizabeth (the pin is actually through the lip). The point, as is common in punk culture, is to refuse and to shock—yet also, paradoxically, to claim. Both Pilar and the Sex Pistols mean to appropriate the very emblems that would exclude them, and each subverts an anniversary—bicentennial, queen's jubilee—celebrated ad nauseam. Thus Pilar seeks not so much to desecrate the icon as to interrogate it, to hint that freedom may herself be hemmed in or interdicted by the barbed wire of convention and custom and ethnocentricity.

Pilar's picture anticipates two later visions of her grandmother. In the first, the artist paints Celia as a flamenco dancer. At first she paints her in red, expressive of Celia's passionate nature, but "mostly . . . I paint her in blue" (233), the color so infinitely varied in Cuba. This true Marian color, suited only to the background of the Liberty painting, seems iconographically right for an unconventionally saintly grandmother. Neither artist nor subject, each an iconoclast in her own way, would be distressed if anyone were to bridle at the conceptual incongruity of the Virgin as flamenco dancer. In Pilar's second, unpainted vision, she imagines Celia "underwater, standing on a reef with tiny chrome fish darting by her face like flashes of light. Her hair is waving in the tide and her eyes are wide open" (220). Here Pilar at once foresees Celia's eventual surrender to the sea and transforms the dead woman into something rich and strange, an alternative, submarine Liberty and, withal, an embodiment of Cuban independence—still on watch, as it were, against invading *gusanos* and Yankees. Insofar as Garcia projects herself as Pilar, one recognizes this valedictory image of Celia as the author's final, complex symbol of the Cuba she left at the age of two: tropical, submerged, vigilant, mysteriously beautiful, whelmed, yet still, perhaps, to be reborn out of some post-Castro sea, a Caribbean Venus Anadyomene, another Virgin, another Yemayá, another Liberty. Ultimately, this vision and the painting it echoes rehearse the two faces that freedom must always wear for the Cuban American. It also represents the submersion, the sinking into the preconscious, of the immigrant's links to the old country.

Having emigrated as a child, Pilar naturally romanticizes the homeland and the remote grandmother with whom she associates it. "Even though I've been living in Brooklyn all my life, it doesn't feel like home to me. I'm not sure Cuba is, but I want to find out" (58). Thus she embarks on what

Bharati Mukherjee calls "that most American of impulses, or compulsions, a 'roots search.'"[19] Her first attempt at "going south" (24) thwarted, Pilar and her rabidly anti-Castro mother eventually return for a visit and discover, as Thomas Wolfe's Eugene Gant does, that one cannot go home again. Pilar encounters the general shabbiness of Cuba, experiences its inadequate plumbing, tastes its wretched food, even gets herself bloodied in the street action by which a few desperate souls seek to get themselves out of the country. Pilar's complicity with her cousin Ivanito's emigration—knowing, as she does, how devastating it will be to their grandmother—hints at a mature recognition of Cuba's political reality, though this epiphany must be discerned within another, which concerns an answer to the question of identity: "I know New York is where I belong—not *instead* of here, but *more* than here" (236). Of course this recognition that she cannot achieve what David T. Mitchell calls "an essentialist core of identity and knowledge"[20] will never assuage the desire to shrink the political and cultural distance that belies the mere thirty minutes' flight that separates her nation from that of her grandmother.

It is important to recognize the looming but never named event toward which this story moves. Garcia expects the reader to remember that the April 1980 occupation of the Peruvian embassy, which she describes, was prelude to a yet more sensational occurrence that figures here only when "Lourdes dreams of thousands of defectors" who "board ferries and cabin cruisers, rafts and fishermen's boats" (238) to escape from Cuba. Between April and October 1980, in fact, some 150,000 Cubans would take part in a mass exodus: the Mariel Boatlift. In omitting any direct reference to this episode, Garcia demonstrates an advanced understanding of the principle of economy articulated by the famous American writer who made his home in Cuba for many years. Hemingway showed that the literary artist gains power in not naming what can be understood without being made explicit: "the dignity of movement of an ice-berg is due to only one-eighth of it being above water."[21] The reader encounters Garcia's economy, her instinct for omission, in small matters as well as great. I have previously noted the importance of the unquoted conclusion to Lorca's "Gacela de la Huida." Although Stevens's "Someone Puts a Pineapple Together" is a presence throughout the novel, only two lines are quoted—and paratextually at that. I conclude with a last, charming example—one in which Hemingway himself figures. Pilar mentions that the legendary author and her grandfather "used to go fishing" together (179), but when she remarks that she was named for Hemingway's yacht (220), the reader smiles at her apparent nescience regarding a more suggestive nominal antecedent: the heroic figure in *For Whom the Bell Tolls*. This Ur-Pilar, a great bulwark against fascism in the Spanish civil war, illustrates the iceberg principle with particular cogency, for in her Cristina Garcia (who would name a daughter Pilarita) summons to her side, as powerful intertextual presence, another version of the grandmother so passionately sought by this novel's most heritage-hungry character.

5 ≋ Korean Connection

Chang-rae Lee and Company

It is painful to be consciously of two worlds.

—Mary Antin, *The Promised Land* (1912)

Americans brought up on standard myths of immigration generally think of the "huddled masses" as victims of oppression, injustice, or terrible poverty, expelled from what was for them paradise poisoned—if not hell itself. The title character of Nora Okja Keller's *Comfort Woman* (1997), for example, makes her way to America only after escaping from a Japanese military brothel. But some writers, less interested in chronicles of victimization than in explorations of the human heart in extremis, examine more flawed immigrants, expelled or fleeing from places where they have committed sins of varying originality. Like Marlowe's Mephistopheles or Milton's great anarch or Jiro Kurohata, the Japanese soldier of Chang-rae Lee's *A Gesture Life* (1999), they carry hell within them. Lee's novel complements Keller's, for Jiro Kurohata—who becomes Franklin Hata—makes his way to the United States after serving as a medical officer responsible for keeping a small band of hapless Korean women healthy enough to "comfort" large numbers of his fellow soldiers.

These two fictions represent especially probing engagements with the tragic complexity of the exilic self, a theme that also figures in Chang-rae Lee's superb first novel, *Native Speaker* (1995). By way of introducing an in-depth discussion of this text, I first consider briefly the ways in which in-vestigations of Asian American difference in *Comfort Woman* and *A Gesture Life* come to center on images of dismemberment and disarticulation, that is, the breaking-up of body, psyche, language, expression, and voice. Con-sideration of these elements will, I think, facilitate analysis of *Native Speaker*, perhaps the finest of the novels scrutinized in this book.

Keller's novel seems much more engaged in trying to recover a Korean past—that of the previous generation as well as something more ances-tral—than in parsing the grammar of new American identity, but because of the motifs it shares with the fiction of Lee (and, incidentally, that of Theresa Hak Kyung Cha), it merits at least brief mention here. A journal-ist who immigrated in childhood, Keller interleaves the Honolulu present of a Korean American mother (the just deceased Akiko, born Kim Soon Hyo) and daughter (Rebecca) with pictures of the mother's past, which in-cludes a tough childhood in a Korean village and a tougher adolescence as one of the hapless *jungun ianfu*, or "comfort women," forced into prostitu-tion by the Japanese in World War II. Keller paints a particularly disturb-ing picture of the life led by these unfortunates. As will be seen, Chang-rae Lee filters their suffering through the viewpoint of a sensitive soldier, but Keller, risking sensationalism, presents the more immediate perceptions of the women themselves. Indeed, she offers an impassioned apologia for women's experience, women's communication, women's spirituality, and women's anguish. Thus *Comfort Woman*'s two narrators, Rebecca and her mother, Akiko, say little about the men with whom they interact. Although the author salutes a husband in her acknowledgments, she seems to make a point of denying narrative prominence to any of the male figures in the lives of Rebecca and Akiko. The reader knows only that Rebecca has or had a lover named Sanford and that Akiko's missionary husband (Rebecca's father) bore the surname Bradley. The other men who figure here—a cen-sus would include faceless Japanese rapists, a couple of callous doctors, a funeral director, and one or two individuals associated with Rebecca's school—are wholly peripheral and largely unattractive.

At the center of her narrative Keller places the near-legendary figure of Induk, whom the Japanese rename Akiko. A thinly disguised personifica-tion of Korea itself, she rebels by denouncing her oppressors, "bellowing the Korean national anthem,"[1] and otherwise making herself a living re-proach: "In Korean and Japanese, she denounced the soldiers, yelling at them to stop their invasion of her country and her body. Even as they mounted her, she shouted: I am Korea, I am a woman, I am alive. I am seventeen, I had a family just like you do, I am a daughter, I am a sister" (20). The outraged soldiers martyr her gruesomely. When they do not bury their victim, her spirit is left to wander as a *yongson*, or "ghost of a person who traveled far from home and died a stranger" (140). It enters her successor, who also inherits the generic Japanese prostitute name, Akiko, by which she will be known for the rest of her life. The new Akiko begins her service in the camp before experiencing her first menstruation. Presently passing the menarche and becoming pregnant, she undergoes a brutal abortion, then escapes. With the help of a half-Christianized old Korean woman, she makes her way to the asylum of a missionary establishment in Pyongyang, where she meets the American who will become her husband. Throughout her ordeal, and on through the rest of her life, this Akiko looks to her predecessor, Induk, as personal tutelary spirit. Indeed, Induk retains her place as first among various strong female figures who keep the second Akiko going through an arduous life that will end with her widowed years in Hawaii, where she develops a reputation—to her daughter's frequent embarrassment—as local sibyl.

The most affecting part of this story lies not in the harrowing account of forced prostitution but in the feelings Akiko experiences at the birth of her daughter, sired by a multilingual American missionary whose lust, though channeled through marriage, links him unforgivably to the Japanese rapists who credited the people of Korea with "an inherent gift for languages, proving" that nation "a natural colony, meant to be dominated" (16). Now Akiko insists on her idea of a language centered on the body, not the Logos: "Each night, I touch each part of her body, waiting until I see recognition in her eyes. I wait until I see that she knows that all of what I touch is hers and hers to name in her own mind, before language dissects her into pieces that can be swallowed and digested by others not herself" (22). This is the "language I know is true" (21), "the language she understands" (18), in part because touching was the only valid language between Akiko herself and—especially near death—her own mother. Keller postpones until quite late in the story the revelation of Akiko's original Korean name, Kim Soon Hyo, and until later still its meaning, which provides a final grace note to the theme of a wordless maternal language of touch: Soon Hyo means "the true voice, the pure tongue" (185). By implication, there is a language of the father, Lacan's Symbolic order in effect, as well as a preverbal language of the mother, which resembles Kristeva's Semiotic or Chora.

Theresa Hak Kyung Cha, another Korean American woman who resists patriarchal language, also imagines a mother-daughter subversion of the Symbolic order. In her strange 1982 book DICTEE, in fact, she seems to invoke the *Nom du Père* itself—

IN NOMINE
le nom
nomine[2]

—and to posit against its notorious "Non" a resistant, affirmational "Oui [We] de la Mère." Organizing various semiotic discontinuities to this end, Cha becomes a latter-day, feminist, postcolonial version of Hieronymo, the Thomas Kyd character Eliot invokes at the end of another great and subversive arrangement of fragments, *The Waste Land.* "Why, then, I'll fit you," declares Hieronymo, who proceeds to write a play in which each character speaks a different language. Cha similarly writes DICTEE in a mélange of English, Korean, and French, with Chinese and *hangul* characters interspersed. From this text, as hybridized as its author, issue varied images of the mother-daughter relationship: Demeter and Persephone, Mnemosyne and the Muses, and Cha herself and her own mother, born in Manchurian exile and long forbidden to speak Korean. Cha's mother shares a name—Soon Huo—with Keller's Akiko (the variant letter represents, as I understand it, only a transliterative vagary), and like Keller the author of DICTEE associates mother, mother country, and the Korean language as sites of resistance to patriarchal and imperial hegemony. "Mother tongue is your refuge," says Cha.[3] Announcing this theme in a characteristically cryptic fashion, the *hangul* graffiti that appear in the illustration facing the title page of Cha's novel, as Chung-Hei Yun explains, were "chiseled on the wall of a mine in Kyushu, Japan, by a young Korean performing forced labor." Yun translates the lines as a secular "de profundis clamo a te": "I want my mother; I am hungry; I want to go home."[4] The book that starts this way will meditate brokenly on those dismembered and disarticulated aspects of the same entity, the Korea—mother and home, mother and mother country—from which history exiles both Hyung Soon Huo and her daughter, Theresa Hak Kyung Cha.

Language, exile, and dismemberment figure, too, in Chang-rae Lee's *A Gesture Life.* The author, who immigrated with his parents at the age of three, presents Franklin Hata, a Japanese of Korean extraction living out his last days in the United States. Affluent and recently retired from a medical supply business, he strives to be the perfect citizen of his pleasant community. Hata's fine house, which he maintains with scrupulous attention (constantly fending off unsolicited offers from would-be purchasers), is a central symbol—of himself and his respectability fetish. When he accidentally sets fire to it, he half admits to a suicidal wish, for his apparent serenity is really affectlessness, something closer to despair.

Before his retirement, a romance had fizzled with a well-to-do Caucasian woman. Unsuccessful, too, has been his adoption of a mixed-race daughter who came to despise him because, as she observes, "You make a whole life out of gestures and politeness."[5] The reader wonders why Sunny so dislikes her father, and Lee, who favors a kind of riddling manner, declines to make plain the grounds of her animosity. Is one expected gradually to see a monster beneath Hata's decent surface? The answer, we are eventually made to see, lies in the past. Predating even the abortion Hata obliged his daughter to undergo when she became pregnant in adolescence, Sunny's resentment and anger become the symbolically appropriate reflection of one man's terribly impaired soul.

Sunny's curtailed pregnancy does, however, take its place within a pattern. Far too indirect to say it, Lee expects his readers to know that a fetus is often dismembered, chopped to bits, during an abortion. This pregnancy and its late termination rank with other dismemberments, other moments of violently canceled or thwarted fruition. Before settling in the United States, Hata had served during World War II as a medical officer in the Imperial Army of Japan. Stationed in Burma, he was responsible for medical supervision of some Korean women the Japanese had forced into prostitution. He falls in love with one of these "comfort women," who attempts to conceal a pregnancy that evidently antedates her servitude. His failure to save Kkutaeh from her fate is harrowing, not least because he is himself Korean by birth. (Though adopted in early childhood by a Japanese couple and seeing himself as wholly Japanese, he is—because he can still understand Korean—uniquely susceptible to the laments of the forced prostitutes.) Kkutaeh is eventually raped and murdered—chopped to pieces—by the soldiers of Hata's unit.

Hata too is "chopped up," but his dismemberment is cultural. His original Korean surname had been Oh, thought to be of Chinese origin (244). The author mentions (235) but does not reveal Hata's Korean first name. His Japanese name, Jiro, is intriguing because it is the traditional appellation for second sons in Japan. Never commented on directly, this detail suggests that the Kurohatas were childless because of the death of a natural son (who would have been an Ichiro, as first sons are named). In addition to his more obvious hauntings, Hata would seem to have an effaced foster brother, a shadowy, fully Japanese ghost self, like the stillborn twin in Wendy Law-Yone's *The Coffin Tree*—or, closer to home, the aborted sibling of his grandson, Thomas (the name means "twin"). When he gathers up what remains of Kkutaeh, he finds a tiny homunculus that is in some strange way his own fetal self, a little Korean untimely ripped from his first home.

The dismemberment continues. Hata's name in America has been chopped out of the original Japanese surname Kurohata. His adoptive Japanese family was descended from apothecaries who took their name from the emblem that announced the need for their services. "Hata is, literally, 'flag,' and a 'black flag,' or *kurohata*, is the banner a village would raise by its gate in olden times to warn of a contagion within. It is the signal of spreading death" (224). Thus the loathsome Captain Ono, in the Japanese military camp in Burma, sardonically makes a black flag the signal that Lieutenant Kurohata, his underling, must attend or guard the woman the senior medical officer seems to have chosen for his personal concubine (223–24; ironically, the lieutenant's growing obsession with Kkutaeh proves merely to replicate that of his superior). That flag seems to be one of the few mementos still in the possession of "Doc" Hata half a century later. His daughter stumbles upon it (147, 222), and on one occasion he fantasizes Kkutaeh wearing it.

What I find striking about this novel (it follows *Native Speaker*, which features somewhat more familiar anxieties of assimilation) is its subtle reframing of the great American conceit of the melting pot. Not comfortably Korean, Japanese, American, or Chinese, Franklin Hata is a casualty of the twentieth century. Like the butler in Kazuo Ishiguro's *Remains of the Day*, he can never, however disciplined, escape the ugliness he has witnessed and—it is hinted—been complicit in. Always already a container of multitudes, Franklin Hata passes through more than one version of the refiner's fire without ever emerging as either ethnic *prima materia* or American alloy. Indeed, none of the familiar metaphors for America's racial mix—melting pot, mosaic, salad—helps to conceptualize the vexed identity of this exile. Rather, Lee intimates, one must imagine some such figure as a membrane stretched over chopped and broken shards—their edges constantly threatening rupture. Such a condition, however painful, has little to do with "postcolonial" postures of victimhood; indeed, Lee focuses on the complicity of this immigrant in acts of victimization in another life.

But in the end the author imagines his character as to some degree reconciled with his daughter, who allows him to play a part in the life of the child, his grandson, that she carries to term and raises alone. Hata also makes certain "gestures" of restitution and reconciliation. He will sell his splendid house and anonymously relieve some of the misery in his immediate purview. He notes "the first fallen leaves of the imminent season" (354) and knows that little time remains, that he will presently enter the yellow leaf and sere. Readers may think of the heartrending lines of Rilke's *Herbsttag*:

> Wer jetzt kein Haus hat, baut sich keines mehr;
> Wer jetzt allein ist, wird es lange bleiben,
> Wird wachen, lesen, lange Briefe schreiben,
> Und wird, in den Alleen, hin und her,
> Unruhig wandern, wenn die Blätter treiben.[6]

"Who has no house now will never build one; who is alone now will long remain so, will watch, read, write long letters, and will wander restlessly to and fro in the avenues, amid the rustling leaves." Having disposed of the house that was one version of his very identity, Hata will resume his wandering, perhaps "to land on former shores." He "will circle round and arrive again. Come almost home" (356). These lines, with which the novel concludes, hint at *nostos*, a return—but they leave in doubt the destination. Japan? Korea? "Home," after all, is for Hata (owing to the circumstances of his childhood) a kind of absconding signified, the entity—only approximated by "Japan" or "Korea"—from which he is estranged by the symbolic order of an entire century of bloodshed and displaced populations. But the ambiguity here, so typical of Lee, also allows the reader to think that Hata will eventually "circle round and arrive again" in America—not a place of perfect fulfillment, perhaps, but a place of second or third or fourth beginnings, where essential decency can still prevail over a dreadful and bloody past. The immigrant's America: almost home.

Immigrant as Spy: *Native Speaker*

Every immigrant knows a season (at least) of the limbo described in Matthew Arnold's famous lines: "Wandering between two worlds, one dead, / The other powerless to be born."[7] Henry Park, the narrator of Chang-rae Lee's *Native Speaker* (1995), finds himself awkwardly situated, early and late, between Korean and American identities. One thinks of "hyphenation"[8] as enabling resistance to subalternity within a "melting pot" rigged always to produce the same kind of alloy, but it delivers no such benefit to Park, who finds himself unhappy on both sides of the hyphen. His stateside birth notwithstanding, he cannot with confidence be American, much less Korean, and thus he engages in a lifelong struggle with the implications of hybridity. "My citizenship," he remarks, "is an accident of birth, my mother delivering me on this end of a long plane ride from Seoul" (310). Born on a cusp, as it were, he embodies a paradox of double consciousness, his Korean self a kind of ethnic pentimento beneath the American. Park lives a distinction at once deterministic and supremely artificial: how could it matter whether his birth takes place before takeoff, during flight, or upon landing? In this small detail the author inscribes difference that is essentially—and ironically—American: few if any other countries grant automatic citizenship to all persons born on the national soil. At the same time, however, the circumstances of Park's birth point to the difficulty of separating nature from nurture in the realm of ethnic identity. Called "Marble Mouth" by peers who have never had to struggle with "a garbled voice," a "bound tongue wrenching itself to move in the right ways" (218), he goes to elementary school with an imperfect ability to speak English; he reaches maturity with a similarly imperfect knowledge of Korean. Nor can he read the language of his parents.

If, as an adult, he speaks English perfectly, the trained ear—that of his wife, Lelia, for example—can nonetheless detect in his pronunciation the vestige of an alien linguistic cunabula. But this trace is not what his wife refers to on the scrap of paper Park finds under their bed after she has left him. On it she has written "False speaker of language" (5), part of the more elaborate list of reproaches she presents to him at parting. This particular epithet seems especially to resonate with the novel's title, *Native Speaker*, which one initially understands as referring to a familiar standard of linguistic mastery. Immersed in the story, however, one discerns a kernel of ambiguity in the phrase, which can also refer to any hapless Caliban who dutifully learns the language of the colonial master. This secondary meaning implies, moreover, a betrayal of something inborn or "native," presumably the special vantage of an untrammeled national identity.

Like an avant-garde poem, the list his wife leaves with him appears as a column of suggestive, fragmentary characterizations, an inchoate catalogue: "You are surreptitious / B + student of life / first thing hummer of Wagner and Strauss / illegal alien / emotional alien" (5), and on through a total of seventeen lines. Postmodern rather than modern, it resists a reader's desire for some totalizing psychological or moral profile. These fragments cannot, it seems, be shored. One recognizes extra postmodern dimensions in what Park does with the list:

> I . . . make three photocopies, one to reside permanently next to my body, in my wallet, as a kind of personal asterisk, I thought, in case of accidental death. Another I saved to show her again sometime, if I wanted pity or else needed some easy ammunition. The last, to historicize, I sealed in an envelope and mailed to myself.
>
> The original I destroyed. I prefer versions of things, copies that aren't so precious. (4)

·Only the second of these purposes seems straightforward or transparent. A spurned spouse naturally fantasizes about future phases of recrimination: "You called me an 'emotional alien!' " But why a "personal asterisk" copy? Park may have in mind something like the strange power and poignancy of what investigators found in the wallet of the martyred President Kennedy: a scrap of paper with a suggestive line—slightly misquoted—from Shakespeare's *King John:* "They whirl asunder and dismember me" (3.1.330). Perhaps, like his father, Park evinces "that small man's folly of sometimes seeing himself in terms historical" (127). Though he calls himself only "the most prodigal and mundane of historians" (16), Park pauses from time to time in his narrative to sketch, as minor motif, a concern with historicity and historical consciousness. The desire to "historicize" that list, in any event, suggests that one ought to situate Park's gestures and remarks within a theoretical economy. In the suggestive circularity of the third copy's transit through the postal system, Lee casually adds a hitch or two to the Gordian knot constructed by Lacan (who asserts that a letter always arrives at its destination) and Derrida (who objects that the postal system figures the signifying chain, its "letters" merely one more illustration of signification's Ponzi scheme). Lacan "reads" Poe's purloined blackmail letter as the signifier or information unit that acquires meaning according to who writes it, fears it, seeks it, receives it. Derrida, mischievously characterizing Lacan's premise as essentially structuralist and logocentric, sees more meaning in the postal system than in the arbitrary units it shuffles. Indeed, the circular journey of the document that Park puts into the mail will rehearse the circularity of language itself, the Symbolic order. But in Park's rationale for posting that third copy of the list to himself, Lee hints at a Jamesonian corrective—"always historicize!"—to the basic language game of poststructuralism. Park evidently realizes that time will furnish him with fresh lists of who he is. If, like the unconscious (in the Lacanian formula), identity is structured as its own Symbolic order, "who he is" must prove as fluid as any other sign system. A postmark, however, will tell him when he was *this* list.

Copies without an original. These documents define or complement much about a life lived at an unclosable distance from authenticity, a life given over to the simulacra of identity. The author's technique here bears a certain resemblance to that of Don DeLillo, who delights in sly manipulation of the categories—"basic reality" and "image"—that constitute Baudrillard's grammar of the simulacrum. As DeLillo gives us atheistic nuns, a mosque that was once a "Moorish" movie theater, a band playing "live Muzak," or a Pakistani who "might be Peter Sellers,"[9] so does Lee present a character who, in effect, impersonates himself. As a private investigator, that is, Henry Park adopts his personal background, experience, and situation as cover: "I was employing my own life as material for my alter identity" (168). The joke extends beyond the obvious fact that Park's cover covers almost nothing (except the crucial element: why he seeks to associate himself with the "subject" in the first place), for it presents an essential thematic point that, like Poe's purloined letter, is hidden in plain sight: Park, a cultural hybrid, cannot ever "be himself" because that essence called the self is in him impossibly splintered.

Having been sentenced to a problematic subjectivity, a life of invisibility, an existence as ethnic other, Park makes his living in domestic espionage. His job, in fact, becomes the novel's basic metaphor for life as a hyphenated American. He is a good spy precisely because he seems in his own eyes not to be assimilated. "Americans generally made the worst spies," declares his boss. "Mostly he meant whites" (160).

Mon Semblable, Mon Frère

Not unique to Chang-rae Lee, the metaphor of alien as spy figures also in a work by Salar Abdoh, an Iranian American. An actual espionage novel, *The Poet Game* (2000) may be of momentary interest here because immigrant writers seldom devote themselves to popular forms (Andrei Codrescu represents an exception—and the example of Joe Porcelli will be adduced presently). The protagonist of Abdoh's novel, Sami Amir, is an Iranian spy, son of an American mother. No ideologue, Sami drinks alcohol and despises "Koran wavers," and in fact he works for The Office, a shadowy Iranian espionage organization keeping its eye on the main Iranian spy outfit, Section Nineteen. Working against the fundamentalists, who stand to gain if a terrorist incident takes place in the United States (the novel was published after the World Trade Center bombing, but before 9/11), Sami must outwit a Pakistani explosives mastermind and tangle with Libyans, a rogue American arms dealer, and (the love interest) a beautiful exotic dancer enamored of Middle Eastern causes. Though the story does not foreground its politics (Sami and his colleagues seem scarcely more appealing than the fundamentalists they seek to thwart), the author slyly includes the occasional glimpse of Western decadence through the Middle Eastern eyes of his hero. At one point Sami stumbles from a violent and sinister encounter with rival agents into the opening of an avant-garde art show: stacks of bricks, studiously banal photographs of a "small white terrier," and "plaster penises with crosses filed into stakes driven through them."[10] Thus, too, he meets the exotic dancer, Ellena Giorgione, at an S/M bar. A fellow agent, she also writes poetry, which Sami sees only when some torn-off scrap swims into his ken. Drawn to this verse, Sami finds it similar, in its ambiguity and reticence and incompleteness, to espionage. Like spy practices themselves, however, the conceit of a "poet game" remains obscure. The story reveals with great clarity, though, a sense of the layered paranoia that spies share with immigrants such as Salar Abdoh—or Chang-rae Lee. Both present protagonists with a knack for betraying their own.

Indeed, Lee's Henry Park succeeds at his work largely because he is willing to exploit in others the vulnerabilities that trouble his own alterity. Repeatedly characterizing himself as invisible (6, 188, 493) and struggling to define the degree of his assimilation (which he simultaneously resists and desires), Park understands what a Richard Powers character calls "the creed of all immigrants: stay quiet, learn all you can, and keep to the middle of the room." Central to the creed: "succeed, adapt, evade."[11] A person of few class or ethnic loyalties, Park spies on his own, especially "foreign workers, immigrants, first-generationals, neo-Americans," including exchange students, resident aliens, and others who may be troublesome in their countries of origin, for instance, anyone "supporting some potential insurgency in his old land, or else funding a fledgling trade union or radical student organization. . . . Maybe a writer of conscience. An expatriate artist" (16). Park ingratiates himself with these individuals in precisely the way he has attempted to establish himself as both dutiful Korean son and legitimate American. "An assimilist, a lackey. A duteous foreign-faced boy" (149), he has sought always to be "a good son, good boy, good citizen, assuring authority" (193). But Park admits also to an "ugly immigrant's truth": that like his father before him (50), "I have exploited my own, and those others who can be exploited" (297). Here and elsewhere, he observes glumly that taking advantage of one's fellow immigrants is the appalling norm, and late in his story a colleague will suggest quite plausibly that the charismatic Korean American politician whose staff Park has infiltrated has been exploiting him as well: "Could it be that the honorable John Kwang is deceiving you, Parky, and not just the other way? Is it possible that through all of your genuine respect and admiration, he is using you?" (271).

"The narrative of the ethnic secret agent," according to Crystal Parikh, "must grapple with both the historical conditions that produce racial meanings and the ethical responsibilities of personal agency and accountability."[12] Park's acts of espionage unfold in social and personal settings that illustrate this pronouncement. "Our mode at the firm was always to resist history, at least our own" (25), declares the narrator. "History," he elsewhere asseverates, "is not a human expression" (228). But of course history has a way of asserting itself as the frame for the acts of "personal agency and accountability" that Parikh speaks of. As undercover investigator, Park tends to get too close to subjects such as John Kwang and, before him, the "Filipino psychiatrist . . . Emile Luzan" (19), whose observations proved perspicacious even though he remained unaware of what had brought this particular "patient" to his office. Park had faltered disastrously in the assignment with Luzan, telling the therapist a great deal about his actual psychological condition and including even the heart-wrenching death of his son (such opportunism would be unforgivable if the genuine therapeutic value were not so much at issue). As Tina Chen observes: "Henry metamorphosizes from impersonating Luzan's patient to actually *becoming* Luzan's patient. The psychiatric sessions take on an air of cathartic confession as the initial irony of Luzan's promise to his 'patient'—'You'll be yourself again'—is supplanted by the literalization of such an occurrence."[13] Luzan flags for Park the issues of "parentage, intimacy, trust," as well as "the larger one of where we live . . . and who you are within that place. Or believe yourself to be. We have our multiple roles like everyone else. Now throw in an additional dimension. A cultural one. Cast it all, if you will, in a broad yellow light" (124). A figure of modest wisdom, a kind of Filipino Tiresias, Luzan hints, in that last figure, at both traditional Eurocentric perceptions of Asian skin color and the cowardice that prevents

Park from quitting his loathsome calling as professional betrayer, the very incarnation of bad faith (at the same time, the therapist suggests illumination warmer than "the whitest raw light" [1] cast by Lelia's list). Luzan also echoes Ellison's Invisible Man, who observes that "if you don't know *where* you are, you probably don't know *who* you are."[14] But where Ellison's generic pronoun—"you"—remains stable, Luzan's does a suggestive shuffle, from "where *we* live," through "who *you* are" and "*we* have," to "if *you* will." (As will be seen, however, the novel as a whole executes a great sweep from the pronoun of isolation to the pronoun of inclusion.) Although Park thinks himself perfectly capable of the "multiple roles" the therapist speaks of ("I had always thought that I could be anyone, perhaps several anyones at once" [127]), they in fact compound the inner division that afflicts him, making yet more problematic the wholeness he desires.

At the same moment that he dodges an opportunity to reflect on his role as son, Park describes for Luzan an elaborate early fantasy about an imaginary or "invisible brother." Readers may recognize a variant of Fa Mu Lan, the narrator's heroic alter ego in Kingston's *Woman Warrior*, in Park's vision of sibling perfection:

> I described . . . his walking before me in the schoolyard, stamping the black-top, announcing our presence with his swagger, his shout. He knew karate, kung fu, tae kwon do, jujitsu. He could beat up the big black kids if he wished, the tough Puerto Rican kids, anyone else who called us names or made slanty eyes. The white boys admired him for his athleticism, how far past the fence he could send a kick-ball. The white girls were especially fond of him. He often kissed them after school, in front of everyone. He knew all about science, about model rocketry, chemistry sets, baseball cards, about American history. He was the lead in the school play. He spoke a beautiful singing English. He made public speeches. My mother and father were so proud of him. He was better than everyone. He was perfect. (191)

Part of the effectiveness of this vision lies in its indirect chronicling of a whole universe of puerile socialization. By implication, Park himself can claim none of these distinctions, nor, sadly, can he see (even now, perhaps) that such perceptions of personal inadequacy are by no means limited to immigrant children. As an adult, Park will meet versions of the more successful and accomplished brother in both Eduardo Fermin and John Kwang.

But before considering how at least one of the text's brothers proves also and more significantly a father (or double), one may pause over Park's dream sibling and note, in passing, his fictive realization in the work of another Korean American novelist. Joe Porcelli's *The Photograph*, which appeared just two years after *Native Speaker*, concerns the experiences of a refugee who, adopted by an American family, goes on to realize various clichés of immigrant achievement before a harrowing encounter, on a battlefield in Vietnam, with the brother he had left behind in Korea. Himself an immigrant (he came from Korea as a child in 1954), Porcelli guilelessly represents displacement as the perfect opportunity for self-realization. Essentially a romance, the novel alternates between the sensational and the sentimental. Its first third, devoted to the hero's initially idyllic, then brutal childhood in Korea, takes place in the period 1950–1954 and reads like a Korean *Painted Bird*. Adopted by an American army officer, who takes him home to Charleston, South Carolina, the young immigrant swiftly and with surprisingly little difficulty comes to terms with the new homeland that he perceives as "one huge banquet, a continual feast of the senses."[15] Bok Chang Kim—now "Joe Rutledge"—appears as a confident and accomplished adolescent who seems never to have experienced any real difficulties with the new language or the prejudices of its speakers. In the third part, Joe returns to Asia to fight in Vietnam, where he meets—and kills—the fraternal shadow self that took a different route out of the Korean War. In the end, the Leviathan that was Vietnam spits him out, an Ishmael, the lone survivor of his Special Forces unit.

Yet the reader knows that he will return to his fashion model girlfriend and a future in Charleston society. In fact, Joe's experiences in two wars bracket a coming of age in America largely untroubled by the puberty, alterity, and familial discord experienced by Lee's more realistic character, Henry Park. (By the same token, John Kwang first comes to the United States "as the houseboy [i.e., not the adoptive son] of a retiring two-star general" [*Native Speaker* 196].) Rather, the American life of Joe Rutledge recapitulates precisely the narrative that Chang-rae Lee characterizes as Henry Park's childhood dream of empowerment. As if guided by this fantasy, Porcelli depicts a character who becomes wholly American with remarkable ease. Translated to the United States (and more specifically to Pat Conroy–land), the former Bok Chang Kim swiftly achieves success at school and in athletics. Deciding against Harvard, he attends his adoptive father's alma mater, the Citadel. Although the book's finest line reflects his understanding of racism, which he characterizes as "ancient without being honorable, automatic without being instinctive" (188), such prejudice as he encounters never seems particularly strong—or, rather, seems directed at others (notably his family's black servants), who suffer worse than he. Looking on racism with cold eyes, he easily rises above it, such are his gifts, his confidence, his knowledge of worse things. "Weighed in the balance with the savagery from whence he had emerged, he gauged everything by a different standard. American discomforts, anxieties, hardships and fears were viewed through distinctly altered lenses" (143). He knows, however, that the racial anxieties of his neighbors may include him, and on the Battery (Charleston's exclusive waterfront neighborhood) he declaims: "This is mine! . . . And I'm yours! We earned each other!" Confident and undaunted, he shouts: "Stand by, you pack of magnificent bigots! I'm here to improve your bloodlines!" (142).

In real life, of course, brothers turn out less like Joe Rutledge and more like Eduardo Fermin, who shares with Henry Park a false filial relationship with John Kwang. In Eduardo, Lee recapitulates and critiques the ideal of fraternal agency introduced as Park's childhood fantasy. A fine singer, an exemplar of immigrant or first-generation striving, a tireless worker for the politics of inclusion, Eduardo is Park's rival in at least two senses: he is Kwang's "favorite" (134), and he, too, is a spy. Like Park, he has infiltrated the political organization—indeed, he may be another employee of Glimmer & Company.

Lee's themes exfoliate with maximum irony, however, in the depiction of the relationship between Park and the man he and Eduardo stalk and betray. "When you met him in person," says Park, "you somehow felt . . . that you were the faintest brother to him" (129). But more than a brother, Kwang is the classic psychological double, and Park recognizes in himself an "outlying version" (129) of the politician. When campaign personnel rehearse for a public appearance by their principal, Park reports, "I played John Kwang" (92). The grief-stricken father of Eduardo Fermin suggestively mistakes Park, paying a condolence visit, for the man who sent him (241). Commenting on "that expression of his, all wisdom and sincerity," Jack Kalantzakos observes, "Sometimes I think you'll look like him, Parky, in fifteen years or so" (33). Park initially observes that "Kwang was around my height, maybe five-ten or so" (123). The narrator's subsequent recognition that the older man is in fact shorter by "two or three inches at least" (125) foreshadows other diminutions for both the politician and his secret sharer.

In investigating and spying on Kwang, Park investigates, spies on, and betrays himself. In time he learns that "in every betrayal dwells a self-betrayal, which brings you that much closer to a reckoning" (292). This modest epiphany clarifies an earlier, enigmatic observation: "Through events both arbitrary and conceived it so happened that one of his faces fell away, and then another, and another, until he revealed to me a final level that would not strip off. The last mask. And what I saw in him I had not thought to seek, but will search out now for the long remainder of my days" (131). What Park recognizes here—something beyond the peculation, the venereal appetites, the complicity in the deaths of Eduardo Fermin and the janitor, Helda Brandeis—at first baffles the reader. The language of this cryptic intimation rises to a kind of tragic intensity, and in fact Park's insight amounts to nothing less than anagnorisis, especially as that term was once glossed by the English essayist Thomas De Quincey: not just "recognition" but "recognition of identity."[16] In Kwang's final mask, then, Henry Park discovers his own face. But how strange the idea of a final *mask*. How could a mask be final? What lies beneath? How could one's deepest self bear the visage of another? The insight seems predicated on a Lacanian view of the ego as merely a site from which to experience perpetual yearning for an illusory psychological wholeness. In affirming that he will henceforth continue the pursuit of self-knowledge, Park seems half to recognize that his problems with identity lie not in the accidents of birth or ethnicity but in subjectivity itself, problematically situated amid imagoes or masks that periodically displace or supersede one another.

Ultimately, delving into the rich humus of the ego's layered compost heap, Park undertakes a version of the night-sea journey chronicled in the poem that supplies *Native Speaker*'s epigraph, Walt Whitman's "The Sleepers." The lines quoted are obscure, as broken in their movement as that of the somnambulist who speaks them:

> I turn but do not extricate myself,
> Confused, a past-reading, another,
> but with darkness yet.[17]

Henry Park has his first extended conversation with the woman he will marry "among the sleepers" (12) in a public park; late in the story he describes sixteen-year-old Chun Ji-yun, injured and comatose after being in a wreck with Kwang, as "the pretty sleeper" (299). Like the Shelley poem that also figures here, "The Sleepers" speaks obliquely to the self-exploration and "past-reading" that Lee's narrator undertakes. Where Shelley's poem momentarily evokes "one in slumber bound," Whitman's catalogues a whole world of sleepers (including immigrants, a catalogue within the catalogue), among whom the speaker wanders, perhaps dreaming himself. Here the night figures the unconscious, the unknown, and death. The speaker embarks on a descent into the self and the self's fears of the night in all its guises, literal and metaphorical. These fears are dispelled at dawn as the poet imagines making peace with darkness and waking to fresh purpose, harrowing knowledge now part of his armamentarium.

As undertaken by the narrator-protagonist of Lee's novel, such introspection may lead to some better understanding of the self or selves sketched in Lelia's cryptic list: "genre bug / Yellow peril: neo American / great in bed / overrated / poppa's boy / sentimentalist / anti-romantic" (5), and so on. Some insights, however, are reserved to the reader, who may discern, for example, that the "anti-romantic" trait refers less to a general outlook than to Park's disagreeable experience with a certain poet. Like Jamaica Kincaid's Lucy, obliged to memorize a British poem about daffodils (presumably Wordsworth's "I Wandered Lonely as a Cloud"), Park has somewhat painful memories of having to recite "Peanut Butter Shelley" whenever he made pronunciation mistakes in grade school:

> Till, like one in slumber bound,
> Borne to [the] ocean, I float down, around,
> Into a sea profound, of ever-spreading sound.
>
> (217)

These lines, from the verse drama *Prometheus Unbound* (2.5), are spoken by Asia, the very embodiment of Henry's ethnicity. Though its author contemplates the world's seemingly intractable evil, including its political form, the poem ultimately concerns prospects for resurrecting the somnolent moral sense and casting off tyranny. As Harold Bloom observes, "Shelley at this point in his career clung to a faith in the capacity of the human mind to renovate first itself, and then the outward world as well."[18] Thus the poem features a famous affirmation of ethnicity transcended, of humanity "equal, unclassed, tribeless, nationless" (3.4.195).[19] Its author imagines the self's prospective deliverance in terms that might, under different circumstances, inspire or comfort a student chained to the rock of grade-school pedagogy and suffering, Prometheus-like, the contumely of a classroom despot.

The poet's moral vision finds its unlikely echoes in John Kwang's probing remarks about the sources, within the self, of both prejudice and its remediation. By the same token, Kwang's speech about recognizing oneself in the ethnic other makes its own ironic comment on the assimilationist drama enacted by Park. The politician characterizes the racism of intraghetto populations as "the problem of self-hate" (140). "Who are they, those who know no justice, no fairness; do you know them? Are they familiar?" (141). Striving to bring together a fractured constituency, he urges his ethnically Korean, Dominican, Puerto Rican, Chinese, Southeast Asian, Indian, West Indian, Central American, and east European audiences to see that "the problem is our acceptance of what we loathe and fear in ourselves" (141). This persuasive analysis goes far toward explaining the divided character of Henry Park, who suffers a kind of internalized racism, the inner Korean at odds with the American—and both at odds with the Korean American. Yearning for psychological integrity, yearning to be truly Korean or truly American or truly some healthy, untroubled hybrid, Henry Park must perforce despise a self perceived as mongrelized. This sentiment emerges most poignantly in his reflection on the outward appearance of his son Mitt (a name surely intended to evoke "Mutt"—as in fact it does among the boy's playmates [96]). One realizes here that Mitt is among the story's doubles, another site or body for the drama of assimilation. Remembering him as a newborn, Park thinks of his pain when Lelia wondered out loud about how little of herself she can see in the child. Thinking "she wished he was more white," Park subsequently recognizes this shameful, half-conscious wish as his own: "I was the one who was hoping whiteness for Mitt" (265).

Elsewhere Park reproaches himself for such "assimilist sentiment" (249). Yet language itself sometimes signals ironic forms of assimilation, as one sees in Park's account of the racial epithet "gook." The term comes, he thinks, from the Korean War, where GIs kept hearing "Mee-gook! Mee-gook!" or "Americans! Americans! 'Mee-gook' means America" (226).[20] As an Asian American, then, Park can say "Me, Gook" in both senses of the word. The irony of the bilingual pun subsumes the whole landscape of ethnic division and prejudice, even as it denies their grounds. Thus when Park, in his valedictory, salutes his wife's thoughtful pronouncing of her students' names, he seems to have recognized something of Kwang's implicit formula for social, cultural, and political harmony. Park articulates a kind of ideal: they immigrate least painfully whose sociocultural difference suffers the least violation. By implication, America realizes itself most perfectly in its willingness to accommodate that difference.

All the King's Horses . . .

When he first hears about his assignment with Kwang, Park calls up casual perceptions, from "media photographs and video," of "an ambitious minority politician and what being one had always meant—the adjutant interest groups, the unwavering agenda, the stridency, the righteousness" (129–30). But Kwang proves far less predictable, for he seems at once to understand and to resist these un-nuanced versions of political purpose. On a couple of occasions Kwang ruefully notes the backlash complaint against certain unimaginative exercises of identity politics, the resentful perception "that this country has difference that ails rather than strengthens and enriches" (256). Thus Kwang constantly seeks to diversify his constituency, knowing the strength that will flow from inclusivity. (In his more rigorous understanding of the political imperative, Kwang may be said momentarily to mirror the author himself, for as a "minor" writer—in the Deleuze and Guattari sense—Chang-rae Lee must also rise above restrictive expectations predicated on the narrow demands of identity politics. In the event, he fashions a work that, never reductive, eschews any and all such easy posturing, especially the tonalities of "stridency" and "righteousness.")

One of this book's strengths is the way it avoids taking its political subject for granted, as merely a plausible frame for a drama of troubled identity. Dallying with Sherrie Chin-Watt, less than scrupulous with the enormous *ggeh* that is evidently something of a pyramid scheme, and complicit in the death of Eduardo (290), Kwang is at last exposed to public opprobrium when he survives the car crash that badly (perhaps fatally) injures the sixteen-year-old girl in his company. If Kwang proves less than the political and moral exemplar for which his community takes him, his downfall remains strikingly archetypal in national terms, for it recapitulates that of the American public figure, especially the politician, brought low by the revelation of poor judgment, bad character, racism, and, above all, womanizing: one thinks of Earl Butz, of James Watt, of Trent Lott, of Bill Clinton with Monica Lewinsky, of Wilbur Mills with Fanne Foxe, and of course, given the accident with a youthful female companion to whom he is not married, of Teddy Kennedy at Chappaquiddick.

Less obvious, perhaps, is the rewriting, from a fresh perspective, of Robert Penn Warren's *All the King's Men.* The narrator of that novel, Jack

Burden, lives again in Henry Park. Both characters interact with a woman on the staff of the politician with whom they associate, and both chronicle that politician's rise and fall. Like Willie Stark, John Kwang is an idealist who surrenders to the temptation to let ends justify means (notably in the death of Eduardo). Believing that "everyone has a secret," Willie Stark sends Burden out to expose whatever his enemies have to hide; in Lee's novel this premise provides the rationale for Glimmer & Company (Park's employer), and it is the politician whose secrets the narrator must ferret out. In a strange way the two narratives converge in their Oedipal dynamics. Judge Irwin, who commits suicide when Burden exposes him to obloquy, turns out to be Jack's natural father. When Stark is assassinated, Jack loses yet another father. Similarly, Henry Park interacts with John Kwang (and Emile Luzan before him) as surrogate for the father from whom he is sundered by assimilation.

Notwithstanding these affinities—and notwithstanding the prominence of the John Kwang subplot—it is important to recognize the subtlety with which Lee has subverted the usual "politics" of identity. That is, from one point of view this work belongs to the sub-genre of political novels—*The Last Hurrah* or *Primary Colors*, as well as *All the King's Men*. With great originality, however, the author of *Native Speaker* allows the politics of politics (vote-getting, fund-raising, interest-group-placating) and the politics of identity to overlap or coincide. Though he weaves together the personal and the political, Lee avoids the more hackneyed and predictable postures of alterity. Readers see the drama of vexed assimilation from both the intensely personal perspective of Henry Park and the highly public perspective of the Korean American politician John Kwang. As Park acts out this drama in bedroom and kitchen and workplace, Kwang acts it before crowds and cameras, masses and media. In the end, as Park recognizes himself in John Kwang, the reader understands the travail of the ethnic other in a powerful new way: not, finally, as some narrow political pursuit of "empowerment" but as the intensely personal struggle to cease being an alien in one's own eyes and in those of the less recently arrived of one's fellow Americans. One aspires, observes Park, "to enter a place and tender the native language with body and tongue and have no one turn and point to the door" (310).

Even as he notes how he answers this definition of the native speaker, Park asserts that he has achieved its "darkest version" (310). He hints, further, that only those willing to enter into a dubious compact with American political pragmatism can hope to achieve the true American "fluency."

Insufficiently ruthless, John Kwang fails, ironically, to meet this standard. He loses in his bid to become the Korean American Willie Stark and so lays himself open to a peculiarly American form of ignominy: whatever their democratic and egalitarian principles, whatever their sympathy for the underdog, Americans respect only winning. Kwang's defeat, however, seems not to lie in the crossing of certain moral boundaries. Even if his acts prove as reprehensible as those of Teddy Kennedy, Richard Nixon, or a host of lesser American politicians, Kwang remains unsuited, at the deepest level of his character, to survival on the tangled bank of American politics. Indeed, one keeps expecting Henry Park to declare Kwang "worth the whole damn bunch of them"—various sordid revelations notwithstanding. Nor does this element exhaust the affinities with *The Great Gatsby:* here, too, the most compelling moral drama is that of the narrator, not the towering figure at center stage. Like Nick Carraway, Park has reached "his early thirties" (85), and Lee's narrator, like Fitzgerald's, might well say, "I'm five years too old to lie to myself and call it honor."[21] Fitzgerald allows his reader to see that for all his talk of standing at moral attention, Nick Carraway has himself been compromised. One makes the related point about Park somewhat differently: though morally flawed, he may yet prove capable of more ethical behavior, but for now, emerging untouched from the collapse of Kwang's fortunes, he bitterly recognizes in himself qualities that make him, he fears, at once a true American and a less than good man.

When the list of supporters without green cards that he compiles for Kwang ironically facilitates an Immigration and Naturalization Service roundup (305–6), Park must face his responsibility for the fate of the illegals. He sees the circles of betrayal widen, and the author critiques the postmodern doxa of the simulacrum to which he has seemed, in the imagining of immigrant consciousness, to subscribe. In the end, the "copy" that falls into the wrong hands is no simulacrum; it "represents" real people who will now suffer real deportation. What especially disturbs one here is the way these plot developments enact the price of "becoming American." Only by some such terrible betrayal of one's blood and instincts and primal identity, only by some adaptive, deeply hypocritical xenophobia, Lee implies, can one become a "native speaker" in the extended symbolic sense the novel proposes and explores.

But always one must historicize. The reader who does so may recognize in the events recorded here a version of the choice traditionally made by every generation of immigrants, however blessed with light skin and round eyes. Each must repudiate—often, as one sees among the immigrants who rebelled against George III, through acts of literal treason—the "native" blood, the "native" self. Some such recognition may have prompted old Park's renaming himself "George Washington Park." That he "never once used" (203) the name, however, suggests the larger failure really to assimilate. By contrast, the son has long since ceased to call himself by his Korean name, and the news that he has one comes as something of a surprise to the reader. When John Kwang addresses him as "Park Byong-ho shih," it becomes a momentary interpellation from a lost world: "I stop. I always freeze for a second on hearing my Korean name" (273).

In the son's struggle for autonomy, Freud meets and bests the Eastern ethic of absolute deference to the father ("as long as you can, you will please the father, the most holy and fragile animal" [285]). To some degree, Park gratifies his sense of filial *pietas* in his dealings with a surrogate father, John Kwang, whose Confucianism the younger man seems to perceive as unproblematic. Park admires "his secular religion of pure hierarchy, his belief that everyone is at once a noble and a servant and then just a man. Its adherents know no hubris. Instead this: you simply bow down before those who would honor you. You honor them back. For you are but ash to their fire. All spent of light" (137–38). But this same Confucianism, in its filial guise, hovers reproachfully over and threatens to scuttle Park's achievement of Americanness. With his own father, a "low master" (47) who never ceased being "a Confucian of high order" (6), Park rebels, decrying the hierarchalism and the straitjacketed familial roles of the paternal ethic: "I know all about that fine and terrible ordering, how it variously casts you as the golden child, the slave-son or daughter, the venerable father, the long-dead god" (6). All the fathers must be betrayed if one is to become a native speaker or American, and in fact the Oedipal drama extends to the relationship with John Kwang, too, for the politician, "slightly younger than my father would have been" (23), is also naturalized, also a paternal presence. It extends even to Mitt, whose vocabulary, before his seventh birthday, includes the word "motherfucker" (104).

Thus Lee offers his readers a psychoanalytic insight into the dynamics of achieving a new national identity. After all, the ethnically problematic self has as its local template the imperfectly Americanized parent, and Park's generational struggle subsumes a host of confused feelings toward the father who, having sacrificed and achieved so much, remains unforgivably an immigrant cliché: the shabby fruit-and-vegetable shopkeeper with his broken English, his killer hours, his exploitation of other immigrants, and his unreflective racism ("we believed in . . . shooting black people" [52–53]). Though he makes a great deal of money and moves to West-chester, the father remains—worst of all—deeply *foreign*, and the American in the son perceives the father's failure to have been born on these shores as irremediable. Yet the Korean in the son honors the father, who becomes something more at his death: an ancestor.

If never perfectly resolved, the conflict of Oedipal and Confucian dynamics here eventually gives way to a vision of the long-alienated self edging toward equilibrium with an emergent national community. Not by accident, then, do the novel's first and last sentences complement each other across 324 pages. The first ends with "who I was" (1), the last with "who we are" (324). Mary Jane Hurst rightly says that the closing sentence "conveys a sense of tragic optimism for the future as it captures with great beauty the linguistic diversity of America at the end of the twentieth century."[22] More broadly, however, the story has at this point modulated lyrically and elegiacally from past to present and from first-person singular to first-person plural. At the outset, Park represents himself as locked in solipsistic confusion, and freshly estranged from his wife—always, according to John C. Hawley, associated with "the traditional idea of America. Park's on-again, off-again relationship with Lelia nicely parallels his ongoing interrogation of his place in American society."[23] At the end husband and wife seem reconciled, and together they take leave of a group of multiethnic children they have helped with speech difficulties. Lelia takes the trouble to pronounce their names carefully, and the moment becomes a small, moving epiphany for her husband and the reader: "she calls out each" child's name, "taking care of every last pitch and accent, and I hear her speaking a dozen lovely and native languages, calling all the difficult names of who we are" (324). The "we" here is powerful, for Park not only recalls his own early difficulties with the English language but also recognizes that he, his white wife, and these children are a part of the great mosaic or quilt of American identity.

Part of the poignancy of this ending derives from the affection that Park and his wife show to their little pupils: "We both hug and kiss each one" (324). Tim Engles suggests that "Henry's emblematic embrace at novel's end of the children of immigrants, connecting as it does with repeatedly sympathetic depictions throughout the novel of various struggling immigrant workers, recalls in its celebratory, sentimental sweep . . . the Whitman of his story's epigraph." But Engles resists any such "warm, fuzzy, White-man-ian embrace of immigrant masses" as the narrator's uncritical response to the interpellative summons of a tendentious ideology: "Lee's final irony . . . is that Henry, believing that he has finally shed his culturally imposed mask of reticent inscrutability, has merely donned another, through which he expresses the distanced affection of liberal pluralism for the struggling masses seeking purchase in America's melting pot."[24] Yet one resists the assertion that the author means to treat with irony his character's Whitmanesque gesture (which implicitly announces that Park himself may "contain multitudes"). Such an argument misses an important consideration or two. Remembering his own acquisition of English as an arduous and at times painful passage to America, the narrator sees himself in these children. At the same time, of course, every child he embraces becomes, momentarily, his own dead son (who had perished accidentally when, at his seventh birthday party, playmates piled on top of him). "When I embrace them, half pick them up, they are just that size I will forever know, that very weight so wondrous to me, and awful" (324). Park's understated recognition that these children are roughly the age at which his own child died is almost unbearable to the reader. Symbolic siblings, these other children of different or mixed ethnicity must themselves, like Henry Park before them, survive being smothered by little Americans.

That Mitt dies on his seventh birthday suggests the intertextual presence of a moving poem by Ben Jonson. Invoking this poem as the merest trace, the author of *Native Speaker* deftly augments the pathos with which his narrator remembers the death of a son. Jonson actually memorialized two of his deceased children in verse; both poems—but especially "On My First Son"—capture and distill grief in the tremendously expressive incoherence with which they conclude:

> Farewell, thou child of my right hand, and joy;
> My sin was too much hope of thee, loved boy;
> Seven years thou wert lent to me, and I thee pay,
> Exacted by thy fate, on the just day.
> O could I lose all father now! for why
> Will man lament the state he should envy,
> To have so soon 'scaped world's and flesh's rage,
> And, if no other misery, yet age?
> Rest in soft peace, and asked, say, "Here doth lie
> Ben Jonson his best piece of poetry."
> For whose sake henceforth all his vows be such
> As what he loves may never like too much.

This boy, like Mitt, is the moribund homunculus at the center of a be-reaved father's embattled sense of self. A literary man who knows that, et-ymologically, the word *poetry* means "making," Jonson sadly notes that the term has a procreative as well as an artistic meaning. The finest thing "made" by the *poiētēs*, Ben Jonson's best piece of poetry, the child is a part of the maker-self. "Thou child of my right hand," the poet apostrophizes, Englishing the Hebrew meaning of the name he shares with his son. Jon-son's poem turns in part on whether the father may see himself or his son as "fortunate," for this is what it means, according to the Hebrew idiom, to be "of the right hand." An early death supposedly translates one to the en-viable heavenly "state." Strangely blessed, too, are those who see their children spared life's misery, which includes "world's and flesh's rage," not to mention simply growing old. Or so the poet strives to convince himself.

But such comforts belong to an earlier age, and Henry Park can only grieve and perhaps moralize, in his own postmodern fashion, a parent's supreme calamity. Even if Mitt had not been characterized as a little spy, complete with recording device (102), the reader would recognize him as a part of Park—the part that cannot live, the part stifled by the ostensibly friendly Anglos all around. Symbolically, this death is the least sparing as-pect of Lee's vision: it implies that hybridity carries its own doom like a virus. Mitt's death at the hands of his playmates anticipates Park's ultimate failure to find a middle way between his American and Korean identities. If there is a way out of the dark wood in which he finds himself, here at the midpoint of his life's journey, it would seem to lie in the understated vision of service with which the book ends. A kind of Korean American catcher in the rye, Park will help his wife register and pay tribute to the linguistic, onomastically inflected differences of immigrant children, children he half-consciously associates with his own dead child, children in whom, un-consciously, he sees himself as youthful stumbler amid the strange conso-nants and diphthongs of English.

6 ≋ Haitian Persephone

Danticat's *Breath, Eyes, Memory*

The wonder is what you can make a paradise out of.... I grew up in a lumpen apartment in Cracow, squeezed into three rudimentary rooms with four other people, surrounded by squabbles, dark political rumblings, memories of wartime suffering, and daily struggle for existence. And yet, when it came time to leave, I ... felt I was being pushed out of the happy, safe enclosures of Eden.

—Eva Hoffman, *Lost in Translation*

"It is a peculiar sensation, this double-consciousness, this sense of always looking at one's self through the eyes of others, of measuring one's soul by the tape of a world that looks on in amused contempt and pity."[1] In this famous sentence W. E. B. Du Bois describes the "twoness" of the African American, but his words can also serve to suggest something of the dual existence, the echoic psyche, of the immigrant. Unlike African Americans, of course, immigrants can remember a prior experience of psychic unity: the time before geographical and cultural displacement. This recollection, however, only makes their diasporic doubleness the more tormented. The exiled Dante's famous line—"Nessun maggior dolore che ricordarsi del tempo felice nella miseria"[2]—gets it only half right, for retrospect transforms even an unhappy past. Indeed, by a perverse logic, the more benighted the nation from which the immigrant escapes, the more difficulty she has in letting it go. Thus the heroine of Edwidge Danticat's 1994 novel *Breath, Eyes, Memory*, beset by "memories of a past that at times was cherished and at others despised," feels the pull of her native land even as she recognizes it as "a place where nightmares are passed on through generations like heirlooms."[3]

But *Breath, Eyes, Memory* invites reading as more than nostalgia, more than a retrospective story of Haiti by an immigrant aware of how swiftly new cultural experience elbows aside old. Readers encounter here an especially rigorous meditation on the survival within the immigrant of the old, pre-American self, the vestigial limb that, no matter how far back the cultural amputation, continues to itch. In the experience of Martine and Sophie, Danticat perpends the Haiti one cannot shake: their struggle represents assimilation at its most problematic. One may think of the exile as an Orpheus, his homeland the Eurydice who fades as he compulsively looks back at her, but Danticat, as will be seen, represents the immigrant as a Persephone never fully reconciled to life in the underworld, to which her mother—the Demeter of this version—has been carried off before her. A Margaret Atwood phrase, "double Persephone," comes to mind here, for in Danticat's story the arms Plutonic claim the mother in one way, the daughter in another.

Whatever the myth invoked, the immigrant writer must devise ways to render the dynamic of doubled identity. Danticat reveals its workings in her story's finer details, as well as in plot and character. Especially deft at the weaving together of motif and detail, she introduces a host of references to daffodils, seeming emblems of immigrant hope for rooting and flourishing in diasporic soils. This figure is all the more interesting in that it so strikingly contradicts the grousings of Jamaica Kincaid on the same subject. Kincaid's Lucy loathes daffodils because she associates them with colonial imposition: they are not native to the island from which she comes, and she resents having had to learn the poem about them so cherished by the colonial master. Danticat's Sophie and Martine, however, outdo Wordsworth himself in their appreciation of this flower. Moreover, its not being native to Haiti heartens them, for they see in its ability to flourish in alien climes a positive model for their own displacement: "My mother loved daffodils because they grew in a place that they were not supposed to," says Sophie (21). But eventually Martine grows indifferent to the flower that once delighted her, and in fact her loss of interest proceeds *pari passu* with her failure to assimilate. When she takes to growing hibiscus, a flower of the Indies, one recognizes a more pervasive inability to face forward into American experience. As in Kincaid but much less tendentiously, the daffodil conceit contributes, in the end, to a complex play on transplantation, rootedness, and postcolonial sensibility.

Danticat may seem guilty of a similar ambivalence with regard to her cultural allegiance, for she sets more of *Breath, Eyes, Memory* in Haiti (richly re-created for the reader) than in America (glimpsed dimly in evocations of inner city, featureless suburb, or ethnically oriented business). Sophie, meeting Joseph, learns something of America's variety (he speaks of Providence, Rhode Island, and the state of Louisiana) but seems unable to possess the nation in which she gives birth to a daughter. In its structure, too, *Breath, Eyes, Memory* seems to enact an immigrant's allegiance to the world she left behind. Of its thirty-five chapters, twenty (along with two half-chapters) concern the heroine's experience in her native country. The remaining thirteen (with, again, two half-chapters) concern the heroine's arrival in the States, her secondary education, her troubled marriage to the musician Joseph, her therapy, and her mother's suicide. Nor do the chapters follow a simple progression from Haiti to America. Rather, the reader first encounters Sophie in Haiti, whence her mother summons her to America; subsequently, as a young mother herself, Sophie flees briefly to her native country, then returns, and is last seen in Haiti again for the funeral that ends the novel.

However desirous of revisiting Haiti artistically, the author herself should not be reproached for her characters' preference for Haitian scenes and Haitian stories, their inability to immerse themselves in America. The immigrant, after all, usually has little leisure for the gleaning of impressions. The writer Junot Díaz describes a fellow immigrant from the Dominican Republic, the fictional Ramón de las Casas, as "angry at the blinkered existence his jobs and the city imposed on him."[4] Thus the settings of *Breath, Eyes, Memory* render the immigrant's sense of space: limited and claustrophobic in unfamiliar America, scaled to person and community in native Haiti. Such formal and thematic considerations go far toward justifying the larger focus on the homeland in this novel, but one notes in passing that from *Krik? Krak!* (1995) to *The Farming of Bones* (1998), *After the Dance: A Walk through Carnival in Jacmel, Haiti* (2002), and *The Dew Breaker* (2004), Danticat has in fact devoted herself to remembering, reimagining, and revisiting Haiti more than to representing the American scene. In this she rehearses a general tendency among immigrant writers active since (and in large measure owing their literary existence to) the inception of "roots" awareness and multiculturalism in the mid-seventies. After first novels set in America, these writers tend to shift their focus toward their native lands—unlike their predecessors, who had perforce to turn their creative backs on the homeland to tell American or international stories. In the older model (itself an aspect of the assimilationist ideal), immigrants with literary aspirations suppressed their ethnicity and moved swiftly toward being perceived as thoroughly American. Those who did not—Carlos Bulosan, for example, whose last novel is set in his native Philippines—entered a literary eclipse, pending revival under the multicultural dispensation. Jerzy Kosinski, who came to the States in the 1950s, wrote one backward-looking (if epochal) novel, *The Painted Bird* (1965), before a series of books largely set in his new homeland, notably *Being There*, with its mordant view of American politics and television culture. But later in the century the paradigm shifts: German-born Ursula Hegi writes two books set in America before re-creating her native Hannover as the Burgdorf of *Floating in My Mother's Palm* (1991) and *Stones from the River* (1994). Both Germany and America figure in *The Vision of Emma Blau* (2000). Julia Alvarez follows *How the García Girls Lost Their Accents*, set partly in her native country, with *In the Time of the Butterflies*, set entirely there. The yet more recent immigrant writers—Ha Jin, Anchee Min, and a host of Indians come to mind—need not bother with fictional treatments of their new homeland at all, so ready is the American readership for undiluted ethnicity.

No doubt many an immigrant artist's retrospection expresses a legitimate preference in subject matter, but considerable marketing pressure forces these writers into commodifying their past, their ethnicity, their difference. Marilyn Halter, in *Shopping for Identity: The Marketing of Ethnicity*, has documented the immense growth of ethnically oriented commerce in recent decades, the marketing of every conceivable commodity, including food, clothing, decor, travel, entertainment, education, and even the fine arts. She characterizes "the possible harm that market forces can do to cultural creativity" as an "ever-present concern."[5] Even those who dismiss as modernist aberration the idea that fine art should be exempt from the marketplace would have to concede that the magnitude and coercive power of commercial forces under an advanced capitalist system must generate questions about the real freedom of any enterprise. In any event, whether through simple personal inclination, through sensitivity to the sociological Zeitgeist, or through the impure motive of pleasing the crowd, many immigrant writers set their later fictions in the homeland and thus unwittingly emulate a widely deplored economic trend in America: more and more "offshore" production.

Sophie Caco, the heroine of *Breath, Eyes, Memory*, recognizes the ability to "flow wherever life takes you" as, on the one hand, "very American" and, on the other, decidedly "not Haitian" (72). The author, like the Bharati Mukherjee of *Jasmine*, knows that to come to terms with the

American flow is the great trial of immigrants from the many countries lacking even a myth of social mobility. Like the Lan Cao of *Monkey Bridge*, Danticat knows, too, the difficulty of identity makeover and revised self-definition—no matter how fully the act of immigration might seem to license such metamorphoses. Commonly, older immigrants have greater difficulty with this aspect of existence in America than their more flexible offspring, but in *Breath, Eyes, Memory* neither the mother, Martine, nor the daughter, Sophie, manages quite to transform herself into a new American woman. So terrible is the weight of the past, and so powerful the cultural force-field of Haiti, that neither can really free herself of the old country and its ways. Neither can neutralize the toxins the old life released in their hearts. Both emigrate at an early age (the one at twenty, the other at twelve), but the psychic wounds they carry with them refuse to heal, leaving them susceptible to further damage in America. Neither seems able to answer in the affirmative when asked, in patois, the traditional question about being free of some heavy burden: "Ou libéré"? (96, 233, 234).

The book opens with Mother's Day at hand; it ends with a mother's funeral. In between readers glimpse a succession of troubled daughters and dead, absent, or rejected husband/fathers, for in Freudian terms the immigrant resembles a child in the Oedipal phase of libidinal development. Its psychic health depends on the ability to renounce the mother and "marry" another. Werner Sollors, in fact, mentions a Scandinavian immigrant who spoke of Sweden as his mother, America as his bride.[6] Inevitably, given this novel's backward-looking bias, the author's characters and the events they experience become a symbolic representation of Haiti itself—or perhaps Haiti as it lives in the troubled hearts of exiles and emigrants. Danticat has denied that the profoundly troubled Martine represents her equally troubled homeland: "I don't see Martine as Haiti because I'm more hopeful for Haiti than that."[7] But this author is by no means innocent of allegory, as one sees in the brief episode in which the Tontons Macoutes murder poor Dessalines, the coal seller. This minor character shares a name with the Haitian freedom fighter Jean-Jacques Dessalines (1758?–1806), who became the nation's first emperor, Jacques I (1804–1806). Like Danticat's coal seller, he came to a bad end, but Haitians still revere his memory only a little less than that of the man he followed, Toussaint L'Ouverture. For the significance of the tableau in which Danticat's latter-day Dessalines perishes, American readers need only imagine members of a thuggish constabulary kicking a character named "George Washington" to death.

If, as Danticat's remark suggests, the reader errs to take Martine as the embodiment of troubled Haiti, some larger symbolism may still be operative here. Indeed, such a dimension would deliver the book from a certain tendency to become soap opera. One grows a little impatient with its sensational elements, notably the mother driven mad by nightmares in which, over and over again, she relives the rape that saw the conception of her daughter Sophie; the cancer and mastectomy; and the suicidal abortion effected through a seventeen-fold self-stabbing (she had sought, unsuccessfully, to abort the rapist's child, too). In her self-defloration with a pestle (88, 130), "sexual phobia" (201), and bulimia (179), the daughter, too, strains credulity. But all of this female suffering makes sense insofar as it suggests the unending violation of a homeland conceived (like Cristina Garcia's Cuba or Lan Cao's Vietnam) as female. The high level of psychopathology here reifies the larger fate of Haiti itself—generally recognized as one of the world's most dysfunctional countries, doomed endlessly to rehearse self-destructive behavior. In other words, Danticat succeeds in finding the human, personal correlative for the social and historical reality of the motherland.

To think about the women of Haiti is also to scrutinize the nation's men, to consider whether the author views any of the male characters here with approbation, for the land, if one insists on symbolic gendering, may well be projected as the brutal father/husband who abandons or—worse—violates his daughters. The absence of a father for Martine and Atie, and again for Sophie, and perhaps even for Brigitte, hints at a much vaster privation or dereliction. Not that Danticat presents all Haitian men as the faceless rapist who fathers Sophie. But if, initially, Monsieur Augustin and Marc Chevalier strike one as sympathetic, they eventually prove feckless or inept figures of the kind who have made little effort, over decades and even centuries, to arrest Haiti's incessant decline. Donald Augustin, a class-conscious schoolteacher, backs out of a romantic involvement with the illiterate Atie, and Marc proves a curiously distasteful "chevalier." His predilection for introducing himself by all six of his names hints at a certain narcissistic self-regard. The word *marc*, in French, denotes the sludge that remains after wine-pressing. As a proper name, of course, it is martial, deriving from *martis*, "of Mars." The surname "Chevalier" is also martial, but rendered absurd by the honorific "esquire"—a term originally meaning a knight's shield-bearer. Etymologically oxymoronic, "MARC CHEVALIER, ESQUIRE" (52) suggests no small fatuity.

As narrator, Sophie seems to want to represent Marc as merely the latest abuser, taker-advantage of Haitian womanhood. Perhaps unfairly, she senses something unwholesome in her mother's paramour. When he officiously makes arrangements for a Haitian funeral for Martine, Sophie violently asserts: "If I died mute, I would never speak to him again. I would never open my mouth and address a word to him" (226). She refuses, too, to sit near him on the flight to Haiti with her mother's body. The author makes no effort to gainsay the narrator's contempt for and antagonism toward this poor, chubby mama's boy (53). She lets stand her viewpoint character's inarticulate perception, which registers the disquiet of a daughter who must recoil at thoughts of the unctuous lawyer's congress with the cancer-ravaged, breastless Martine. Yet the reader ought also to realize that he is thus strangely disgusting only in the eyes of the emotionally damaged and perhaps unreliable daughter, whose condition may be most visible in her inability to appreciate what may in fact be an admirable and attractive steadiness (in French, fine brandy is also *marc*). This dynamic colors perceptions of Sophie's husband, Joseph, as well, and in a more obvious way. Tremendously patient with the troubled Sophie, Joseph seems rather admirable. As a character, Joseph helps Danticat frame her picture of Sophie's suffering. To put it another way: Sophie's difficulties with such a decent and sympathetic husband become an especially effective gauge of her alienation, not to mention the physical and spiritual damage she has suffered. In Joseph, apparently in his mid- to late thirties and roughly the same age as her mother (74), Sophie has, ironically, the ideal husband and father so conspicuously rare in Haiti.

Ultimately, the author locates what troubles Martine, Atie, Sophie, and Grandmè Ifé, the old matriarch in Dame Marie, in a constellation of causes centering in a kind of "virginity cult, our mothers' obsession with keeping us pure and chaste" (154). Haiti, according to the author, is one of those cultures in which brides must bleed. Consequently, young, unmarried women must suffer the odious practice of "testing"—a less lurid antitype of the genital mutilation practiced among certain African tribes and agonized over by Alice Walker in *Possessing the Secret of Joy* and Gloria Naylor in *Bailey's Café*. (Like Naylor's Miriam, Danticat's Buki, who shares group therapy with Sophie, is a displaced daughter of Ethiopia.) The digital testing for virginity is so traumatic that it calls into existence a psychological defense mechanism: the "doubling" required, Danticat implies, of every Haitian woman. In that it denies autonomy and freedom, testing fosters its own kind of slavery. Like the slave who takes refuge in spiritual twinning, the Haitian woman survives psychologically by living at a distance from the body that is in bondage. She may even embrace the rape or self-mutilation that will obviate further testing. Destroying her own hymen becomes for Sophie "like breaking manacles, an act of freedom" (130). Yet the habit of doubling remains, as a destructive form of repetition compulsion, emotional slavery after the fact.

Densely woven into the narrative, the doubling conceit lies behind and complicates the Freudian circumstance of being "my mother's daughter and Tante Atie's child" (49). Like Freud's Leonardo, in other words, Sophie is a bastard who has two mothers and experiences considerable psychosexual disorientation. Testing compounds the mental disarray: Sophie doubles when tested, doubles in the marriage bed (she finds intercourse painful), and doubles even as citizen. Like virginity itself, as will be seen, doubling becomes the figure for problematic identity. Doubling figures, more broadly, as a varied trope that frames and characterizes considerably more than the experience of women under patriarchy. In addition to the furcation of immigrant consciousness, it subsumes, in former times, a people's problematic survival of slavery and, in the present day, the standard mode of Haitian politicians. This pathology, replete with self-contradiction and destructive circularity, links up with and ramifies outward through all of Haitian history, religion, and culture. Thus Haiti worships, in Erzulie, a dual goddess: at once voudou *loa* and the Christian Mother of God, at once maternal nurturer and siren/temptress, "the desire of all men" (59). Replicating itself in ironic ways, this gyno-spiritual doubling finds debased expression in the fable of the Marassas, which Danticat explains as "actually part of the African tradition where there are twin deities. In the tradition of the Ibegi in Africa, twins are considered very special, in some cases to be very powerful. . . . *Marassa* in common language means twins."[8] Sophie learns the lore of Marassas concurrently with her initial experience of testing. Her mother on this occasion indulges a profoundly ironic fantasy of their becoming as close as twins, and indeed, in their psychological afflictions, the two women will be twinned forever—and twinned, even, within themselves. Asked in therapy about her pregnant mother's "state of mind," Sophie says: "It was like two people. Someone who was trying to hold things together and someone who was falling apart" (218). She is also, of course, describing herself. Martine's pregnancy is as disturbing to her daughter as to her, and Sophie's therapist remarks, "I think you have a Madonna image of your mother" (220). "As a child," in fact, Sophie "had imagined" a parent "like Erzulie, the lavish Virgin

Mother" (59), but for burial she dresses Martine in crimson and notes her resemblance to the other Erzulie, the "Jezebel," the "hot-blooded" goddess (227).

Doubling multiplies the identity confusion and general misery of the Haitian immigrant, who discovers a whole fresh realm of double consciousness. I began with the suggestion that an immigrant such as Martine or Sophie must live with some version of "double consciousness," W. E. B. Du Bois's acute term for the psychology of African Americans. Sophie Caco's doubleness is itself doubled if not, indeed, pleated, for she becomes both immigrant and African American. I suggested, too, that Danticat represents her heroines as Persephone doubled. This symbolism emerges in the story of the lark and the little girl (124–25). An example of what Bruno Bettelheim calls a "beast-groom fable," this one does not have the expected outcome, in which Beauty discovers and accepts an eligible mate in the bestial other. As told here, the story replicates more than one element in the larger diegesis. It turns on whether the lark can persuade the little girl to bring along her heart to the distant land to which he proposes to take her. She outwits him, and her heart remains in its childhood home. At one level, the little girl is Sophie, the lark Martine, who carries her daughter off to America but never succeeds in getting her to bring along her heart. (When Martine dies, Sophie declares her, among other things, a lark in a tree.) The pomegranates with which the lark entices the girl recall a detail in the classical myth of how winter began: Persephone eats seeds of the pomegranate in the underworld and so must spend part of every year in the realm of Hades. Both Sophie and her mother are Haitian Persephones (the one actually raped by a violent stranger who suddenly materialized beside her, the other compelled periodically to shuttle between the sun-drenched world and chthonic America).

The novel's interpolated or embedded stories, parables, and songs flesh out a picture of Haitian mores, customs, and folkways that provide a commentary, often bitter, on the central narrative. Nancy Gerber argues that the storytelling binds generations of women, that the storyteller—and especially Sophie—is empowered to write new scripts of womanly possibility.[9] But in my view the text is far less sanguine about the stories and songs. The relations between them and Sophie's narrative tend to be less redemptive than ironic. A technique with roots in both oral and literary tradition (in the novel its etiology goes back to Cervantes and Fielding), the interpolated stories in *Breath, Eyes, Memory* should not, then, be mistaken for mere "color," nor are they the expression of benign folk consciousness.

"Somehow, early on, our song makers and tale weavers had decided that we were all daughters of this land," Sophie declares, but the "something . . . essentially Haitian" that "had given all the mother-and-daughter motifs to all the stories they told and all the songs they sang" (230) is not a benevolent force, for the songs and tales are heavily freighted with oppressive traditions. Of the twelve or so stories introduced into the text, three at most (the people of Guinea [25], the little girl born from roses, water, and sky [47, 61], the song about the mermaid who married a fisherman [229]) do not seem tendentious. The others all exhibit something like the duality that so pervades Sophie's world; that is, a fairytale quality proves over and over again to mask a dark social or personal reality. The stories rationalize folk customs that perpetuate one kind of bondage or another.

In her lifelong affliction, for example, Martine mirrors the protagonist of more than one of these stories. Sophie conflates two of them in a valedictory declaration: "My mother was like that woman who could never bleed and then could never stop bleeding, the one who gave in to her pain, to live as a butterfly" (234). A rape victim who never had a wedding night, Martine "was like that woman" who, failing to incarnadine the bridal sheets, is cut by her husband, only to bleed to death (154–55). In another story, a kind of sister or twin of this hapless bride goes for years "with blood constantly spurting from her unbroken skin." Like the biblical woman afflicted with an issue of blood (Mark 5:25–34, also in Matthew and Luke), she appeals for divine deliverance, only to learn that "if she wanted to stop bleeding, she would have to give up her right to be a human being" (87). The goddess Erzulie transforms the sufferer into a butterfly. But the meaning of both fable and reference is dark, for the butterfly is an emblem of transformation traditionally associated with the soul, *psyche*, which only death can liberate. Over the bier of her mother, Sophie pronounces Martine a butterfly as well as a lark.

When Sophie notes that the secret police, the Tontons Macoutes, take their name from the fairytale bogeyman invoked to foster children's deference to grownups, she hints bitterly at the enormities the Haitian "respect your elders" (138) ethic can encourage and excuse. The custom of testing and the cult of virginity are part of the same spectrum, the same acceptance of how things have always been done, that precludes cultural liberation. The brutality of the Tontons Macoutes—one is thought to have raped Martine, a group of them murder Dessalines—reveals just where such uncritical deference to "tradition" leads. More than personal violation, then, testing is emblematic of women's mindless complicity in the patriarchal order and, more broadly, of whole cultures' appalling abuse of women's sexual futures. In other words, though testing may have its roots in an oppressive patriarchal system, its custodians are women, and the reader recognizes such complicity as one of the larger constellations in the phallocentric heaven. Atwood underscores it in the militancy of the "aunts" in her dystopian Republic of Gilead, and Maxine Hong Kingston, in *The Woman Warrior*, sketches its historical actuality in the strictures of Brave Orchid and other Chinese women. As Gloria Anzaldúa observes, "[m]ales makes the rules and laws," but "women transmit them": "Son los costumbres que traicionan."[10] Thus Danticat represents the problem of Haiti as a deep-seated pathology most easily seen in the experience of certain Haitian women.

The women of Haiti—at least as represented in this novel—have embraced an ideology that they cannot break out of. The real horror, of course, is that the women themselves promulgate the practices that breed psychopathology. "My grandmother, and her mother before her," Sophie tells her therapist, "had all been *tested*" (207). Yet these women are not in fact victims, in Althusser's sense, of unconscious or unexamined ideology (except insofar as the ideology by which they live presents itself as natural or normative). That is, they are perfectly capable of bringing the ideological underpinnings of their cultural practices to consciousness, as Martine explains: "'I did it,' she said, 'because my mother had done it to me. I have no greater excuse. I realize standing here that the two greatest pains of my life are very much related. The one good thing about my being raped was that it made the *testing* stop. The testing and the rape. I live both every day'" (170). Sophie makes a similar point regarding the violation that ends violation (130). Both tested, both violently deflowered, both frightened and insomniac (193), both afflicted psychologically, mother and daughter are presented as twinned, like the Marassas in the folktale, especially in that "when they cried, their tears were identical" (84). Sophie's bulimia finds its complement in Martine's great hunger, which cannot outpace the wasting effects of cancer (179). As Buki says in an apostrophe to "the dead grandmother who had cut off all her sexual organs and sewn her up, in a female rite of passage" (202): "It would be easy to hate you, but I can't because you are part of me. You are me." In a ceremony poignant in its very impotence, Buki, Sophie, and the others "wrote the names of our abusers in a piece of paper, raised it over a candle, and watched as the flames consumed it." Sophie will later see, caught in a tree, the balloon that Buki releases on this occasion. It suffers the same fate as all the kites back in Haiti, artificial butterflies that sooner or later tumble from the sky to clutter the cemetery. Still, knowledge fosters healing, if only in a future generation. Thus Sophie understands that her own suffering and that of her mother

> were links in a long chain and if she hurt me, it was because she was hurt, too.
> It was up to me to avoid my turn in the fire. It was up to me to make sure that my daughter never slept with ghosts, never lived with nightmares, and never had *her* name burnt in the flames. (203)

Though one feels reasonably sure that this mother will not put her daughter through the mortification of "testing," little Brigitte will grow up with a suicide in the family attic and (if Sophie cannot bring herself to live with Joseph) an absent father. In the novel's conclusion, outside the Haitian cemetery, the reader hears nothing about Sophie's returning to her husband in the States. The flames, then, may yet devour more names, and this is the saddest thing of all. The only hopeful note here at the end is the recently concluded business of deeding the family freehold to all of its women. Martine explains the newly notarized deed to Sophie: "The land"—again, symbolically, Haiti itself—"is equally divided between Atie and me and you and your daughter" (167).

Danticat has been criticized by Haitians and Haitian Americans for what they perceive as overstatements or distortions of the culture's puritanical enforcement of female chastity. It is not clear that "testing" is any kind of widespread practice (and the author's italicization of the term is, stylistically, no small miscalculation). But this conceit and the theme of sexual purity and impurity figure more, here, than anthropological exotica. Virginity becomes a metaphor for the essentialist identity that cannot survive emigration. Martine's literal emigration merely formalizes a deracination or spiritual departure that dates from her violation. Sophie's self-defloration is similarly an announcement of the travail of balancing between the behaviors her mother seeks to impose on her and the rebirth of the self awaited by Joseph—and America.

7 ≋ Assimilation and Adolescence

Jamaica Kincaid's *Lucy* and Lan Cao's *Monkey Bridge*

Who can depict the feeling of desolation, homesickness, uncertainty, and anxiety with which an emigrant makes his first voyage across the ocean?
—Abraham Cahan, *The Rise of David Levinsky*

The disorientation of the immigrant bears considerable resemblance to that of the teenager, and adolescence vies with infancy as a standard metaphor for the experience of changing countries. Some immigrants actually make this change during the years of adolescence. Landing in a different country with hormones in a stew, these hapless individuals literalize and compound the conceit that puberty (as someone once remarked) resembles finding oneself marooned on an unfamiliar planet without passport or travelers' checks. Of course the word "alien" applies to someone who comes from either another country or another planet.

The two fictions discussed in this chapter, Jamaica Kincaid's *Lucy* and Lan Cao's *Monkey Bridge*, introduce autobiographical heroines: a Vietnamese who spends most of her adolescence in her new country, the United States, and a West Indian whose twentieth year sees a removal from sun-drenched Caribbean to variable-seasoned metropolis. Each struggles to differentiate herself from a mother who represents the old life and the obstacles it erects to assimilation. Each heroine-narrator sees the good and bad of the country left behind at the same time that she keenly observes her new environment. But they differ in the extent to which they can affirm the new world's promise. Kincaid's *Lucy* sees too much continuity between the British imperium and its North American clone. Cao's Mai, though acutely aware of the enormous gulf between Southeast Asia (however superficially Americanized) and the United States of America, nonetheless represents something like the eutectic ideal. These characters also exemplify familiar models of the adolescent passage, the one defining herself as perennial rebel (almost to the point of arrested development), the other the dutiful daughter who adjusts to life in America and gains admission to an elite college on her way to an honored place in the adult world. This may sound like a pair of stereotypes, the black rebel with a cause on the one hand, the notorious ideal (Asian) minority on the other, but as one contemplates the ways in which Lucy and Mai negotiate their passage to America, concrete instantiation transcends type and cliché.

Angry Young Woman: Kincaid's Rebel Angel

Readers who saw *Life of Brian*, the Monty Python movie set in ancient Palestine, will recall that it satirizes more than the four gospels. It also targets the Jewish firebrands who sought to rally resistance to imperial Rome. One droll sequence begins with a disgruntled native posing what he intends as a rhetorical question: What have the Romans done for us? In a series of responses (each cheerfully acknowledged by the would-be revolutionary) the answer materializes and becomes an embarrassing catalogue: aqueducts, sanitation, roads, irrigation, medicine, education, wine, baths, public order, peace.

Such satire must not blind one to the fact that a world of such benefits cannot compensate for freedom and independence denied. In our own time many voices among the formerly colonized insist that no amount of aqueducts, sanitation, and roads can make up for the ills fostered by empire. Prominent among these voices, Jamaica Kincaid laments—in fiction and nonfiction—the damages colonialism inflicted on her native Antigua. In *A Small Place* (1988) she deplores "the millions of people, of whom I am just one, made orphans: no motherland, no fatherland, no gods, no mounds of earth for holy ground, no excess of love which might lead to the things that an excess of love sometimes brings, and worst and most painful of all, no tongue. For isn't it odd that the only language I have in which to speak of this crime is the language of the criminal who committed the crime?"[1] As Shakespeare's Caliban observes (the quotation is a favorite in postcolonial theory), "You taught me language; and my profit on't / Is, I know how to curse"(*The Tempest* 1.2.365–66).

But what pristine version of Antigua would the author embrace? That of the Arawaks, who displaced the aboriginal Siboney—or that of the Caribs, who displaced the Arawaks? If the Siboney had not been wiped out, might they not lament the destruction of their gods, their language, their sacred places, and so on by those who came after—whether Arawak, Carib, European, or African? Though rooted in legitimate grievance, postcolonial reproaches to empire often fail adequately to historicize and contextualize; sooner or later they trip up on unexamined myths of a somehow less burdened past. To recover a lost heritage, someone like Kincaid's autobiographical character Lucy Josephine Potter would have to separate the Carib, African, and perhaps European streams of her own blood, consigning each to its primal, god-given sphere. But perhaps she would do better to differentiate colonialisms—or to ask what peoples have not at some point been colonized. Would Antigua have fared better at the hands of Catholic Spain or Portugal? In more modern times, does the Antiguan not see in England a colonial mother preferable to Belgium or Germany or Japan? Might Lucy—or Kincaid—not recognize that the rapacity of the English was, more than that of other colonizers, tempered by civilized restraint? By the same token, might she not see that Antigua derived as much benefit from its English conqueror as the Saxons derived from their Norman conqueror or the British Celts from the occupying Romans? Perhaps not. "Even if I really came from people who were living like monkeys in the trees," declares the unmollified Kincaid, "it was better to be that than what happened to me, what I became after I met you" (32).

In 1991 Kincaid told an interviewer: "I'm not an American citizen. . . . I have no intention of becoming an American citizen."[2] According to the statement inside the cover of her novel *Lucy* (1990), Kincaid "remains a citizen" of Antigua. As an expatriate, she excoriates both societies, frequently lashing out at England as well. She has subjected Antigua to some of her most vitriolic denunciations, asseverating in *A Small Place* that its independence has not turned out particularly well. The Antiguans, she declares, have turned to tourism, making a spectacle of their own backwardness; they have neglected the commitment to education and literacy that could have promised a better future. Expressing her anger and contempt thus forcefully, Kincaid seems to have made herself persona non grata in her native country, where reaction to *A Small Place* was not friendly. "Reviews," according to the South African journalist Maya Jaggi, "were harsh."[3] The author even claims to have discarded the appellation Elaine Potter Richardson to deflect the enmity of those at home: "I changed my name . . . so that they wouldn't know I was writing."[4] If Kincaid had been acknowledged and embraced as an "articulate survivor"[5] of colonialism's abuses by those remaining in Antigua, one might be more willing to grant her the moral ground she claims. Yet whatever the resistance in Antigua (not to mention England) to her denunciations, many readers in the United States seem almost too willing to declare their culture guilty of complicity, at least, with colonial exploitation. Thus it is with some trepidation (and a recognition that I am in a minority, at least among academic readers) that I register a modicum of resistance to the way Kincaid has been read in this country. I think American readers ought, perhaps, to learn from their shocked cousins in Antigua a certain judicious resistance to this author's more intemperate pronouncements.

In her highly autobiographical novel *Lucy*, Kincaid gives her narrator, the title character, a great deal of her own rage (as expressed in *A Small Place*). "You are a very angry person, aren't you?" asks Lucy's employer, Mariah. "Of course I am. What do you expect?" Lucy replies.[6] Though she might, as sympathetic employer, expect civility and some deference, Mariah seems not to question the legitimacy of Lucy's general resentment. Similarly, most critical readings of *Lucy* defer to an idea of postcolonial license, an idea that the subaltern, when she speaks, must be attended to by a guilty Western ear. This conscience-stricken abjection uncannily reproduces the postures and tones of the old dispensation, with roles reversed. Caned by the previously victimized, white guilt says, "Thank you, Ma'am, may I have another?" No doubt justly: those ignorant of or indifferent to the bloody and unconscionable origins of their affluence need shaking up from time to time. Still, I wonder if the standard critical response to *Lucy* does not diminish it, make it one-dimensional. Resisting the idea that any politically valenced discourse by the cultural other automatically has literary merit, I argue that *Lucy* succeeds only to the extent that its author has done something more than air her personal anger.

The novel has not wanted for thoughtful analysis—notably by Gary Holcomb, Moira Ferguson, and Helen Tiffin. Holcomb argues that Kincaid shows "how a postcolonial author may deploy tropes of travel as a means of deconstructing the imperialist ideology written into the very genre of travel literature."[7] Especially acute on the subject of Lucy's sexuality as it intersects with and confounds stereotypes of the exotic other, he shows how the references to Paul Gauguin call into question a host of colonizing postures. Ferguson, for her part, notes a meaningful progression between the story's opening, in a gray mid-January emblematic of a post-colonial transition, and its springtime close, with Lucy, who has allowed the word "history" to figure in her narrative with increasing prominence, now recognizably a symbol of her native island (or any such former colony), "a territory freeing itself from the colonizer." Thus, says Ferguson, "the death-like, gray-black and cold January of the opening . . . has been transformed through Lucy's awakening and agency into the blood-red, milk-white, Caribbean-blue colors of her writing."[8] In other words, as Lucy writes with blue ink on the blank white pages of the red journal given to her by Mariah as a parting gift, the colors of empire (whether Union Jack or Stars and Stripes) have in effect been reinscribed as a new post-colonial subjectivity. Helen Tiffin, finally, probes the "four pervasive metaphors" that "structure the novel: imprisonment (and punishment); daffodils and the colour yellow; tongues; and hearts."[9] Parsing the figuration of articulate subjectivity, she is especially cogent on tongue and heart, arguing that sexuality and sexual liberation are linked to liberation of the tongue, which includes the simple right to speak for oneself:

> Lucy uses her "tongue to manipulate male sexuality, never letting any of the boys she experiments with touch her "heart." In thinking "of all the other tongues I had held in my mouth" (82) Lucy associates sexuality, colonialism and recitation; and, resisting that fatal connection between "tongue" and "heart," she converts recitation to resistance. The two sections "The Tongue" and "Cold Heart" precede the final appearance of "Lucy" and the attainment of rebel angel status. By manipulating the tongues of others—putting her tongue in their mouths—Lucy takes back control of her own voice and body from capture by European texts of all kinds."[10]

Or thinks she does. These critics falter in their tendency, on the one hand, to ignore the nastiness of the eponymous narrator and, on the other, to grant her too much autonomy, authority, and insight. Her anger, her contumely, derives as much from adolescent circumstance, from the universal need to escape from home and family, as from sober political evaluation. Like Joyce's Stephen Dedalus or Lawrence's Paul Morel, Lucy keeps discovering the renewal, within herself, of the entities she wants to escape. By the same token, just as Joyce or Lawrence or Pound (in "Hugh Selwyn Mauberley") critiques a version of himself, so does Kincaid make of Lucy an instrument of the examined life. The strength of *Lucy*, I would argue, derives from Kincaid's ability to represent and sublimate her own anger in that of a narrator of limited reliability whose real subject is less political outrage than the travail of adolescence and leaving home and coming of age. A thoroughly unpleasant young woman, Lucy arrives in the United States a disgruntled teenager—with all the narrow tetchiness and lack of civility characteristic of that genus. Neither Holden Caulfield nor Malcolm X, she resembles the ill-tempered Mary Grace in Flannery O'Connor's story "Revelation." If, like Mary Grace, she is the vehicle of a legitimate reproach to white middle-class complacency, she is also, like the O'Connor character, a monster.

Indeed, a Caliban whom readers persist in identifying as Miranda. Lucy's general unattractiveness may, of course, be taken as a gauge of just how the colonial experience has warped her. Whatever its justification, readers err to pretend that her truculence makes her admirable. Lucy insists over and over on being as sullen and contemptuous as she can be. She announces "thoughts centered, naturally, on myself" (26), characterizes the love of her mother as a "burden" (36), and repeatedly causes Mariah anguish as she rebuffs attempts to establish friendship or common ground. She considers efforts to preserve the environment pointless (49) or at least irremediably hypocritical (72). "I was not," she asserts, "the sort of person who counted blessings; I was the sort of person for whom there could never be enough blessings" (110). In her perversity Lucy compliments herself on her strong body odor (27) and declares that she delights in halitosis, for she fondly remembers a youth named Cuthbert, whose "breath always smelled as if it were morning and he had just got out of bed—stale and moldy" (116).[11] One finds especially suggestive the figure by which she describes the contrast in outlook between her employer, who is like someone who knows "that the world was round and we all agreed on that," and herself, certain "that the world was flat and if I went to the edge I would fall off" (32). This from someone whose birthplace had an early visit from Columbus. The world is in fact round, and viewing it from a pre-Columbian or postcolonial perspective does not, even figuratively, make it flat. But such a view does identify one as a crank.

The story takes place, significantly, at the height of the sixties youth rebellion, between January 1968 and the spring of 1969. Born, like Kincaid, in 1949, Lucy sketches for the reader her first full year in the United States, during which she turns twenty. Though she does not name her native island, its size ("twelve miles long and eight miles wide" [134]) and the circumstances of its naming (by Columbus "after a church in Spain" [135]) identify it as Antigua, which at the time of the story had recently become

self-governing (full independence would not come about until 1981). Lucy
comes to the United States as a "servant" (95, 143)—but an observant one.
Mariah's husband, Lewis, calls her "the Visitor," a sobriquet that hints at
the instinct for euphemism and even hypocrisy on the part of her employ-
ers (denied the surname that Lucy eventually supplies for herself, they
constitute what Gilbert H. Muller calls a "generic American household").[12] But a visitor, etymologically, is one who "goes to see." A visitor
can also be one who performs a formal inspection. Thus Lucy, who
presently takes up photography, is very much the walking eyeball, inspecting—and generally being unimpressed by—the mores of the nation in
whose shadow she grew up and of which, presumably, she will become a
citizen.

But the real country in which Lucy must be naturalized is adulthood,
with its surrender of "attitude" in all the evolving meanings of that word.
The chief example of her eye-rolling impatience (of a peculiarly American
variety) is the sequence in which the naïvely enthusiastic Mariah introduces her to the daffodils that, as a number of critics have pointed out,
gradually become a large-scale motif, an emblem, supposedly, of colonial
oppression. Not native to the islands, often cultivated by servant or coolie
labor of one kind or another, daffodils can only be, in Diane Simmons's
phrase, "a brilliantly disguised weapon of imperial domination."[13] Lucy recoils in disgust. Made to memorize a poem by her colonial master, about a
flower *he* liked, as part of an education dictated by a colonial government,
she swells with resentment. She recalls her brilliant success at reciting the
poem publicly as "the height of my two-facedness" (18). But real two-
facedness seldom occasions such candor, and this particular pronouncement sounds disingenuous. In fact, the true height of her two-facedness
occurs much later, when she disguises adolescent rancor as postcolonial
pique. After her public recitation, Lucy recalls, she dreamt of being chased
and smothered by daffodils (18). No longer emblems of vernal beauty,
tranquil recollection, and romanticism (that vernal phase of Western culture itself), Wordsworth's daffodils have gone malign, become associated
with—so Lucy claims—a tendentious, coercive colonialism.

Ferguson reminds us that Wordsworth also wrote five poems about a
girl named Lucy.[14] As his friend Coleridge might say, the author of "I
Wandered Lonely as a Cloud" includes this later Lucy unawares. Kincaid's
Lucy would not see a daffodil until years later, when she is nineteen (the
daffodils that Mariah shows her now are in fact the first she has ever seen:
"I was glad to have at last seen what a wretched daffodil looked like" [30]).

Her resistance to daffodils, at any rate, seems to make the color yellow especially prominent in her tale of life in America. She mentions yellow sunlight (5), yellow linoleum, yellow hair, yellow skin (notably of Mariah [27]), the yellow house near the lake (35), the yellow roses Paul brings to Peggy and Lucy's new apartment, the yellow ground over which she is chased in her first dream, and, most suggestively (given her intuitive desire, upon seeing daffodils, to scythe them), the "six yellow-haired heads" of Lewis and Mariah's family "bunched as if they were a bouquet of flowers" (12). As Muller explains, the prominence of things yellow, especially flowers, works with the foregrounded abhorrence of the Wordsworth poem to reinforce the idea that "Lucy perceives the American Empire as an extension of the milieu created by the British Empire in the West Indies."[15]

When she first encounters Mariah's enthusiasm for daffodils, Lucy asks herself a question that becomes a motif: "How does a person get to be that way?" (17, 20, 26, 41, 137). How, that is, does one come to love flowers that others loathe? How does one become oblivious to views directly contrary to one's own? The reader is expected to admit: by being the scion of European "winners"—so far removed from actual conquest or exploitation as to romanticize the survival of the exploited races in one's own blood (39–40). Absent any doubt of the narrator's reliability and authority, one must concur with the critic who sums up Lucy's hosts as "a WASPish family whose insistent happiness and fervent liberalism mask their superficiality; their ignorance of history; their misunderstanding of class, racial, and gender divisions; and their complicity in the colonial condition."[16] But a more resistant reader may reflect that Mariah, who "spoke of women in society, women in history, women in culture" (131), has herself gone to some trouble to raise Lucy's consciousness. At pains to treat her au pair with every consideration, Mariah and her husband, evidently the kind of people with a social conscience, the kind of people who have done their best not to look at the world through a racist lens, receive only contempt.

But Lucy is herself a distorting lens, and her narrative invites comparison with such artfully managed autobiographical fictions as Alice Walker's "Everyday Use" and Joyce's "The Dead," both of which display great subtlety in the handling of point of view. In the Walker story, two sisters—one sophisticated, the other uneducated and self-effacing—vie for possession of some old quilts that embody their African American heritage. Brilliantly projecting herself into both figures, Walker critiques the superficial politics of racial identity. Joyce, too, insists on treating politics as subordinate to issues of identity and self-knowledge. Not that he shies away from direct treatment of politics: in "Ivy Day in the Committee Room," he makes something rich and strange—and engaged—out of a political theme. Like Kincaid, after all, Joyce is an exiled writer from an island under the English thumb. *Pace* the new school of postcolonial Joyce criticism, however, the author of "The Dead" rightly understood Irish politics as a minefield for the artist and so tends to make that subject only one strand within the artistic weave. One shudders to imagine "The Dead" told from the point of view of, say, Molly Ivors, the Irish nationalist who baits Gabriel Conroy at the Twelfth Night party given by his aunts. Yet this is precisely—and daringly—what Kincaid has done: she foregrounds the character with tunnel vision, gives her direct access to the reader's attention. If that reader takes the angry narrator as exempt from the author's irony, then the story founders, for *Lucy*, like any Joyce fiction, stands or falls by the success with which the author develops the complexity of the central character and the action in which she is engaged: negotiating the new world, assimilating or failing to, *growing up*.

Lucy, then, somewhat disingenuously disguises her youthful rebelliousness, not to mention her taste in poetry, as politically charged anger. Her political cathexis of the Wordsworth poem is suspect not least because, in damning a frail yellow flower, she breaks little more than a butterfly on the wheel of her ill humor. Nor is the poem itself much sturdier (however durable in anthologies). Disliking "I Wandered Lonely As a Cloud," after all, is not so rare—even among academics who, far from delighting in having memorized it in childhood, find it, years later, little more than a treacly trifle.

In fact, Lucy is selective in her literary repudiations. Thus she does not inveigh against Shakespeare—or the Milton that Annie John is made to copy out.[17] In fact, having also memorized parts of *Paradise Lost*, Lucy identifies with Milton's Satan, who becomes for her, as for Blake and the romantics and Stephen Dedalus, an example of nonconforming, redemptive, *artistic* energy. In interviews, Kincaid admits to loving English literature.[18] Like Jean Rhys, in fact (another Milton reader), Kincaid revisits Charlotte Brontë, telling a story about a fiery little governess who interacts with, dreams about, and observes the amours of a handsome and dissolute master.[19] Like both Charlotte and Emily Brontë, not to mention Rhys again, she weaves symbolic dreams into her story. Like Austen's Elizabeth Bennet, moreover, Lucy must deal with an impossible mother who favors the heroine's less worthy siblings. Lucy's family name derives, she imagines, from some English slaveholder—a figure who may call to mind

Sir Thomas Bertram in Austen's *Mansfield Park*. Small wonder that "the names of the authoresses whose books I loved" include "Emily, Charlotte, Jane" (149).

Although I have insisted here on an immature narrator's disagreeable qualities, my point is not to argue that *Lucy* is a failure. On the contrary, *Lucy* succeeds precisely because its author swaddles polemic in literary subtlety. The reader finds sorting this narrator out more interesting than listening to her preach and strike poses of moral superiority. Perhaps, too, the reader recognizes the better person in Lucy—the person glimpsed in her occasional admissions of fondness and even love for those she is at such pains to chasten. Examples include Lucy's expression of love for Miriam, one of her little charges, or the moments of compassion for Mariah on Lucy's part: "A sadness for her overcame me, and I almost started to cry— I had grown to love her so" (46). All along, Mariah has been a handy lightning rod for Lucy's conflicted feelings about her mother, and the longer Lucy stays with her employer, the more she loosens up, transferring filial sentiments that occasionally veer toward the positive. Indeed, Lucy's violent feelings toward her mother are clearly overdetermined. As Queen Gertrude says in *Hamlet*, the lady does protest too much.

Kincaid allows Lucy's mother and mother-surrogate to blend with the colonial "mother," England. The reader glimpses this conflation most clearly in the passage in which the mother sews with the colors of the Union Jack (131)—colors that return, freshly cathected, at the end. If Lucy's relationship with her mother and Mariah recapitulates the relationship between colonial "child" and its mother country, the point remains: it is the adolescent passage that is foregrounded. As colonial parent, England trains her children in the ways of British virtue and righteousness. When the children rebel and want their independence, "stony-face, sour-mouth" (136) England tries to reassert her authority, only to yield in bitterness. This colonial valedictory, so familiar in the years after World War II, is echoed in Mariah's grudging relinquishment of Lucy, for their anaclitic relationship has always strangely mirrored that of England and its colonies: "Mariah spoke to me harshly all the time now, and she began to make up rules which she insisted that I follow; and I did, for after all, what else could she do? It was a last resort for her—insisting that I be the servant and she the master. She used to insist that we be friends, but that had apparently not worked out very well; now I was leaving. The master business did not become her at all, and it made me sad to see her that way" (143). Mariah gives Lucy "a cold goodbye . . . her voice and face . . . stony" (144).

Mariah's face, in other words, has come to resemble the visage appearing on colonial postage stamps: that of the British monarch.

The novel's final image and final declaration carry considerable weight. They speak not to the narrator's politics but to her emotional life. Lucy's tears follow the writing of a first entry in her journal: "I wish I could love someone so much that I would die from it." At these words she experiences "a great wave of shame" (164), and this I take to be a kind of palinode, the repudiation of much of the disagreeable posturing that has gone before: she feels shame at her churlishness with Mariah, and she regrets the failure to treat her mother with consideration (she has gone out of her way to make plain her loathing and disgust, her inability to forgive the older woman, a product of her culture and her day, for favoring her male issue and failing to appreciate her daughter's intelligence). Perhaps, too, she regrets her negative view of the opposite sex (men are to be desired and used but never trusted, for they "have no morals . . . they do not know how to behave . . . they do not know how to treat other people" [142]). Thus her steely disinclination to love any of the men in her life was never sensible caution or mature discretion or tough-minded, feminist recognition of masculine failings—only some fear of allowing herself to risk emotional involvement, with its inevitable imperfection and compromise. Indeed, Lucy's absolutism is the chief exhibit in the case for her having been, from first to last, more the unhappy teenager than the voice of justified feminist or postcolonial ire. Lucy takes her leave of the reader at the moment she becomes human. In her end is her beginning, and her narrative, read properly, shows her rebelling as much against a parental colonization as against the usual kind. After that rebellion, one comes to terms with the reality principle, yields up the moral priggishness of adolescence, becomes a citizen indeed.

Between Karma and Manifest Destiny: Lan Cao's *Monkey Bridge*

In former times, many of those who came to the United States from abroad—Chinese laborers in the nineteenth century, Filipino laborers in the twentieth, migrant farm workers from Mexico—were allowed to work but not to stay. Readers of Carlos Bulosan's *America Is in the Heart* (1943) and John Okada's *No-No Boy* (1957) discover the misery of immigrants and even the children of immigrants never allowed to call themselves Americans. But the history of indignities coexists with the more mythic narrative of the myriads who—making a life, becoming citizens—came and over-came. In his memoir *South Wind Changing* (1994), Jade Ngoc Quang Huýnh tells a fairly representative story. After great misery in postbellum Vietnam, he and his brother escape to Thailand, then seek "resettlement in any free country that would have us." From his refugee camp Huýnh imagines a "third country, wherever it would be," where he "would have a chance" at education and employment.[20] Eventually the brothers go to the United States, where initially they must shelve their dreams in the struggle to make a living. Exploited in his first job, Huýnh is alternately made to work long hours without overtime or sent home when the supervisor does not need him (287). Eventually, however, his hard work enables him to arrange for four more siblings to escape from Vietnam to Indonesia and thence to America. Despite these successes, he cannot deliver his "parents and two older brothers" (289), and the difficulties of exile lead him nearly to despair: "Why did I come here in the first place? I wished I could go home, to a place where at least my skin and culture, my morals and values were the same as others'. A place where I was born and spoke the language. I wished I could die there someday, coming back to my roots, to the taste of the water and the air" (289–90). But these effusions mark the end of his regrets, and presently the family arrives, like Cather's Bohemians, in "the land of the good life, Nebraska" (292). Thereafter he makes good on his dream of an education—first a B.A. at Bennington, then an M.F.A. at Brown.

When Lee's *Gesture Life* appeared in French translation (as *Les sombres feux du passé*), a reviewer for *Le Monde* observed that "the twentieth century with its wars and its catastrophes, its lands and countries alternately privi-leged and devastated, has caused to be born an unprecedented literature of immigration," with emphasis, always, on themes of "identity, belonging, return to roots, assimilation, integration, repudiation, betrayal, guilt."[21] But not all the permutations of exile are negative. Though often frowned over as a painful passage, immigration can and does issue in physical, men-tal, emotional, and spiritual renewal. Nor is the renewal experienced only by the newcomers: the benefits of immigration flow to the adoptive home-land as well as to those debarking from steerage. Also psychologically ex-emplary, immigration sooner or later reverses the polarization of self and other. Despised at first, exploited, even brutalized, the alien presently be-comes part of a national self that, never subjected to these fresh integra-tions, would inevitably drift toward, at best, an unvital or insular compla-cency—or, at worst, a xenophobic or racist isolationism.

Immigrants resemble the "individual talent" that Eliot famously situates within an existing literary tradition. Indeed, the terms in which Eliot discusses the accommodations of tradition to new art lend themselves to any description of the ways in which American society accommodates new immigrants:

> What happens when a new work of art is created is something that happens simultaneously to all the works of art which preceded it. The existing monuments form an ideal order among themselves, which is modified by the introduction of the new (the really new) work of art among them. The existing order is complete before the new work arrives; for order to persist after the supervention of novelty, the *whole* existing order must be, if ever so slightly, altered; and so the relations, proportions, values of each work of art toward the whole are readjusted.[22]

As the immigrant subtly changes the larger American society, so does the art of the immigrant writer make a place for itself within the tradition of American literature. I propose to show how both of these accommodations, these displacements, figure in one especially deft fiction, Lan Cao's *Monkey Bridge* (1997).

In this novel about Vietnamese immigrants and their troubled memories, Cao places between herself and the reader a somewhat autobiographical narrator, Mai Nguyen, who comes to America in 1975 at age thirteen (as did the author). "We were . . . a ragtag accumulation of unwanted, an awkward reminder of a war the whole country was trying to forget."[23] Young enough to move swiftly toward mastery of English, success at school, and assimilation into American life, Mai is yet old enough to know and remember Vietnam and its travail. She also remains Asian enough to accept "the Confucian covenant that kept us forever connected to our ancestors" (59)—though it is precisely this covenant that survivors of a civil war will find most difficult to honor. She had come to the United States ahead of her mother, through the sponsorship of a sympathetic American military officer, "Uncle Michael" MacMahon (a French- and Vietnamese-speaking colonel, a veteran of World War II and six years in Vietnam). That MacMahon's relationship with Mai proves more than avuncular turns out to be part of a complicated meditation on Vietnamese American paternity and familial relationships. Mai learns only toward the end of the narrative that Colonel MacMahon had in fact become her adoptive father by a formal arrangement put into place before she left Vietnam—and evidently not revoked when her mother also comes to America (258). The mother, Mrs. Nguyen, will eventually reveal that she, too, has more than one father. Such revisions to the filial perception of kinship complicate the traditional Confucian piety and duty toward parents and ancestors—ancestors that include Vietnam itself, variously refracted through the characters' stories, their bodies, and even, in an elegiac moment at the end, the heavens: "Outside, a faint sliver of what only two weeks ago had been a full moon dangled like a sea horse from the sky" (260). This seahorse shape or attenuated *S* recurs as the emblem that marries the topography of Vietnamese land and Vietnamese body. Thus Mrs. Nguyen's "S-shaped spine twisted like a crooked coastline" (205). Her ravaged body iterates that of Vietnam—and vice versa. Her face, said to have been burned in a kitchen fire (3), was in fact burned by napalm, and she characterizes herself as a "woman . . . with all the signs of a ravaged battlefield on her face, a face of war" (230). Mai echoes this description when her mother lies recuperating from a stroke in an American hospital: "Her body had become a battlefield" (7).

Symbolism edges toward allegory. As the land repeats itself in the body, so does the recent history of Vietnam distill itself into the experience of a single, representative family. Nor is the history only that of a generation or two. Repeatedly in her narrative, Mai recalls what she has learned about the larger passages of the Vietnamese past, notably its proud history of resistance to foreign invasion. But this linchpin of national identity and collective remembrance becomes problematic when the Vietnamese, rid at last of the Japanese and the French (not to mention, much further back, the Chams, Mongols, and Chinese), cannot agree that a new invasion has taken place. Who are the new invaders—the Americans or the North Vietnamese? Can a fifth column—the Vietcong—be said to "invade"? Warring camps in the south have tragically different answers to these questions.

Mai spends much of her adolescence troubled by what she is allowed to believe is her mother's Confucian distress at having left behind in Vietnam a beloved parent, Baba Quan. Supposedly "they had missed each other at their place of rendezvous on the 30th of April, 1975" (4). On that day the war ended as the victors rolled into Saigon amid the last, frantic airlifts of American civilians and loyalist Vietnamese took place. Appearing in the text at least nine times (and obliquely referred to several times more), the date represents a transition, a climacteric, in the life of a family and a country. Hereafter, the search for the father, a venerable literary motif in the West, becomes something more Asian, more Confucian, more broadly ancestral—a search for the father/grandfather that comes to be a search for one's heritage as a refugee from the great, decades-long cataclysm of the Vietnam War. Only at the end, in a letter Mrs. Nguyen writes shortly before her suicide, does Mai learn the truth about her grandfather, which is in large measure the truth about a whole country's identity and fate. "Baba Quan . . . is a Vietcong from whom I am still trying to escape" (227). A drunkard withal, Baba Quan had pimped his wife to "a rich landlord known in the Mekong Delta as Uncle Khan" (229). Several thematic threads converge in Mrs. Nguyen's epistolary retrospection. She tells of attempting to inter the body of her mother in their village graveyard, which lies in an interdicted area, a "free-fire" zone occupied only by the Vietcong. Here she happens upon fragments of her own strange history in violent confrontation: she sees two Vietcong—one of them Baba Quan, the man she had for years accepted as her father—murder her real father, the abusive landlord. This remembered agon between fathers provides the novel's climax and crowns a cumulative revelation about paternity and other ancestral antecedents. Khan, ironically, had risked returning to the village to visit the grave of his mother, grandmother of the woman who witnesses his end. With the body of the woman shared by Quan and Khan literally strapped to her back, Mrs. Nguyen is gravely injured by napalm when an air strike is called in.

One might object to this scene on the grounds of its dubious plausibility were it not part of a larger strategy of symbolic representation. As they take their roles in the familiar drama of immigration, the vast pageant of exile and vexed assimilation, the narrator and her family enact an archetypal version of the transition from Asian to Asian American. Shuttling between her memories of the homeland and the present American reality, Mai registers her own cultural duality, incorporating the American perspective even as she penetrates or occupies it in a kind of reverse colonization. "My dilemma was that, seeing both sides to everything, I belonged to neither" (88). Like those pictures that shift and change when held against the light, the narration here constantly executes a kind of perspectival shimmer. As Pynchon speaks of muffin-tin images in aerial reconnaissance photographs that tease the eye, seeming from moment to moment to shift from convex to concave and back, so does the viewpoint in this narrative shift, in its cultural valence, from one side of the Pacific to the other. Mai's mother speaks of the "very young Americans" who first came to Vietnam, "a little frightened, perhaps, because everything must have looked and smelled as new to them as their country, fourteen years later, looks and

smells to us" (238). Mai's late father "had insisted on adopting a Viet-
namese perspective by calling the 'Vietnam War' the 'American War' or
the 'Second Indochina War'" (126–27). Much later, asked about "the war,"
Mai puzzles over the appropriate response. "Which war? I wanted to ask.
America was just beginning to stare at its own bruises. The war about
America's loss of innocence? About the American rite of passage and the
American experience gone wrong?" (126).

Such observations represent candor, not disparagement, and if Cao, in-
tent on thoughtful analysis, does not engage in sentimental apologetics for
the Land of the Free, neither does she dwell on American xenophobia.
Mai's encounter with a somewhat oafish apartment manager (Cliff) does
not seem particularly oppressive, and he is balanced, as it were, by Americans (notably Bill and "a gaggle of other GI regulars" [207] at the Mekong
Grocery) who seem capable of imagining the point of view of the cultural
other and even happy to embrace on their own shores what they had come
to know in some of the most intense passages of their lives. Aware of the
Vietnamese "color of mourning, the standard color for ghosts, bones, and
funerals" (1), Uncle Michael even repaints, in pink, the white ceiling of
Mai's room. No one, however, can alleviate the oppressive whiteness of the
hospital in which Mrs. Nguyen recovers from her stroke.

Having come at a still malleable age to "a country in love with itself,
beckoning us to feel the same" (31), Mai can look at her fellow refugees
with an "anthropologist's eye . . . step back and watch with a degree of detachment the habits and manners of Little Saigon" (146). She characterizes
the older Vietnamese as "adolescents," for she recognizes the classic immigrant reversal of parent-child roles and on one occasion refers to her
mother's "undramatic transformation from mother to child" (44). In violation of every Confucian precept, "all children of immigrant parents have
experienced these moments" (35) of filial reversal and have, presumably,
noticed "the peculiar and timid way" that adult immigrants "held their
bodies and occupied the physical space, the unfailing well-manneredness
with which they conducted themselves in public—their foreigners' ragged
edges." Mai's observations conclude with an insight worthy of Baudrillard:
"They had never managed . . . the eye-blinking, arm-folding maneuvers
needed for a makeover. . . . [T]hey continued to present themselves as reproductions from the tropics" (146). In other words, unable to master the
cosmetic adjustments implied in the word "makeover," the immigrants
cannot pose as Americans. Unable by the same token to be authentic

Asians, they remain only tragic "reproductions" of something more ethnically grounded. A study in the attenuation of signifieds, they exist under erasure, less substantial even than simulacra.

But some immigrants learn to play the game of identity simulacra all too well. In Falls Church, Virginia, Mai and her mother reside in a refugee enclave that includes a collection of draft dodgers and deserters, many of whom, in the spirit of immigrant self-fashioning, have become

> decorated veterans of battlefields as famous as Kontum and Pleiku and Xuan Loc. It was the Vietnamese version of the American Dream; a new spin, the Vietnam spin, to the old immigrant faith in the future. Not only could we become anything we wanted to be in America, we could change what we had once been in Vietnam. Rebirthing the past, we called it. . . . Even those with identification papers burned them before any authority could see. There was, after all, something awesome about a truly uncluttered beginning, the complete absence of identity, of history. (40–41)

Thus when Mary MacMahon tells Mai, "Be yourself," the narrator reflects that her foster mother "couldn't possibly understand that immigration represents unlimited possibilities for rebirth, reinvention, and other fancy euphemisms for half-truths and outright lies" (124). The dark irony of such pronouncements reveals itself when Mrs. Nguyen, in the letter she leaves behind at her suicide, admits how fruitlessly she had "tried to extinguish the imprints of my life and create alternate versions that suit my imagination and heal my soul" (227). The karmic cards allow no such reconfiguration of the self, and in the end both identity and history cling to and burn her—and by implication all immigrants—like napalm jelly.

Part of the irony includes the suggestiveness of draft dodging and the burning of identity documents—a strange mirroring of American behaviors during that much-hated war. Indeed, the novel has opened with young Mai enacting a variation on the flight to Canada that was so much a feature of the Vietnam era for young American men. Because her new homeland offers no telephone service to Vietnam, Mai and a friend drive to the Canadian border in hopes of being able to telephone Baba Quan in his village, establish that he survived the harrowing last days of the American presence, and thereby provide some comfort for his supposedly tormented daughter, Mai's mother. But Mai loses her nerve before entering Canada, and the truth about Baba Quan must await the revelation supplied later, in Mrs. Nguyen's posthumous letter.

Actually, the truth has been emerging all along: reading the private papers of her hospitalized mother, Mai begins to see the complexity, the moral wilderness, of a past that is at once her own and her country's. She also discovers fresh perspectives on herself and the experience of immigration. That Mai can read and understand—but not write—her own native language (46) may be taken as a gauge of her deracination (or, shifting the angle of view, her acculturation). Part of the genius of introducing the mother's journals and correspondence into the text is that, rather than the stereotype of the aged, dark-clad, English-impaired "Mamasan" (23), the reader encounters educated, allusive, trilingual fluency. (Nabokov similarly allows his bumbling Pnin to appear in a series of scenes in which the reader understands that he is speaking his elegant native Russian, not his broken English.) The journal entries of Mrs. Nguyen afford the older immigrant, the adult, her own voice, which is often skeptical, less willing blithely to embrace the new country and its mores.

Prying into the previous generation's secrets, Mai in fact does what her mother had done before her. On the day she marries Mai's father, the scholar Binh, Mrs. Nguyen finds and reads Uncle Khan's "book of debts" (232), the ledger that reveals to her the secret of her parentage and the mutual villainy of Baba Quan and his landlord. Perhaps these violations of privacy, however justified in the name of truth-seeking, discover the karmic legacy of prior transgressions. It is of course the book of *karmic* debts that every Vietnamese daughter must read on the eve of her marriage—characterized as a kind of immigrant prolepsis by Tran Thi Thanh, Mai's mother, whose marital "exile" (186) at age fifteen seems to parallel or set the pattern for the literal exile of her daughter at age thirteen.

The emphasis on karma here—so important to Asian consciousness— corrects for any tendency an American audience may have to read monoculturally. Americans lack a sense of karma, but for the Vietnamese it amounts to a kind of "ethical, spiritual chromosome . . . as much a part of our history as . . . DNA" (170). Even language buttresses the awareness of karmic reckonings: "Our reality, you see, is a simultaneous past, present, and future. The verbs in our language are not conjugated, because our sense of time is tenseless, indivisible, and knows no end" (252). Immersed in America as "the great brand-new" (60), Mai notes how her mother and other Vietnamese "saw life in terms of centuries, millennia" (60–61). Mrs. Nguyen passes on "this terrible truth—the long, deep line of karma carved by a world which precedes you—the truth of sin, illegitimacy, and murder"

(228–29). But even as she characterizes karma as "the antithesis_of Manifest Destiny" (55), Mrs. Nguyen articulates the classic immigrant expectation: that her child will enjoy "a different inheritance, an unburdened past, the seductive powers of an American future" (254).

Lan Cao's story of private papers rifled and heritage reassessed make her something of an Asian American Faulkner. Testing ideas of "inheritance," to use Mrs. Nguyen's terms, against a past that proves never to have been "unburdened," Cao seems to write with the author of *Go Down, Moses* looking over her shoulder. Where Cao tests the American Dream against the karmic debt so troubling to the Asian heart, Faulkner meditates on the American Eden and its fate. Faulkner's viewpoint character, Ike McCaslin, gradually comes to a recognition of his southern heritage through a kind of research that is directly parallel to acts of familial espionage undertaken by both Mai and her mother. Ike's major discoveries come in his reading of plantation ledgers that reveal to him the record of a whole people's unspeakable violation. Just as Ike discovers the contamination, by the circumstances of its realization, of the heroic southern past, so does Mai's mother, then Mai herself, piece together the karmic antecedents to her present life situation. Like Cao's Mai, Faulkner's Ike discovers the depravity of a grandfather. In slavery, and especially in the depredations of Carothers McCaslin, Ike is compelled to see a primal transgression, an original sin, that forever contaminates posterity. Old Carothers not only raped his slave but also raped his daughter by that slave. Guilty of incest as well as miscegenation and rape, the patriarch leaves to his descendants a "legacy" of primal corruption, and the phrase "southern heritage" takes on the full, crushing weight of modernist irony. Ike must recognize his own kin, his own flesh and blood, among those violated by his grandfather. In much the same way that all white southerners must sooner or later come to terms with the true dimensions of their heritage (the recognition that the imperfectly liberated other is in fact the self), so must Mai—and her mother before her—discover the sordidness of familial and national identity.

But *Monkey Bridge* makes its readers self-conscious about ethnocentric literary analogues. The text invites readers to recognize or look for specifically Asian antecedents to Mai's story, to see, for example, the irony behind allusions to *The Bionic Woman* and *I Dream of Jeannie* (9–10, 38, 69–70). The American references take on additional meaning as the reader sees them overtaken by the narrator's elaborate fantasies of becoming Trung Trac, "a sword-wielding Trung sister, the greatest warrior of all

Vietnamese warriors" (29), who heroically resisted Chinese occupation of Vietnam two thousand years ago. Like Fa Mu Lan, the "woman warrior" of Maxine Hong Kingston (an important influence here), this "first fighter, along with her sister, to elevate guerrilla warfare and hit-and-run tactics into an art of war, the first Vietnamese to lead a rebellion of peasants against the Chinese empire" (118–19), proves inspirational on shores far from Asia. Going into the "battle" of a "dreaded college interview," Mai imagines herself the undaunted Trung Trac, the heroic figure who sets the example for a whole history of resistance, enabling a modern Vietnamese to say, "We had driven back five Chinese invasions, three Mongol, and two French" (118). Of course, as Mai understands, this very history may well lie behind the perseverance of the communists. When, victorious, they "re-name most of the major streets in Saigon," they leave one street name un-changed—"the Street of the Trung Sisters" (124). Whereas Mai tells how her parents regaled her with stories of the Trung sisters, Lan Cao herself learned the heroic myths and legends of Vietnam from her Uncle Nhung, the family Vietcong who served as the model for the fictional Baba Quan.[24]

One other incident from this period—1979—is worth pausing over be-cause it hints at what a different perspective allows one to see in the expe-rience of others. Mai describes watching, with Uncle Michael, a movie about the Vietnam War in which American soldiers play Russian roulette—first under coercion by their Vietcong captors, then as a strangely driven compulsion in the back alleys of Saigon. The movie, obvi-ously *The Deer Hunter* (1978), elicits from the usually perspicacious Uncle Michael a puzzlement that was widespread among literal-minded viewers at the time of its release: "I was in Vietnam for six years and I've never seen or heard of anyone doing this before, at least on this massive scale." But Mai seems fully to understand this element as a metaphor for what Amer-ica was doing all along in Southeast Asia: "The roulettelike spin of a gun as arbitrary and senseless as Vietnam would dictate the life and death of American innocence" (100–101).

The perspicacity of the daughter contrasts with the vulnerability of the mother. Mai and Mrs. Nguyen define not so much the cliché of intergen-erational conflict as the constant poles of immigrant experience. Trapped between cultural paradigms, unable to cross the figurative monkey bridge between a painful past and an impossible present, Mai's mother might seem to exemplify a point made by Lisa Lowe in her study of Asian Amer-ican culture, *Immigrant Acts:* "The cultural productions emerging out of the contradictions of immigrant marginality displace the fiction of reconciliation, disrupt the myth of national identity by revealing its gaps and fissures, and intervene in the narrative of national development that would illegitimately locate the 'immigrant' before history or exempt the 'immigrant' from history."[25]

But such arguments beg questions predicated (as Lowe herself notes) on little more than journalistic myth, and any assertion regarding "a political fiction of equal rights . . . generated through the denial of history" (27) strikes one as being, itself, insufficiently historicized. No doubt the attempt to recuperate painful immigrant narratives to a vision of American homogeneity involves some denial or ignorance of history (not to mention contemporary social reality), but the culprit at this juncture is less likely to be some reprehensible desire to sweep the institutionalized injustice of the past under the rug of spurious "reconciliation" than the simple and much-discussed attenuation of the historical sense under the postmodern dispensation. Notwithstanding the fantasy of (re)inventing a self exempt from history (a fantasy that, as noted previously, Cao registers and critiques), the return of repressed history was always a fact of individual immigrant experience—one that can be recorded without necessarily indicting the new homeland's moral conscience. Certainly in *Monkey Bridge* the emphasis is not, as much postcolonialist theory would have it, on how becoming an American citizen is to be coerced or inveigled into forgetting past racism and imperialist exploitation. The emphasis is rather on the true complexity of personal and national history among those immigrating from a place fought over for two thousand years before the advent of the American imperium. Moreover, the author of *Monkey Bridge* balances the unhappiness of Mrs. Nguyen against her daughter's prospects on the eve of matriculation at a first-rate American college. Like Cao herself, Mai will attend Mount Holyoke, and perhaps she will eventually become—like the author—a professor at one of America's elite law schools. In these details Cao seems to refute Lowe's assertion that "narratives of immigrant inclusion . . . are driven by the repetition and return of episodes in which the Asian American, even as a citizen, continues to be located outside the cultural and racial boundaries of the nation" (6). Such formulations, intended as reproaches to the blinkered bigotry of a supposed American mainstream, actually tend toward a bizarre (though widespread) nostalgia for older, essentializing narratives of racism, cruelty, oppression, and exploitation. But books such as Cao's *Monkey Bridge* or Lee's *A Gesture Life* should not be mistaken for *Uncle Tom's Cabin* or *Up from Slavery*.

In a way more intimate than what readers steeped in reportage of the Vietnam War might expect, Cao's novel makes them see how American history must accommodate Vietnamese history. Having been to war in Vietnam, that is, Americans know that it will figure in their annals. But those who read *Monkey Bridge* learn also that the category "American" now includes large numbers of immigrants, Vietnamese Americans, who can remember calling this conflict, from their transpacific vantage, "the American war"—as, from that perspective, it was. The dual consciousness of the immigrant and the immigrant's narrative is something of a commonplace, but this story seems more resourcefully than most to integrate or incorporate or subsume the American perspective in the perspective of the "other," the colonized, who turns out, after all, to be the face in the mirror. As Carlos Bulosan long ago insisted, "All of us, from the first Adams to the last Filipino, native born or alien, educated or illiterate—*We are America.*"[26]

8 ≋ Ethnicity as Pentimento

Mylène Dressler's *The Deadwood Beetle*

> As long as the harbors are dark, herds flee out from Asia, wearing her necklace of skulls, doomed Europe and her ovens full, Mother Russia scouring the back steps with wire and broom, the fly-bitten eyelids of Africa...
>
> —Li-Young Lee, *The Winged Seed*

Mylène Dressler's *The Deadwood Beetle* concerns the troubled soul of an immigrant, Tristan Martens, who left his native Holland a few years after the end of World War II to make his way in the place of new beginnings, America. Here he has married, got an education, become a university entomologist and a citizen. But when the reader meets him, old Martens has little for which to congratulate himself. His wife has left him, his only child has become a Jesus-crazed survivalist, and he has a heart condition that is both literal (he has undergone a triple-bypass operation) and figurative, for he is troubled by what he takes to be his failures as husband, father, and brother.

Martens's profession as entomologist may put the reader in mind of *Cat's Eye*, the Margaret Atwood novel whose narrator grows up in the household of an entomologist father (as Atwood herself did). Martens specializes in the order *Coleoptera*, which includes beetles and weevils, and Dressler's epigraph reminds us of an ancient culture's curious association of beetles with troubled hearts: "In ancient Egypt . . . [h]eart scarabs were placed on or near the chest of the mummy . . . admonishing the heart not to bear witness against its own master on judgment day." The story that follows concerns an unhappy old man who, all too ready to bear witness against himself, must struggle in his heart to live down a dark heritage: as the child of wartime collaborators in Holland, he committed an act of betrayal for which he cannot forgive himself. The betrayal, however, is not what one might expect.

Something of a crisis is precipitated when, over half a century after the war, Martens stumbles upon his mother's sewing table in the New York antique shop of Cora Lowenstein, an attractive woman in her fifties. She points out the childish inscription on the table's underside: "Als de Joden weg zijn is het onze beurt," which she translates as an echo of Pastor Niemöller's powerful homily, "When the Jews are gone, we will be the next ones."[1] But Martens knows better. He knows that the children who penciled these words deep into the wood of that table—he and his sister—were merely transcribing the Nazi slogan their collaborationist father had parroted: "When the Jews are gone, it will be our turn" (177). Profoundly disturbed, Martens wants to remove this table from the public eye, but Cora has no intention of selling. In undertaking a campaign to persuade her to part with it, Martens finds himself enamored—especially when he learns that her husband, Sandor, languishes in a life-care institution with physicians who "insist he's dead, that he has no higher brain functions" (89).

Equal parts German and Dutch by birth, Martens might be called a halfling, but he also reveals himself to the reader as a *Häftling*, a prisoner of his past. This novel disrupts the common depiction of the immigrant as a kind of moral tabula rasa whose sufferings are conspicuously undeserved. *The Deadwood Beetle* resembles Chang-rae Lee's *A Gesture Life* in that here again a narrator-protagonist gradually reveals a guilty conscience that interestingly corrects for the tendency to see the immigrant as exemplary or blameless—and all too willing to discard a painful past. Each novel focuses on a person implicated in atrocity, and each of these central figures is of what we might call peripheral ethnicity. It is the Korean blood of Lee's Franklin Hata that complicates his relationship with the pathetic "comfort women" he is charged with keeping healthy for the pleasure of his fellow soldiers in the wartime Imperial Army of Japan. By the same token, Tristan Martens cannot, in his heart, make amends for his family's associations with the Germans who occupied his homeland.

The life odyssey of Tristan Martens in fact gives the lie to certain cherished myths about fresh starts in America. Thus he does not move from old world fatalism or determinism to the new world paradigm of self-fashioning. Rather, he becomes the testing ground for what immigration theorist Werner Sollors calls "descent" and "consent" models of ethno-social integration. "Descent relations," Sollors explains, "are those defined by anthropologists as relations of 'substance' (by blood or nature); consent relations describe those of 'law' or 'marriage.' Descent language empha-sizes our positions as heirs, our hereditary qualities, liabilities, and entitle-ments; consent language stresses our abilities as mature free agents and 'architects of our fates' to choose our spouses, our destinies, and our polit-ical systems." Sollors characterizes "the newcomers' rebirth into a forward-looking culture of consent" as a "classic American idea."[2]

In the problematic Americanization of a European, Mylène Dressler in effect reframes Henry James's characteristic theme of American innocence encountering the much older and more complicated descent culture of Europe. For Dressler's Martens, however, the fabric of consent begins to unravel toward the end of his life. Never fully assimilated into the Ameri-can consent model, he increasingly perceives his European past as dictat-ing his present and what future remains to him. The consensual relation-ships with his environment and with other people have proved difficult to sustain, as if a terrible determinism must inevitably figure in the post-immigration existence of certain Europeans—those unable finally to cast off the bitter memories that would seem to be their inalienable heritage. Now, in his twilight years, he renews his struggle with the implications of what shaped him, what he descended from.

Not to mention what descends from him. Has he, after all, been merely the carrier, the passer-on, of certain dark genes? One of the novel's bitter-est ironies is that Martens's wholly American son seems bent on reinvent-ing the half-baked fascism of his old world grandparents. "Greetings from the land of milk and honey" (180), writes this well-armed fundamentalist, unaware that his characterization of Texas as Promised Land echoes the figure used by his grandmother to characterize her native Germany (174, 175). Neither the Dutch Nazi nor the Christian fundamentalist seems to give any thought to the phrase's Jewish provenance. Bracketed genera-tionally by dangerous ideologies, poor Martens cannot seem fully to es-cape the kind of blood or kinship determinism characterized by Sollors as the "descent" paradigm of ethnic identity.

America, too, is a promised land, and Martens himself, "among the cho-sen" (160) allowed to immigrate after the war, unconsciously echoes the language of Hebraic election. But even though he acquires a substantial education, an academic career, and a family, Martens becomes at best a problematic American. Late in life he has shed job and wife, and any sense of promise in a new world identity or nationality seems attenuated as his mind circles around certain events in his European past. Martens remains that familiar figure of twentieth-century fiction, an exile, but he does not, like Nabokov or one of his characters, pine for a literal homeland. Rather, he yearns for the innocence cut short by the circumstances of his childhood.

Richard Eder, reviewing W. G. Sebald's *Vertigo*, observes that "the Holocaust, lethally radiating in every temporal direction, contaminates in its foreshadowings and rememberings all human chronicles, not just those of the Jews."[3] This novel is a case in point. Like Sebald, Dressler has an instinct for registering the way the Holocaust poisons human relationships long after the fact. Yet she avoids the mistake of equating one gentile's personal tragedy with the Holocaust (the mistake Styron makes in *Sophie's Choice:* he invites the reader to care as much about the puerile narrator's coming of age as about the horrific suffering of Sophie, her children, Nathan, and the rest of the 6 million). Engaging the century's central horror with taste and caution, Dressler makes the emphatic point that Martens's experience does *not* equate with that of Holocaust victims. She does not seek to represent the Holocaust; far less does she make the mistake of suggesting that Martens's misery is on anything like the scale of those who suffered at the hands of the Nazis. She seeks rather to represent the small-bore tragedy of one whose suffering is—like a candle beside the sun—completely overwhelmed by another, far greater tragedy. "There are occasions when sins are drowned in other sins" (210), says a priest to the young Tristan. This is one key to Martens's tragic misery. His crime—the destruction of his sister's one chance at love—cannot be dealt with because of the circumstances in which it transpired: "What right did I have to speak, when I had killed some faint hope for her, and the bodies had already been piled so high, in Birkenau, in Dachau, in Buchenwald?" (224). In other words, dwarfed by concurrent horror on a vast scale, his one small cruelty and its sequel cannot be expiated. Guilt follows him across the Atlantic and down through the years.

Being an immigrant is always, in a novel such as this one, more than a given. Tristan Martens was seventeen when he immigrated to the United States, "this land of re-invention" (24) in which "everything was possible" (68). His mother, on her deathbed, makes a curious remark: "All this dying, it's got nothing to do with you anyway. You're an American" (162). By this she may mean to reproach her son for abandoning his native land, but she also airs the perception that even death must defer to American

virtù: Et in America *non* sum. When he attends the funeral of this last surviving old-world connection, grief eludes him, and he cannot weep. He assures himself that he need no longer remember the war years and their
thoroughly unpleasant aftermath for collaborators: "I was a grown man. I
was married. I had a young son. I lived in the United States of America, I
had become a man of education and profession and distinction. . . . I had
escaped. I had made good. There seemed to be no reason, then, to think of
such events anymore, or to try to stir what lay dead and buried" (170). This
description may remind the reader of Camus's affectless Meursault: "Au-
jourd'hui ma mère est morte." Like Meursault, too, Martens tells his own
story, which will include a revelation about the blood on his hands.
Presently as disconnected from American wife and son as from Dutch
mother, father, and sister, Dressler's Martens sees himself, citizenship
notwithstanding, as some kind of eternal outsider. Indeed, such contemporary dramas of the immigrant's problematic metamorphosis reverse the
conceit behind all those mid-century novels of alienation: where a Camus
or a Salinger or a Bellow compares a protagonist's anomie or accidie to the
confused otherness of the foreigner, the Mosaic stranger in a strange land,
the contemporary novel of immigrant experience invokes a now familiar
psychological estrangement as referent for the disorientation that complicates or precludes assimilation. It is as if, half a century after the fact, these
writers were making a point of the alternative translation of that familiar
Camus title *L'étranger:* the foreigner.

However indifferent to the death of his mother, Martens finds himself,
some years later, curiously moved upon discovering, in the Lowenstein
shop, the sewing table she had once owned. And oddly enough, the image
that swims into his ken is that of the original, biblical stranger in a strange
land: "I edged toward it, feeling something, I couldn't help it, it must have
been like the confusion and hope and longing of the woman who crept
toward that improbable baby's basket nestled in among the reeds" (32). At
first, the figure seems incongruous, even when one considers the extent to
which the table witnesses to the Holocaust—the horror inflicted on the
descendants of that baby in the basket among the bullrushes. But the table,
like Moses, is of divided provenance, belonging now to collaborators with
the century's supreme anti-Semites, now to preterite Jewish survivors
of the cataclysm. Nor is an old man's momentary association of himself
with the finder of the basket inappropriate, for Martens identifies, miser-
ably, with Pharaoh, not the Hebrews.

Yet the table is also his childhood self, "inscribed" with the unspeakable. The adult self has its own inscriptions and, indeed, its own furniture. The sewing table seems to be complemented by Martens's extensively "scratched" dining table, "one of the relics of my divorce" (22). As the one table documents a benighted childhood, so does the other, glass one, "spotted everywhere with . . . fingerprints and haloed with the ghosts of medicine-bottle caps and Pepto-Bismols and blotted and Rorshached with coffee rings and spills" (148), bear mute witness to a miserable old age. A last inscription is at once the most incondite and the least ambiguous: the scars from his triple-bypass operation record the "heart trouble" that, as noted before, is more than physiological. Martens's body is inscribed, as it were, with his crimes against the heart. Written on the body, the scars make him, in his own eyes, a version of Dr. Frankenstein's hideous monster (21).

The reader may also think of the miserable inmates in Kafka's penal colony, where a device called the Harrow brings a slow death as it inscribes their crimes on their bodies. But even more suggestive are the parallels between Dressler's story and Kafka's "Metamorphosis." Each work exploits an analogy between a main character and an insect to express modern ideas about alienation. Kafka famously literalizes the analogy, as Gregor Samsa actually turns into a large bug—indeed, into a beetle, according to Vladimir Nabokov, who emphasizes a central irony: "Gregor is a human being in an insect's disguise; his family are insects disguised as people."[4] Nabokov also notes a strangely conflicted relationship between Gregor and the sister, Grete, who eventually fails him.

Dressler expands the Kafkaesque conceit, developing extensive insect and beetle analogies, reversing the dynamic of sibling betrayal, and perhaps even welcoming some of the psychoanalytic interpretation so abhorrent to Nabokov. Where Kafka's insect metaphor projects the isolation and alienation of the sensitive individual or artist vis-à-vis bourgeois complacency and philistinism (the story of "coleopteron Gregor," says Nabokov, is that of "mediocrity surrounding genius"),[5] Dressler's gauges only the isolation of an immigrant, albeit one much troubled by guilt. But if Dressler deploys this metaphor to less profound or sublime ends, she allows it considerably more reticulation, for she—or her narrator—also invites readers to discern suggestive insectival features or traits among the secondary characters. When Tristan Martens first encounters Agnes, the woman who will marry and divorce him, she has fallen while skiing and is struggling on her back, like an upended bug (67–68). Similarly, Martens briefly perceives Cora Lowenstein as a water weevil (146). Cora's institutionalized husband, braced in a wheelchair, does not strike Tristan as completely vegetative; he finds himself thinking of "that vulnerable stage when a creature is struggling to molt" (107). This perception proves prophetic, as presently Sandor will begin to recover—and heart-dead Tristan may undergo a similar resurrection by story's end, a spiritual or affectional ecdysis.

Tristan is often characterized as a beetle, "a desperate burrower, a borer," survivor of open-heart surgery that leaves him with a "cracked carapace" (155). Like the *Cassinidae*, the subfamily of tortoise beetles that is his scholarly specialty, he is adept at pulling in his head, sheltering within or behind his shell. Although the reader never encounters a direct explanation of the book's title, it presumably refers to its narrator and main character. But what is a deadwood beetle, and what does it mean to call Tristan Martens one? Many beetles inhabit dead wood, but one searches the literature on *Coleoptera* in vain for a particular "deadwood" beetle. Evidently, the significance here is more general: Martens is at once a human beetle and, in the old figurative sense, dead wood. He is superannuated, no longer professionally vital. He is also, apparently, impotent (154–55).

Every character seems to have an insect identity, though at times the author allows the human analogue to remain obscure. Thus the reader puzzles at first as to just who—Tristan himself or his tiresome and smug son—finds his likeness in the "New Guinean fly" whose "armored, spearlike" proboscis often proves so overdeveloped and weighty as to become a fatal disability. Since the business of these flies is "thrashing and stabbing at one another" (60), it would seem that both father and son resemble them, for theirs is a continuously combative relationship. Tristan, however, is the one most obviously exhausted by this battle and the labor of wielding his own metaphorical spear. As infant, too, he is characterized as fastened to the maternal "breast like a fly to a spigot" (141).

Martens's student Elida, another ostensibly buglike character, fears at one point that her irascible old adviser will pinch her head off (205). Martens describes her braid as "like a thick split chrysalis" (16), and he recognizes "the successful academic's hunger" in his protegee, "the ambition that narrowed life to a single stalk: a green reed to be gnawed on and chewed and grasped with all available limbs and climbed, up and up and up" (18, cf. 24). She studies a particular beetle native to the desert: it has become wingless to provide "insulation" (14), and it "stridulates," she thinks, "using the air-space above the abdomen" (15). The reader recognizes in Martens a version of this creature: he dwells in an emotional desert, and above the abdomen a figurative void occupies the space of his heart. Elida proposes to write a thesis on "insect deceivers" (13, cf. 15, 128), creatures that have taken certain forms of mimicry to extraordinary lengths. Early in the story she reports to Tristan about a "trick beetle" (18), a "species that avoids predation by mimicking wasps" (13; cf. 128). Even at this point the reader can see that Tristan himself belongs to this species, his vespine disposition calculated to keep the world—including Elida—at bay. In fact, human versions of the trick beetle abound here. Thus Tristan does his best not to look like the "lamentable, lonely character" (119) he is, and Elida disguises her memories about her father and his untimely death. She also resorts to deception when she invites Tristan to Christmas dinner, pretending that she needs his advice (118). Tristan characteristically operates by indirection, by variously appearing to be the thing he is not or to pursue the thing he does not actually want. His oblique, roundabout pursuit of the sewing table is itself part of the theme of deception and protective counterfeit. "Should a woman . . . ever come my way," he thinks, she would have to "be tricked into spending some time with me" (22). In this he resembles his oafish father, whose mimicry of distinction, posing deceptively beside a motorcycle that he does not own, contributes to his securing a mate: Tristan's mother.

As narrator, too, Tristan is a trick beetle—not least because he is, so far as the reader knows, the source of the insectival imagery. In a story so fraught with personal and historical pain, one welcomes the slight comic exaggeration of a character given to a particular channel of rhetoric. But Dressler does not depict Martens as another Uncle Toby, ever ready to mount an entomological hobbyhorse. Nor does she mean to undercut his perceptions, however colored they are by professional habit and disillusionment with human relationships. Rather, she exploits the entomological imagery and lexicon as a means of creating a distinctive narrative voice and realizing a Kafkaesque gauge of his alienation. Elida obliges the narrator "to participate in common human rituals . . . [b]ecause you keep forgetting, Martens. We're human" (142).

Most of all, the rhetoric deployed by the narrator defines a psychologically plausible defense mechanism. Martens's unreliability, such as it is, chiefly reflects the half-unconscious desire to disguise a terrible psychic wound behind the ultimately less significant concern about that sewing table's languishing in the wrong hands, its inscription constantly miscon-strued. For this very reason Martens insists through much of the story that the table and the Holocaust guilt it evokes are what most trouble him. But this is a piece of psychoanalytically plausible misdirection. In fact (and to some degree he manages to deceive even himself) it is the betrayal of his sister and her subsequent suicide that lurks in his heart as the most psy-chologically and spiritually oppressive of memories. In this rhetorical cam-ouflage, of course, he exemplifies a familiar precept of psychoanalysis: trauma screens itself with false clues and repression.

Seconding the trick beetle theme is the play of parallels among charac-ters and incidents. At one point Elida wonders, "Do you think it's possible everything mimics everything else?" (204). The story variously exempli-fies the implied postulate, for everywhere in it the reader discerns sugges-tive replication. Tristan immigrates to the United States at age seventeen. His mother had immigrated from Germany to the Netherlands shortly after encountering his father for the first time at the age of sixteen. Tristan breaks a dish while lunching with Cora (51), another while dining with Elida's family (143). Like Cora Lowenstein, Elida's mother, Rocío, must live without her husband. Tristan and Elida were naturalized in the same year. There is a suggestive parallel between Tristan and his Nazi-sympathizer father, characterized now as a "drone" (152), now as "*Gymno-pholus lichenifer*, the walking-garden beetle, a species which carries with it an entire household on its back" (44). Years later, the son will also appear to be "carrying all his possessions" (40). The image of Tristan's father standing beside a motorcycle prefigures the photograph of Cora and San-dor leaning against a sports car (43, 76). Indeed, there appears to be some kind of parallel between Tristan's parents and Cora and Sandor Lowen-stein. Subsequently Sandor in the care facility reminds Tristan of his ter-minally ill mother in her hospital ward (91). The dead calf Tristan's mother had seen as a girl in Germany (21, 97) finds its echo in the dead goat that Tristan sees there (219). More portentously, the Martens family enact a mirror image of the Jewish deportations with which, as collaborators, they have been complicit: Westerbork, cattle car, stripping, delousing, labor camp, barbed wire (168–70). Tristan's disappointments at love—the di-vorce from Agnes, the abortive affair with Cora—parallel the experience of his sister, whose love also came to naught. At the heart of this weave of paralleled motifs, this textuality, lies the inscription under the table and the opposed meanings of "once the Jews are gone." Ironically, Tristan never brings to consciousness the relevance to his present situation of that equivocal phrase: once a particular Jew is gone—Sandor—it will be "his turn" with Cora.

In this text, at least, "everything mimics everything else." Steven G. Kellman suggests one thematic rationale for the prominence of this textual mimicry: "imitation," he remarks, "enables immigrants to assimilate, children to mature, and subject peoples to thrive under Nazism."[6] Perhaps, too, the parallels model textuality more directly, a weave of self-referring signifiers that constantly defer representation of the signified, constantly refuse to yield up the first causes of an individual's (or a century's) pain. In other words, this fine reticulation functions as language in miniature—the language that, in the Lacanian formula, discovers the very structure of the unconscious.

But the parallels model repetition and structure that invite reading from an older psychoanalytic perspective. Unlike Lacan, who saw the contents of the unconscious as inaccessible within the Symbolic order of the very language that models its structure, Freud believed that the repressed secrets of the unconscious reveal themselves obliquely in dream or parapraxis—and yield themselves to analysis. Tristan Martens, probing for what the pursuit of an embarrassing table screens, in effect undertakes a kind of self-analysis and takes himself and the reader back to a highly cathected moment in his own psychological history, a primal scene, as it were. Freighted with the narrator's obsessive, overdetermined pursuit of the maternal table, the text's fine weave of echoic repetition and parallel intimates the very web of fatality that circumscribes an exile such as Tristan. Insofar as neurotic iteration actually structures the text, it hints at meanings in the realm of psychopathology. Like all such repetition, it invites understanding as sophisticated *fort-da* game. It was in contemplating his grandson's curiously repeated enactment of loss and recovery of a toy that Freud recognized how the mind copes with trauma. It seeks to ritualize and thus control loss—even though to do so it must absent itself from felicity and violate the pleasure principle. Freud discerned a disturbing drive in the repetition paradigm, a death instinct, "an urge inherent in organic life to restore an earlier state of things."[7] In a sense, all immigrants play some such *fort-da* game, for they must often yearn for a prior condition—if not the "inorganic state" that Freud's death instinct targets, then some equally problematic anteriority to the painful growth and becoming of exile or immigration, a state fraught, of course, with the very pain that drives them into exile.

At the end, having completed his self-indicting narrative, Tristan knows that Sandor Lowenstein will recover and that Cora will remain only a friend. But he takes his leave of the reader with a phrase as ambiguous as the one on the underside of his mother's sewing table: "The truth would have to be left behind, on this night" (226). Perhaps he means that he has finally left the truth about his own past behind, in the shop, with the table. Or perhaps the surrendered truth is simply the love that, never to be communicated or realized now, must be left behind in what remains of his life's journey. If Martens does not find love, however, he seems to undergo his own kind of resurrection, a complement to that of Sandor. The story has observed a progression from an autumn that embodied Martens's decline, through a secular Christmas, to a springtime of reawakenings (in this last the author also recalls and gently revises Kafka, who is bitterly aware that insects revive in spring). If nothing else, Martens has discovered in himself the redemptive ability to care about and love others—Elida, Sandor, and especially the desired Cora. Although he does not recover the table, he discloses its history and the real meaning of its inscription, and so experiences some relief from his guilt. A remembered childhood confession with nothing to confess recurs now, as he confesses everything to Cora, who offers absolution: "You were just a child" (225) then; "you're a good man" (158) now. She articulates the insight of the ancient Egyptians: the guilty heart must not be allowed to bear witness against itself.

Whatever the renewal, Dressler does not encourage the reader to see it in a religious light. Cora declares herself a nonbeliever, and Tristan declares himself "finished with faith" (87). Lamenting "how little the mechanical chances and outcomes of the universe take us into account" (158), he characterizes "randomness" as "incapable of even the smallest concessions" (200). Nevertheless, he sees latitude for personal connection in the midst of history's brutal indifference and so distances himself from the despair that another twentieth-century literary character glimpses in another disturbing Nazi-era inscription. The shell-shocked Sergeant X, in Salinger's "For Esmé, With Love and Squalor," looks into a copy of Goebbels's *Die Zeit Ohne Beispiel* in which the previous owner has written, "Dear God, life is hell." Sergeant X writes Dostoyevsky's words below: "Fathers and teachers, I ponder what is hell? I maintain that it is the suffering of being unable to love."[8] This insight, expressed in negative terms, becomes at once more positive and more tentative in Dressler's novel. Martens seems to recognize that, "implicated in each other's fate" (49), we remain capable of love, even when love proves elusive. It is never too late, apparently, to learn this lesson: "I wanted her to remember history and that it teaches us nothing if not the panoramic triumph of human failure, interrupted only by small moments . . . small communions, when one of us reaches out imperfectly and selfishly toward the other and says, Be with me" (87).

9 ≋ Immigration as *Bardo*

Wendy Law-Yone's *The Coffin Tree*

I was a wanderer when I came here
Thinking of my home in far-off Ch'ang-an.
From inside Yellow Crane pavilion
I heard a beautiful flute playing "Falling Plum Blossoms"
In the late spring, in a city by the river.
—Li Po (trans. Sam Hamill)

Wendy Law-Yone, in *The Coffin Tree*, omits few of the classic elements one looks for in novels by immigrant authors, but at times the familiar features figure in unusual ways. One expects characters in immigrant fiction to suffer from a pronounced and often debilitating double consciousness, for example, but here the least healthy character of all—the narrator's brother Shan—seems fatally incapable of such duality. Therein lies the pathos of his fate. It seems significant that Shan had a stillborn twin. As the stillbirth suggests, he can only be one self, and that self, once transplanted, is doomed. His sister, the narrator, paradoxically experiences double consciousness when she attempts to end consciousness altogether. Proximate death is attended by a moment of ultimate doubleness: "I felt myself lifted onto some dim, distant plane where I could split myself off, quite painlessly, from that awful lonely thing I was watching."[1] The eating disorder that often figures in fictions by immigrant women appears here in a somewhat attenuated fashion. Janie C. Har draws attention to the curious dynamic of Shan's pathetic and disgusting gluttony, abetted and enabled by a sister who offers "food as a substitute for affection."[2] Less ambiguous is the compulsion to eat on the part of Helga, the narrator's fellow patient—and fellow immigrant—in the mental institution, 3 East. Evidently German or Austrian, Helga contributes to the subtle intimation that this asylum contains a suggestive density of aliens (several bear names—Paddy, Winston, perhaps Maria—infrequently conferred on the native-born).

Elsewhere in this novel the author arranges the building blocks of immigrant narrative in more familiar ways. Before and after the main characters' departure from Burma, the reader gets glimpses of old-country customs and mores in urban, postcolonial Rangoon, as well as among the hill tribes. The unnamed narrator takes on maternal responsibility for her half-brother Shan: "I was turned into the mother of the child he had become" (74). Ten years older than she, he is that much less adaptable to life in a new social and cultural environment. These characters leave behind their actual mothers (dead or deranged before their children's emigration) and their father, whose death, five years after the narrator begins her transformation into an American, signals some final dissolution of old ties. Like the mothers of his children, he embodies the lost homeland—but less forcefully with every passing year. As the parents become a fading memory, the immigrant Orpheus must relinquish the homeland, his Eurydice, to infernal powers that turn it into "Myanmar," another of the rogue states that enlarge the kingdom of Hades.

Arriving in America, Law-Yone's Burmese immigrants make their way only with great difficulty, but after two years some progress has been made—at least by the narrator: "It was at the point when I was beginning to feel some mastery of life in America, when I had learned to drive a car and file a tax return, when I had found steady work and made acquaintances, when I could look around me and consider all the possibilities the new world had to offer—it was at this point, two years after our arrival in the States, that I was taken captive for the next two long years in which my brother fell apart" (70). "Taken captive," she and her brother now serve a "two-year sentence," which for him proves "a death sentence of the mind" (75). The carceral imagery recurs insistently. When she characterizes herself and her brother as "escapees from an imprisoned land," the narrator signals her awareness that the homeland, their native Burma, has become a police state, replete with "fear, privation, arrests, confiscations, deaths, despair" (149). Its exiles, ironically, suffer a different kind of incarceration, and in characterizing the last two years with her brother, the narrator mines the penal lexicon for words expressive of their plight. Carceral rhetoric figures with particular prominence in the chapter describing the final months with Shan and in the chapter in which his sister languishes in the mental institution. Here, declares the narrator, "I felt a prisoner" (86). However benign the motives of those who have committed her, she declares herself "still a prisoner" (87). "Weeks passed in that prison," she says (171).

In a way, all of the references to incarceration are subsumed in a line or two of the Buddhist verses introduced in the novel's closing pages: "the gods of death" are said to be "nothing but the phantoms / Imprisoned in your soul" (189, 190). This text, like *The Tibetan Book of the Dead*, which it condenses, constantly exhorts the soul, during its *Bardo* or journey toward reincarnation, to differentiate spiritual reality from *maya*—the world of illusion that imprisons it. As will be seen, however, this spiritual counsel proves ineffectual for the novel's two central characters. Shan never really grasps it, and his sister comes to resist supernaturalism on principle, whether it present itself in Christian or Buddhist guise. But she does embrace a secular version of the precept trumpeted on every page of Buddhist doctrine: Avoid illusion.

Framing this precept (in both its secular and spiritual signification) is the most problematic of the standard features I have been recapitulating: the folk material with which the author ostensibly renders authentic the picture of her native Burma. This element, however, resists easy interpretation. In the deployment of a remembered Burmese mythology and Burmese folk tales—of golden pheasant and the coffin tree itself—readers discern Law-Yone's special perspective on the immigrant experience. But rather than some rich, lost tapestry, some "ocean of story" easily navigable by anyone who grew up in Burma, these tales prove obscure, curiously character-specific, and of dubious provenance. Their positive meanings difficult to affirm, they resemble the similarly ambivalent folk material in *Breath, Eyes, Memory*.

For information about an actual coffin tree, one turns to the explorer-botanist Francis Kingdon-Ward, who in *Burma's Icy Mountains* (1949) describes the various species from which artisans construct the heavy, elaborately enameled coffins bespoke by rich Chinese. He identifies the rare *Taiwania cryptomerioides* as the true "Chinese coffin tree" but notes that "*Libocedrus, Cunninghamia* and at least one laurel (a species of *Machilus*)" can also supply the prized hundred-pound planks essential to the manufacture of the "weighty oblong box" considered ideal for interment. Law-Yone takes from Kingdon-Ward details about the weight of the planks, the rarity of the trees, and the riches to be gained from their discovery and harvesting. When the narrator beholds in a dream what she takes to be a coffin tree "crowned by a graceful pagoda of leaves" (194), she echoes Kingdon-Ward's description of a fine specimen's "pyramidal top," which "had rather the look of an idealized Christmas tree." When the tree in the dream turns out to be not the long-sought rarity but a common juniper, one notes another detail from Kingdon-Ward: "Ever since the first decade of this century, rumours of the Chinese coffin tree have come out of the remote corner of Burma, the timber being at one time identified with *Juniperus recurva*."[3]

Although trees figure in the mythology of both East and West (the Christian rood, the Norse Yggdrasil, the *bodhi* under which Gautama achieves enlightenment), the narrator of Law-Yone's novel can make little of the coffin tree myth, which seems a kind of *hapax legomenon* of folklore. First spoken of by Shan, it is finally explained as a detail in the book he had from "the old coffin tree merchant" (119), an "opium addict" (124) and "soothsayer" (119) who on one occasion tells the heroine's fortune with considerable accuracy, like his counterpart in the opening pages of Mukherjee's *Jasmine*. But does recovery of the coffin tree myth—and with it awareness of esoteric Buddhism (Tibetan, that is, rather than Burmese)—empower or enlighten the nominally Christian narrator? It does not seem an altogether positive influence on her brother, after all. I have already noted that the book culminates in verses quoted from the curious volume that, according to his sister, Shan had cherished and studied. Based on the never named *Tibetan Book of the Dead*, the verses contain repeated reference to something never mentioned in that source: "the Spirit / Of the Coffin Tree" (191). Whence this factitious myth, and why does the author make it so central to her tale? Is it "a piece of chicanery, a fake map leading to a bogus treasure" or the "legend of other-worldly concerns" (192) by which one might reshape a literally errant life? Perhaps, as John Barth says, the key to the treasure is the treasure.

Nostalgia and Madness

The presence of nostalgia—or rather, say, its relative foregrounding—tends to differentiate novels of exile from novels of immigration. A Nabokov character, watching newsreels of the Russia to which he can never return, finds himself suddenly overcome with emotion: " 'I must not, oh it is idiotical,' said Pnin to himself as he felt—unaccountably, ridiculously, humiliatingly—his tear glands discharge their hot, infantine, uncontrollable fluid."[4] Part of the poignance of this little moment lies in Pnin's speaking to himself in imperfect English. In the rich music of his native Russian he would not be so verbally clumsical. But he has become an American citizen, and the English language helps to control feelings that threaten to unman him. If, like other émigré characters in Nabokov (not to mention the author himself), Pnin engages his Russian past with powerful emotions from time to time, he has learned, along with many an immigrant before him, that undue surrender to nostalgia merely compounds his anguish.

Like the word "nostology" (the medical field—now called geriatrics—devoted to treatment of those at the point of returning whence they came), the word "nostalgia" has at its etymological heart the Greek *nostos*, meaning return or homecoming—especially that of Odysseus to the arms of Penelope. The twentieth-century literary imagination found the Odysseus story particularly compelling, and *Pnin* occupies a space midway along the shelf of *Odyssey* redactions that stretches from "Canto I," "Hugh Selwyn Mauberley," *Ulysses*, and Cavafy's moving poem "Ithaca" to Kurt Vonnegut's *Happy Birthday, Wanda June* (1970) and Charles Frazier's *Cold Mountain* (1997). These treatments tend to be ironic, and *Pnin* is no exception. Joyce parodies Homer, and Nabokov parodies the parody: his eponymous protagonist is another Leopold Bloom, complete with faithless Penelope and a Telemachus unrelated to him by blood. Another Odysseus manqué.

The narrator of *The Coffin Tree* never reveals her name—perhaps to encourage readers to see her as a female version of the wily and resourceful hero who includes strategic anonymity in his repertoire of survival tricks. Captured by the Cyclops Polyphemus, the hero calls himself "No one" (a pun on his name in the original). Stuart Gilbert, commenting on Joyce's treatment of this episode in *Ulysses*, observes that "anonymity may be identified with nonentity" and quotes the historian Georges Contenau, for whom "une chose n'existe que si elle a un nom."[5] A thing exists only if it has a name. Declining to name herself, then, Law-Yone's narrator paradoxically expresses her sense of nonexistence at the same time that she invokes an identification with the wandering hero of Greek lore. Marooned between two economies of identity, between the death of one self and the rebirth of another, she is archetypally nobody, negotiating survival with the new world Cyclops. Like Odysseus she descends to the underworld (the mental institution), and, like him, too, she ends her journey stripped of companions. But eventually the identification with Odysseus fades: an immigrant rather than an exile, she cannot aspire to some triumphant homecoming, for in her Ithaca the suitors have long since prevailed. Thus the narrator of Law-Yone's novel renounces *nostos* and expresses particular scorn for nostalgia, its enervating simulacrum.

In the rag and bone shop of immigrant memory, as it happens, nostalgia occupies less shelf space than one might think. By the same token (though the point may seem counterintuitive), nostalgia enjoys little play in the semiotics of immigrant fiction. One might think it a truism of immigrant experience and thus too commonplace for literary emphasis—or inclusion in a typology. But immigrants such as Law-Yone's narrator can see, like Pnin, how uncurbed nostalgia precludes the mental adjustments that promote recovery of something like a normal life. Exiles, by contrast, make of nostalgia the whetstone by which they keep ever sharp the dream of recovering the lost life and the lost land. Because immigrants seem to realize that nostalgia undermines acculturation, it figures in their stories—for the most part—in fairly cautious ways, if not altogether under erasure. Which is not to say that immigrants ever become immune to this undertow; it is what Richard Rodriguez, speaking of his Chicano childhood, calls "the hunger of memory," a hunger no repast—least of all the past itself—can satisfy. But writers who face it squarely—Law-Yone, for example, and Rodriguez himself—risk and achieve much, in terms of literary power. The author of *The Coffin Tree* not only foregrounds and critiques this feature of immigrant experience but also reveals its pathology, its affinity with madness.

Like her narrator, then, Law-Yone takes a dark view of nostalgia. Writing in *Time Asia*, the author describes a visit to the British Museum, where she contemplates Burmese paintings of the Buddhist spirit world, including hell. In the glass that shields this work, she recognizes

> a metaphor . . . Exiles are beings with their noses forever pressed to the windows of the past, fogging up the panes with sighs of inchoate nostalgia and guilt. Yet the sigh I breathe as I step back from the glass is mostly one of relief. Exile, I am reminded, can be an escape from hell, a form of salvation, and not necessarily the state of privation and alienation it is often cracked up to be. With half the world in a state of dislocation, with not just intellectuals and revolutionaries but whole populations in search of such salvation, exile nowadays suggests quite other states of being. Freedom, for instance. Or privilege. Or even prestige.[6]

The narrator of Law-Yone's novel speaks of herself and her brother as having been "exiled from the past" (149) as well as from a place. An exile's unsanctioned return to the homeland—to a place—may well result in imprisonment or death. By the same token, any attempted temporal return, any mental revisiting of a proscribed past, can result in comparable suffering. Certainly this is the case with Shan. But the immigrant's mental inventory of the old-world past, if scrupulously non-idealizing, can also lead to the kind of recognition experienced by Law-Yone—and by her narrator.

In *The Coffin Tree*, Law-Yone divides the expected picture of painful acculturation between a brother and sister. The growing instability and paranoia of the one represent the immigrant in extremis; the other, though driven to attempt suicide, survives by schooling herself in acceptance of reality, however painful. In retrospect, having seen the downward spiral of her brother, having attempted to join him in death, and having spent four months in a mental institution, the novel's narrator recognizes in nostalgia the insidious crippler of immigrant resolve. As Mukherjee's Jasmine observes, "To bunker oneself inside nostalgia, to sheathe the heart in a bulletproof vest, was to be a coward."[7] Law-Yone, by contrast, sees in uncritical retrospection a kind of primrose path to neurasthenia—at least for individuals who, short on mental toughness to begin with, must make their way in a new land. Both of these immigrant authors see nostalgia as dangerously solipsistic. Twinned with the isolation commonly suffered by the immigrant, it can only breed further alienation.

Law-Yone's own immigrant experience, incidentally, was not particularly difficult. Why, then, the misery of her characters? In an interview she explained that "history . . . is the version of the victors. The history books are slanted in favor of the successful conquerors. Literature, on the other hand, documents the version of the conquered. I'm on the side of literature."[8] In these remarks the reader discerns what may be one rationale for the iconoclastic lugubriousness of Shan's story. We hear too little about immigrants who simply go under: Can that fate be as rare as the myth would have us believe? Getting their bearings and making their way, immigrants undertake an arduous and life-wrenching passage. Some do not make it, and their failure, the narrator suggests, may stem from an uncritical, weak-minded surrender to nostalgia. What really destroys Shan, according to his sister, is the accelerating psychosis that announces itself, in part, in dubious effusions regarding their former life. "I hated his nostalgia for a past that never was," she declares, "his view of the world we'd left behind as an idyll destroyed by the present. I hated his language of sentiment and triviality—a language of empty catchwords. He talked of old friends who gave him 'love and respect'" (77). Before he completely loses touch, then, Shan delivers himself of a whole litany of spurious recollection, which the narrator characterizes as a species of self-abuse, an onanism of memory.

All immigrants are "strangers" (the word's root means "foreign") or "aliens" ("others"), and the two encountered here see themselves, early on, as space travelers. At one point the narrator observes all around her "people who had become extraterrestrial in their obliviousness to me" (156). Arriving in America in 1969, the year of the first moon landing, she bitterly characterizes herself and her brother as "men on the moon" themselves: "Finding our footing was nearly as awkward as the astronauts' first steps in the atmosphere of the moon" (50, 44). The moon's traditional association with madness may lie behind this conceit—for presently these immigrants lurch toward lunacy and death, one actually perishing, the other immured in a mental institution after an attempt at suicide.

The refugees find life in the United States hard, even though their first decade sees the passing of traditional models of assimilation—at least among post-immigrant generations. Those newly arrived, like Shan and his sister, find little latitude for the ethnic pride rapidly—in the 1970s—becoming the norm. Some reviewers and critics see America reproached for its unfeeling treatment of immigrants. Ebony Adams, for example, observes that "the narrator and Shan . . . experience first-hand the indifference, or utter cruelty of an American society ill-equipped to deal with difference. It is treatment that will send Shan spiraling into paranoia and death, and the narrator into a suicide attempt and a mental hospital."[9] Yet no one in the new world treats Shan as harshly as his own Burman father. The narrator dismisses Shan's "calculating" (74) allegation that he has been raped as less a paranoid delusion than a play for sympathy, a claiming of victim status.[10] Although Shan's claim may remind the reader of America's historic feminization of Asian men, the new world in fact treats these two arrivals with more accommodation than harshness. The reader can trace all of their most serious reverses to Shan's increasingly dysfunctional behavior.

Thus the author depicts in Shan a pathology that links him to the patients institutionalized at 3 East (whose afflictions, by the same token, she does not depict as brought on by conditions endemic to life in America).[11] If this novel were a musical composition, one might think of its representations of mental vulnerability as a kind of ground bass, a context for specific figures or themes of immigrant alienation. Or one might say, more simply, that the author marshals two metaphors, according to which she represents the immigrant now as a mental case, now as a soul in transition from death to rebirth. The additional psychological and spiritual depth afforded by this strategy, however, takes an unexpected turn or two. Neither psycho-analysis nor religion will provide much help to Law-Yone's characters.

Developing the first of her metaphors, the author insists on a basic pre-cept: accurate knowledge of the past facilitates maturity and psychological equilibrium; inaccurate knowledge perpetuates dependency and neurosis. The narrator makes a point of juxtaposing her reflections on Shan's illness with her observations of psychotherapy in the mental asylum. Chastened by her experience with a shameless idealizer of the past, she resists the model of therapy that encourages patients to regress to their childhood as a necessary first step toward working through the repressed memories that make them neurotic. "We were free to pry open the trapdoors to memory and feeling," says the narrator, "to descend into the unknowns of our-selves" (97). However warped it may have been in actuality, their lost childhood invites the exercise of a disenabling nostalgia, as patients view their past and their parents through the idealizing lens of retrospection. Like Shan, the more the patients indulge, the closer they come to break-down. Thus the narrator registers considerable disgust at what group exer-cises dredge up:

> The tears, the outbursts, the unsettling revelations that we could indulge in with impunity all exposed our yearning to be children again. After all we had been through to gain that costly freedom from sanity's pretenses, we were drawn, it seemed, only to memories and acts of childhood.
> Our Groups often turned into play groups, where we reveled in kinder-garten chaos. (97–98)

In time she recognizes her suicide attempt as a retreat from maturity, "the child in me crying out for attention" (157), a reversion that appears to be recapitulated every day in group therapy, where any such return to child-hood seems merely to reaffirm and prolong the neurotic's already disabling abdications of autonomy.

Late in the story, after "years" as "a creature caught in the amber of the present" (149), the narrator speaks of experiencing "the oceanic flood of the past" (185). Whether or not she means to echo a specific psychoanalytic lexicon in her choice of adjective (Freud commonly disparages transcen-dent religious feelings as "oceanic"), it seems clear that any such flood must threaten the frail bark of self. Certainly Shan's increasingly desperate representations of his old life overcome his sense of present reality. Weltering in tidal illusion and progressively estranged from the reality principle itself, the narrator's brother comes to resemble the desperate figure whose fate the poet William Cowper compares (in one of literature's most powerful characterizations of conscious madness) to that of a man washed overboard and lost at sea. The desperate figure is the poet himself, in anguished contemplation of his own faltering reason, his own sense of mental drowning: "But I beneath a rougher sea, / And whelmed in deeper gulfs than he."[12]

Law-Yone suggests that every immigrant must experience a kind of lunacy, a taking leave of reason. She or he must spend a season in quarantine, as it were, as "patient" in a sometimes literal asylum (one thinks, too, of the two institutionalized sisters in Alvarez's *How the García Girls Lost Their Accents*). Immigrants emerge from their quarantine, whether literal or figurative, only when they come to terms with their situation, only when they recognize and repudiate the insidious workings of nostalgia. The narrator comes to understand nostalgia by observing its pernicious effects on her brother and on her fellow inmates at 3 East, who suffer a different kind of exile. Although Shan does not survive to enter an asylum or receive treatment, he seems almost to live again—as the narrator twice observes—in a fellow patient, Paddy, who, like her brother, is given to game-playing and a scattershot interest in religion (103, 176). In reaction to her brother's condition, the narrator learns to despise sentimentality, to "avoid it at all costs, to fix on reality a hard, unblinking eye" (78). She recognizes in nostalgia a simple failure to engage with the actuality of either the present or the past. In its extreme form, this failure verges into madness. Like all psychoses, then, the psychopathology of exile involves maladjustment to the reality principle. As will be seen, the exile's recovery of mental equilibrium depends on either letting go of the past or allowing it to occupy a carefully circumscribed emotional space.

The Future of an Illusion

If nostalgia and unredeemed exile can lead to breakdown, to what does immigration lead? Law-Yone remarked in an interview that "America has something of an aura of the hereafter."[13] To the figurative conflation of immigration with madness, then, she adds a second ingenious metaphor for immigration's dark passage. The immigrant, she suggests, undergoes a version of the *Bardo*, the journey of the soul from death to rebirth as described in *The Tibetan Book of the Dead*. The story does not lack for appropriate imagery. The birth of the narrator causes the death of her mother: "I had come into the world with a death (my mother's) on my hands, and it seemed increasingly a duty—a family obligation almost—to leave the world the same way" (154). The loathsome grandmother's death effects a rebirth. The deaths of father and brother occasion yet more rebirths. But of course it is the narrator's own symbolic death (the failed suicide attempt) that eventuates in a true rebirth—indeed, a rebirth more palpable than what the Tibetan doctrine promises.

Every immigrant undergoes a death, and the period during which she or he struggles to be reborn, to be reincarnated as the citizen of another country, resembles the *Bardo*, or process of torment and confusion described in *The Tibetan Book of the Dead*. Like the religion of ancient Egypt, which has its own book of instructions for the soul newly freed from its body (one recalls the emblematic scarab invoked in the epigraph to Dressler's *The Deadwood Beetle*), the Tibetan belief system features an elaborate and detailed picture of the transitional state. New immigrants make their way through what in her version of the Tibetan text Law-Yone calls a "shadow world, / The world between death and resurrection" (187). In their nostalgia, in fact, one recognizes a secular equivalent of the disembodied soul's misguided yearning for its old body.

Some account of the source material of the book Law-Yone's narrator describes and quotes from in her closing pages might be in order. The accordion-pleated document the narrator finds among her brother's effects is not a complete copy of *The Tibetan Book of the Dead*; rather, it is a kind of cobbling together—evidently Law-Yone's own—of certain passages from that text. The lines reproduced by the narrator of *The Coffin Tree* appear as four pages of verse that distill, depending on the edition and on the amount of scholarly paraphernalia, some 70 to 125 pages of prose (only ancillary prayers and invocations are versified in the original). Probably not able to read archaic Tibetan, Law-Yone could have consulted any of three English-language translations available in the years during which she worked on *The Coffin Tree*. As often happens when a poetic sensibility takes over a prose crib, her rendering is actually more graceful and lucid than the original in any of these versions. So far as I can tell, she mines book one, part two (in which, in the *Chönyid Bardo*, the newly dead soul must struggle with a host of "*karmic* illusions") and book two, part one, of the *Sidpa Bardo* ("the intermediate state when seeking rebirth"). I offer, below, some comparisons of Law-Yone's language with that of the original as translated by Lāma Kazi Dawa-Samdup, edited by W. Y. Evans-Wentz, and first published in 1927.

About this time [the deceased] can see that the share of food is being set aside, that the body is being stripped of its garments, that the place of the sleeping-rug is being swept; can hear all the weeping and wailing of his friends and relatives, and, although he can see them and hear them calling upon him, they cannot hear him calling upon them, so he goeth away displeased.[14]

> You will see the offerings of your kin:
> The clothes they have stripped off you,
> The place they have swept for you.
> Unaware of your own death,
> You will call to them;
> But they, in tears,
> Will be deaf to your words,
> And you in misery
> Will go your lonely way.
> (*Coffin Tree* 188)

Even if thou couldst enter thy dead body nine times over—owing to the long interval which thou hast passed in the *Chönyid Bardo*—it will have been frozen if in winter, been decomposed if in summer, or, otherwise, thy relatives will have cremated it, or interred it, or thrown it into the water, or given it to the birds and beasts of prey. (*Tibetan Book* 165)

> But your body by then
> Will lie freezing in winter snow,
> Or rotting in summer steam,
> Or burning on the family pyres,
> Or buried in the ground,
> Or covered in water,
> Or flung to the birds and beasts of prey.
> (*Coffin Tree* 189)

The visions of males and females in union will appear. If, at that time, one entereth into the womb through the feelings of attachment and repulsion, one may be born either as a horse, a fowl, a dog, or a human being. (*Tibetan Book* 178)

> You will see the mating
> Of men and women;

> You will feel the storm of raucous rain.
> This will be the moment
> You could be born
> A horse, a fowl, a dog, or a man.
>   (*Coffin Tree* 190–91)

What Law-Yone adds to the original is the tutelary "spirit of the coffin tree" (187), which she depicts as a kind of Buddhist psychopomp that conducts the soul through its trials. Why this departure, this modification? She may have felt, as storyteller, the need for some agent that would draw together and order the chaotic tribulations detailed in her original. Thus she makes supernatural (and internal to the text) the human *yogin* or guru who, reading the scripture over the dead, functions as spiritual guide in the funerary ritual as it would actually be observed. But I suspect that she also wanted to place a judicious wrench in the works, lest anyone misunderstand and think she was, in invoking Tibetan Buddhism, actually "recommending it to faith" (to paraphrase Wordsworth's remark about a similar appropriation). The point of the narrator's discovery, in other words, is not some pietistic epiphany, not recovery of a lost religious heritage. By hybridizing *The Tibetan Book of the Dead* (and not mentioning it by name), she presents a text stripped of historical cogency, a text that remains only the subtle analogue for the immigrant experience of illusion and reality—and perhaps, more narrowly, the marker for one immigrant's fruitless engagement with esoteric doctrine.

With her troubled protagonist, her dark vision, and her skeptical invocation of lines from *The Tibetan Book of the Dead*, the author of *The Coffin Tree* rewrites and supplements well-known texts by Joseph Campbell, Thomas Pynchon, and, as Kathryn VanSpanckeren has pointed out, Maxine Hong Kingston. In "*Coffin Tree* and *The Woman Warrior* alike," observes VanSpanckeren, "mystical, pure mountains and a remote, all-powerful father are associated with an Asian childhood and an Asian source of strength." Both works, she adds, explore "loss, separation, culture shock, mental illness, and suicide in America."[15] Similarly, in introducing the language and images of the Tibetan holy book at a climactic moment, Law-Yone follows Joseph Campbell's practice in the magisterial *Oriental Mythology* (1962), which concludes with a powerful reading of Chinese communist atrocities in Tibet against the horrors described in that country's most sacred text. To great effect, Campbell abandons all semblance of scholarly detachment as he describes the migration of horror after horror from the imagined afterlife to the all too real here and now of Chinese aggression. Law-Yone seems also, finally, to echo Thomas Pynchon's *The Crying of Lot 49*, a story named to invoke both the forty-nine days leading up to Pentecost and the forty-nine days of the Tibetan *Bardo*. Pynchon grapples with the pervasive Western perception of "exitlessness," of spiritual and cultural dead ends, of "the absence of surprise to life" in a drearily secular contemporary world. Oedipa Maas, Pynchon's heroine, undergoes a sensitizing to alterity, and people like Shan and his sister—the American Dream's insomniacs—are what she comes to discover. Like Law-Yone's characters, Oedipa struggles with paranoia and a burgeoning sense of alienation from "the cheered land" all around her. Her story ends with the passionate vision of America as a grand legacy diverted from its rightful heirs. "The only way she could continue, and be at all relevant to it, was as an alien, unfurrowed, assumed full circle into some paranoia."[16]

Where Oedipa's paranoia is one of the great red herrings of postmodern fiction, the problematic sanity of various characters in *The Coffin Tree* invites interpretation in both literal and figurative ways. Shan, of course, is the figure of major interest in this regard. His connection to madness may be genetic, for his mother becomes the hill country's Crazy Jane or Mad Kate (another of Cowper's studies in insanity). From his father, by the same token, he inherits more than the severe dyspepsia that carries both off: he learns to think of mental incapacity—even his own—as wholly despicable. His sister, however, eventually manages to move beyond the unexamined deference to paternal and other forms of power. Indeed, she proceeds to an indictment of all paternal totalitarianism. Though disinclined to join in the histrionics of her fellow patients, the narrator undertakes, in the privacy of the mental or written discourse on which the reader eavesdrops, a thoughtful assessment of her own relations with a male parent at once tyrannical and charismatic.

In the sequence with the mad beggar in chapter 10, the author deftly introduces a kind of historical perspective on the suffering of both the narrator and her brother. The narrator recurs to this figure from her childhood, that is, only after she has chronicled the trials that she and Shan go through as adults. As the author remarked to Nancy Yoo and Tamara Ho, the book had its genesis here: living in Kuala Lumpur in the early seventies, Law-Yone "wrote a little story about the brutal treatment of a madman, a basically harmless character. . . . [I]t got enclosed in another, bigger story that grew over time."[17] Like Odysseus making his way to Ithaca, she eventually spent ten years tending that fictive acorn, watching it become not oak but "coffin tree." The beggar compels our attention because his mental state proves part of a thematics of madness developed in the story and because his interaction with the narrator and her household reveals certain important dynamics of family, nation, and culture. The violent treatment of this figure, the reader learns, has its mirror in similar brutality with the youthful, balbutient Shan: the father tries "to knock the stutter out of him" (108), and the reader can imagine how this parent might deal with a son's schizophrenia. "I came to associate madness with power," Law-Yone remarked to Yoo and Ho. "The irrationality of power, the power of irrationality."[18] In *The Coffin Tree*, Shan's irrationality becomes a form of power over his sister, who subsequently interrogates the power exercised at 3 East, notably the encouragement of allegedly therapeutic forms of regression. But she first learns how madness can impose on sanity in her encounter with the beggar, who embodies the poverty and mental illness into which she and her brother will themselves descend. Though born to economic privilege, the narrator responds to the beggar's plight with sympathy that may generate karmic capital with which to stave off, a few years later, her own mental bankruptcy.

The story of the beggar ends with the vignette of the narrator, as child, balancing on her father's hands. Every child stands with the help of a parent, and what child does not delight in the Pisgah view from a father's shoulders? But the precarious support supplied here becomes emblematic of the shakiness, the limited reliability, of this particular father's aid. How long can one balance there? How long can the sustaining arms, however strong, bear the stress? In the end, of course, standing on someone's hands is a fundamental perversion of all four extremities (like the rebellion of the body's several parts beloved of political metaphorists in the Renaissance). Rachel Lee contrasts the elevated perspective enjoyed by the child on this occasion to the demotic, ground-level view she had with the beggar.[19] The supporting hands, in other words, figure the foundation given children of privilege. But the view achieved by this means will be false, unstable. Artificially lifted up, such children may lack resources when the privileged life disappears. The support may even postpone the painful process of learning truly to stand on their own—not to mention achieving the kind of elevated perspective that one associates with the seasoned "outlook" of maturity.

Significantly, this act of remembering accommodates a judicious veneration of the father (the narrator recalls his selfless attendance during her illness) without sacrificing mature perspective; it is part of her coming to tempered terms with inevitably erroneous perceptions of the parent whom, in childhood, she "worshiped" (144). From her later vantage, she sees that in her extravagant regard for the father, she linked him to the deity he "was so good at impersonating" (141). She experienced both father and Christian god as temperamental, absent. "Chance had singled me out to side with a God who was foreign to my world, but whose power over me was unanswerable. It was not unlike Father's power. I could never have challenged him, either. Or counted his secrets" (28). Eventually, however, the narrator pierces the veil of filial awe: "I came to see my father in a truer field of vision than was possible through the warping lens of a child's unre-quited and unquenched love" (185–86). By implication, she comes to a bet-ter understanding of the heavenly father as well. At the end, even though she recognizes that Shan had needed and found a spiritual "crutch" (192) and that she herself suffers "the absence of a dream to live by" (184), she af-firms a personal resistance to all forms of supernaturalism:

> If I accepted the world, it was this rootless, chaotic world I inhabited and knew; no other. If I believed in life, it was not life after death, but *this* life; nothing less, nothing more.
>
> Yet it was clearer to me now that just to continue in this immediate world, this terminal life, I needed my own version of the coffin tree—some story to tell myself, some illusion to shape the future, some dream to lighten the days.
>
> But maybe the only dreams I would have were the ones in my sleep, when "that old fool, the unconscious," went wandering through the country of the past. (192)

The past, as H. E. Bates famously observes, is a foreign country. The state-ment holds, paradoxically, for the immigrant, whose concept of alterity or "foreignness" must perforce undergo a curious reversal. Meanwhile, a "dream to lighten the days," which this immigrant cannot yet name, may promise some future balm for the sleep disorders that recur here with sug-gestive frequency, especially among the population at 3 East (Paddy and the narrator are insomniacs [125], Winston dozes off during group therapy [95–96], Helga suffers from narcolepsy). But Law-Yone resists the tempta-tion to end a story of such travail with any hint that the morrow will bring the narrator's long-delayed initiation into the celebrated cultural dream of America, a dream to compensate for the painful night passages on which this tale has centered.

Rather, the narrator takes leave of the reader with a last dream of her doomed brother, a grimly symbolic recapitulation of Shan's fate and the sidelined witness of the dreamer. Her valedictory mixes recognition that

Shan "had found a crutch" (the word deconstructs itself) with a yearning for some dream that she knows cannot take the form of religion. She concedes, however, that her brother's quest was at least more spiritual than materialistic: "All along I had taken the book on the coffin tree to be a piece of chicanery, a fake map leading to a bogus treasure. Instead, I discovered a legend of other-worldly concerns" (192). Still, she cannot embrace his inchoate belief system: "I could not divine the promise held out by this legend, but I suspected it helped him flee the persecutions of the moment and gave him a story to calm his terrors." The narrator relates a dream of seeing her brother as a "hairy mountain man" in the cloudy uplands, where she beholds him "encased in ice, hanging from the top" of what she takes for the mythic tree he has sought. But she learns, still in the dream, that it is only "a juniper, often mistaken for a coffin tree" (194–95). The point of this oneiric recognition is that the juniper is, among trees, a nonentity, largely innocent of mythic associations. It does not figure in the classic tree catalogues of Ovid (*Metamorphoses* 10.90–105), Chaucer (*Parliament of Fowls* 176–82, "Knight's Tale" 2921–23), or Spenser (*Faerie Queene* 1.1.8–9). Nor does the reader find it named in the lengthy *Câd Goddeu* or "Battle of the Trees" in the Welsh *Book of Taliesin*, so exhaustively analyzed by Robert Graves in *The White Goddess*. Admittedly, these are all Western texts, but Eastern mythology, whose meaningful trees include the *bodhi* (i.e., the peepul or banyan) and the mulberry, affords no hermeneutic rationale for the juniper either. One finds nothing in Asian lore that makes of the juniper anything more than an inconsequential shrub—unless it be a passing reference in the *Encyclopaedia Britannica* to a tradition that Tibet (source of Shan's book and the myth he embraces) emerged out of an ancient sea as a stand of juniper trees.

Thus the "dreadful revelation" (195)—that Shan has sacrificed himself not on a real tree of knowledge, not on some Asian Yggdrasil, but on a spiritual misconception—tells the narrator that such mythologies cannot deliver her. Whether one hangs on the tree, like Jesus or Odin, or merely sits under it, like the Buddha, the mythology has become moribund, no longer meaningful or efficacious. If not quite a tale told by an idiot, it finds a place only in the vaporous, New Age ramblings of an asylum inmate: "Did you know that all religions are more or less the same? Look: The Bhagavad Gita and the Bible and the Koran are much alike, do you see? There is always a prophet, and there is always a dying god. And God will expose himself in all religions" (169). Yes, rejoins another, less reverent inmate: as divine flasher. From her later vantage of recovered mental health, the narrator will conclude that any such divine self-exposure will reveal the deity only as one more tyrannical parent, a celestial bully, an embodiment of patriarchy, a fraud.

Buried here are a number of deliberately inchoate echoes or distant invocations of various sacramental ideas. In many cultures twins are taboo—now a sign of divine parentage, now a curse, now evidence of maternal unchastity. The women attending on Shan's mother view the birth of her twins as "a bad omen" (21). The stillbirth of the older twin, however, obviates any future need to reenact the sin of Cain. Given his paternity, Shan is effectively a *saohpa*, a prince, and Burmese and Shan successions, according to E. R. Leach, routinely involved the wholesale elimination of siblings ("eighty or so" in one famous instance) who might have their own claim to throne or title.[20] In times not so ancient, a Shan prince would have been regarded as semi-divine and expected to marry a half-sister.[21] But to this story's unhappy siblings any such cultural recollection of hierogamy is unknown and, indeed, unthinkable. The narrator's calling herself her "brother's keeper" (76), by the same token, seems more than the casual deployment of a familiar expression. The phrase originates with Cain, who impudently answers the deity's question with another question: "Am I my brother's keeper?" (Genesis 4:9). The echoing of this Old Testament line hints at the narrator's feelings of guilt at not being able to protect Shan from his miserable fate. Like Cain, the sister faces continued existence as a wanderer on the face of the earth, an exile, a person quite literally denied death. More important, perhaps, the remark identifies Shan as Abel, the innocent victim who becomes the archetypal *pharmakos*. In the dream the narrator describes at the end of her story, Shan's appearance as hanged man hints at the supreme fulfillment of the archetype, especially insofar as he seems to perish at an age appropriate to a dying god.[22] (The narrator attempts suicide at the age of twenty-five—apparently in the second year after the death of her brother, who was ten years older than she. Thus Shan seems to have died at the age of thirty-three, that messianic threshold.) But the metanarrative sketched in these details grows increasingly vestigial, on its way to becoming as obscure as the belief system of those Easter Islanders whose religion long since disappeared into the Pacific mist. Thus the narrator, said to resemble "an Easter Island head" (143) herself, sets her story in a spiritual wasteland that, in its very aridity, comments on the characters' painful experience of dislocation.

10 〜〜 Closet and Mask

Junot Díaz's *Drown*

> The more I see and remember the more their story is the same. The story is mine. How I come by plane, come by boat. Come climbing over a fence. When I get here, I work. I work for the day I will finally work for myself. I work so hard that one day I end up forgetting the person I am. I forget my wife, my son. Now, too, I have lost my old mother tongue. And I forget the ancestral graves I have left on a hillside of a faraway land, the loneliest stones that each year go unblessed.
>
> —Chang-rae Lee, *Native Speaker*

Julia Alvarez, Walter Abish, Anchee Min, Bharati Mukherjee, Ursula Hegi, Mylène Dressler, Li-Young Lee, Chang-rae Lee: as noted before, the authors examined in this study are often, as immigrants, atypical. Some arrive in the company of educated parents with professional credentials. Others arrive privately well schooled, often in English. Even at the secondary level, many poor countries offer fairly rigorous education. Such circumstances enable a perhaps surprising number of immigrant writers to move swiftly into the front ranks of American letters. All the more remarkable, then, the truly disadvantaged immigrants who learn English more or less from scratch, acquire an education, and somehow become proficient writers of fiction. Junot Díaz, who at the age of seven moved from the Dominican Republic straight to one of those hellish public housing projects in New Jersey, writes about both "third-world childhood" (as he calls it in his story "Fiesta, 1980")[1] and life in the American barrio. So powerful and mythic that they often coerce their tellers, such stories dictate their own telling, but Díaz rejects the template, resists procrustean diegesis. He will tell his own story, it will not tell him. Rather, in a laconic yet sensitive style, he strives for an unsparing representation, neither romantic nor clichéd, of the conditions in which great numbers of immigrants find themselves. Iconoclastic in treating class, race, and identity, he manages even to provide an altogether fresh view of machismo, that much-stereotyped feature of the many cultures subsumed under such generic terms as "Latino" or "Hispanic."

A French interviewer once asked Aleksandar Hemon, who began to write fiction in English after immigrating to the United States from his native Bosnia: "What is the relationship between the experience of emigration and the act of writing? Are you, as émigré, the bearer of a message?" Hemon affirmed that writer and immigrant view the world from similar perspectives: "the writer is already, as such, a migrant," a "traveler," as it were, "who ignores every kind of border." By the same token, "in a world marked by the migration of labor and by the perpetual redrawing of geographical borders," it is "the immigrants, émigrés, and refugees" whose "stories . . . need to be told and retold, more than the obsolete myths that represent the bulk of national literatures."[2] Presumably Hemon means with this remark to impugn only the viability of the national literatures that flourish (or once flourished) in immigrants' countries of origin, for the writers who share their passage and tell their story can hardly avoid engaging one of the most fundamental of American narratives. "I truly appreciate the special qualities that America and American national myths offer me," remarks Bharati Mukherjee.[3] Grappling with the fact of displacement, the immigrant writer tells of struggle in and with the new land, and that has always been an archetypal American story. Certainly it remains so in the hands of Hemon himself, an author who puts his most memorable character, the Bosnian émigré Josef Pronek (he appears in the centerpiece novella of *The Question of Bruno* [2000] and in the novel *Nowhere Man* [2002]), through a fairly standard set of coming-to-America experiences: menial jobs, shabby lodgings, borderline health, linguistic travail, and ultimately frustrating brushes with a cisatlantic Eros.

Such material can make for some jagged fictive edges, and so it is in the fictions collected in *The Question of Bruno*. Characterizing these stories as "multiple," "autonomous," and "heterogeneous," the French interviewer asks Hemon about the collection's architectonics: "What was the objective of this multiple narration? Can one see in it a mirror of the fragmentation [*déchirures*] currently seen in your country, of the ethnic ruptures that have led it into chaos?"[4] Hemon demurs, preferring to describe the multiplicity of his technique with reference to the Bible, *Ulysses*, and other classics that assemble various stories and points of view. The interviewer's notion that a collection of stories might be other than discontinuous strikes one as odd. Suggesting that the immigrant writer must perforce produce fragmented pictures, regardless of the fictive scale or form, the interviewer seems to imply that a long fiction by such a writer would necessarily be too chaotic, replete with an immigrant sensitivity and vision somehow at odds with representation. The unstated assumption is that immigrant writers, fresh from painful experience, must lack formal control, must be unaware that a direct, unmediated rendering of their personal travail will not succeed as literary art (which requires some degree of "artful" indirection). But of course the short story collection is by its very nature a jumble, and one errs to assume that an immigrant's collection must necessarily exceed norms of formal discontinuity. (Only the occasional *Dubliners* or *Go Down, Moses*, after all, invites reassembly of its component fictions into some larger, integral exercise in modernist storytelling.) That said, insofar as it presents itself as one kind of fiction writer's debut, a short story collection can obviate or forestall the perception or expectation that immigrant writers must be overwhelmed by the dislocations of their passage to America.

For whatever reason, Junot Díaz makes his debut with *Drown*, a collection of stories that do in fact strive, with a lack of success at once ironic and instructive, to gather themselves into a whole, some version of the very blend so much commended as American mosaic. Although the stories resist the reader's desire to recuperate a novelistic integrity, Díaz has taken considerable pains with what he calls "the architecture of the collection . . . Emotionally, it forms a tapestry."[5] Thus pictures emerge as from a weave, now of life in the immigrant underclass, now of the toll of displacement on psyches already damaged by native poverty, parental dereliction, and, at times, the lingering effects of colonialist actions on the part of the colossus to the north. (The United States exercised direct control over the Dominican Republic from 1905 to 1941, with marines occupying the country from 1916 to 1934 and again in 1965.)

Discerning certain specific lives here, the reader strives to fix names, ages, and dates. Half consciously, one may try to connect all the fictions and to collapse several narrators into one, and in fact the stories in *Drown* commonly concern the experiences of a single viewpoint individual (who usually narrates). Perhaps because the narrators all sound alike, one of Díaz's interviewers had the impression that the stories collectively concern a "young man searching for identity, and a family struggling against its own demise."[6] But the young man, Yunior, is in fact part of a large, extended, and connected family (like that of Elida, the Mexican American graduate student in *The Deadwood Beetle*). At best the implicit protagonist of the collection and perhaps fairly close to Díaz himself, Yunior provides these stories only a teasing modicum of continuity. After all, he narrates only half of them: "Ysrael," "Fiesta, 1980," "Aguantando," "How to Date a Browngirl, Blackgirl, Whitegirl, or Halfie," and "Negocios." Yunior, whose real name is Ramón (as the reader eventually learns), may or may not be the pool table deliverer and college dropout who narrates "Edison, New Jersey." The narrator of "Aurora" is a drug dealer, Lucero, but not the same drug dealer who narrates the title story, "Drown," and mentions this rival in passing. Also unnamed, also different, is the narrator of "Boyfriend." All of the narrators report on the lives of Dominican immigrants in the Washington Heights section of New York City and in the slums of New Jersey, but only Yunior tells of life back in the Dominican Republic as well. Probably, then, he is the narrator of a sixth, somewhat anomalous story, "No Face," which returns the reader to Santo Domingo and the disfigured boy first described in "Ysrael." In this sixth story, however, the teller remains unidentified, the narration a much more distant third person.

Machismo Revisited

Díaz dispenses with the expected saga of the difficulties attending his characters' early encounters with English, for he recognizes that readers of ethnic fiction have become overly familiar with such passages. As he told an interviewer, "I have read a thousand stories where we see the kid learn how terrible English is, how hard it is."[7] Consequently, other than a brief reference or two to the struggle of Yunior's father, Ramón Sr., with "the awful crunch of sounds that was English" (173), Díaz contents himself with an epigraph that telescopes lifetimes of linguistic dislocation:

> The fact that I
> am writing to you
> in English
> already falsifies what I
> wanted to tell you.
> My subject:
> how to explain to you that I
> don't belong to English
> though I belong nowhere else.

In these lines, the "Dedication" to his own memoir of immigration from Cuba, Gustavo Pérez Firmat artfully restates the familiar postcolonial reproach: empire has colonized even my tongue. In its self-contradictory premises, his verse recalls the famous paradox of Epimenides, who declares that all Cretans are liars. But since he is himself a Cretan, how can he be speaking the truth? By a similar paradox, Pérez Firmat suggests that whatever he expresses in English—and especially on the subject of his own tongue—involves a fatal displacement of immediacy and legitimacy. Like Richard Rodriguez (and *contra* Derrida), he hints that writing itself represents an estrangement from authentic, unlettered speaking. The implicit contrast here between "writing" and "telling" seems to invoke the older theory of language that preserved the illusion of a presence in speech that the removal into writing traduces. But the mechanics of the signifying chain and the logic of deconstruction are inexorable: writing is in fact the very model for speech, and presence remains elusive to both. One ought, then, to recognize that the oft-heard lament for a lost tongue depends for its cogency on a construction of language as instrument of social and cultural intercourse ("it is sad when I speak English and others of my blood speak Spanish"). In strictly linguistic or phenomenological terms, however, the language of the "sign" brings it no closer to the "referent." The displacement out of one language and into another merely widens, a bit, the unclosable gap between signified and signifier. By the same token, the identity belied by attempted representation in a new language is always already obscured by one's primal entry into the Symbolic order. "The fact that I / am writing to you in English already falsifies what I wanted to tell you" invites a deconstructive gloss: "The fact that I am using language in any way already falsifies what I wanted to tell you—falsifies, indeed, my own desire."

Whether or not "the fact that I am writing to you in English" compounds *différance*, it effectively announces a thematics of absence, for "the inner narrative of any Diaspora," as Eli Gottlieb observes, "is the story of absence—of landscapes, habits, and individuals above all. The family portrayed in many of Díaz's stories is fatherless, and the father's ghost-presence is the core of the book, a kind of ground tone or ambient noise which shades the narrator's whole childhood."[8] In other words, the one condition (fatherlessness) compounds the other (displacement), and in fact the absentee parent recurs in immigrant fictions. Sophie Caco, in Danticat's *Breath, Eyes, Memory*, has never known her rapist father; Lucy Potter's father, in Kincaid's *Lucy*, seems hardly to figure in his daughter's life; and

Mai Nguyen's father, in *Monkey Bridge*, dies before emigrating with what remains of his family. The loss of one or both parents renders the essential condition of loss and displacement all the more poignant (and often the lost parent stands for the lost homeland), but in the case of a male Latino writer such as Díaz, the dysfunctional element is almost overdetermined. The viewpoint character and frequent narrator "Yunior" struggles to survive in an especially harsh landscape, whether in his native country or in the United States.

The spareness and precision of the language in the stories—one thinks of Joyce's "style of scrupulous meanness"—make for a kind of minimalist lyricism that affords an approach (at least) to emotional continuity. Like a Hemingway of the barrio, Díaz contrives to convey a sense of strong emotion that has been contained, channeled into a rhetoric of understatement easily misunderstood as ghetto sangfroid (or *only* ghetto sangfroid). The dominant tone of all the narrators betrays a vulnerability inadequately shielded by what one calls "heart-leather" (112, 114)—and undisguised by verbal postures of insouciance, indifference, or truculence. Over and over again the reader encounters tough young drug dealers or homeboys, at or near the genius level of street smart, who cannot help sounding wistful about the ephemerality of paternal regard ("Fiesta, 1980," "Negocios"), love ("Aurora," "Boyfriend," "Edison, New Jersey"), and friendship ("Drown"). This dynamic casts fresh light on their seemingly stereotypical machismo. Literary genius commonly manifests itself in the ability to subvert or transform cliché (to make it new), and Díaz invites recognition for a radical reconfiguration of Hispanic culture's most notorious element, that "cult of virility" described by Evelyn Stevens in terms of "exaggerated aggressiveness and intransigence in male-to-male interpersonal relationships and arrogance and sexual aggression in male-to-female relationships."[9] Even as Díaz serves up the expected female servitude, his narrator seems to question it: "The women laid out the food and like always nobody but the kids thanked them. It must have been some Dominican tradition or something" (36). Thus Yunior, Rafa, Lucero, Cut, and the rest all exemplify the machismo supposedly widespread among Latinos at the same time that they force reconsideration of received ideas. The bigamist Ramón, the errant husband and father, also confounds expectation. Yunior calls him "a voracious reader" (36). Within an ethnic group known for opening and operating restaurants, his culinary abilities excite comment. He even prides himself on washing and ironing his own clothes (170).

One could easily say that Díaz thematizes identity and manhood in cultures in which, historically, such qualities are endangered by a general powerlessness vis-à-vis the rest of the world, especially, of course, the geopolitical colossus on Mexico's northern border. But he seems to be after something less predictable. No purveyor of stale, politicized sociology, he merely allows each story its ironic dimension and makes each narrator's language self-questioning. Repeatedly, then, the subject matter addressed by these narrators forces them into postures of unexpected sensitivity. The loss of a lover recurs with some frequency—in "Aurora," "Boyfriend," "Edison, New Jersey," and "Drown." In "Boyfriend" the author doubles this figure of loss: troubled by the departure of his girlfriend, the narrator eavesdrops on and tries to connect with a woman whose lover has walked out. In "Drown" the parted lovers are both male.

These figures of lost love adumbrate more, I think, than adolescent heartache and narcissism. Collectively they subvert certain premises of the culture of machismo. In the collection's title piece, in fact, Díaz offers an especially good example of machismo belied, turned inside out. Here another sensitive narrator-protagonist deals dope and thinks bitterly of the high school friend, his partner in seasons of youthful delinquency, who had gone off to college and a change of destiny. A reader who abhors teachers and education generally, the narrator views the departure of his friend Beto for Rutgers (Díaz's alma mater) as pure betrayal. "He's a pato now but two years ago we were friends" (91). The dialect word means "fag," but one finds the adverb "now" more interesting: a small universe of self-deception lurks in it. The narrator means to suggest, however absurdly, that his friend was not always gay—and that he himself never was. Immured in a closet he cannot recognize, the narrator protests too earnestly that he allowed himself to be seduced only two times: "Twice. That's it" (103). Now he stays in shape, running three and four miles at a time, and dodges the local army recruiter, whose "photos of . . . skinny filipino girls sucking dick" (100–101) do nothing for him. Though he ogles the Rutgers coeds when he and his friends go into New Brunswick, one doubts that he would know what to do if one responded. He finds himself in a kind of sad pseudo-marriage with his mother, watching TV with her, escorting her to the mall, bankrolling her shopping there, policing her telephone contact with the man who deserted them, alleviating her concerns about the security of their apartment.

Sexuality here seems intimately related to changing one's circumstances, but the story has little to do with gay apologetics. Rather, Díaz brilliantly devises a set of images and situations that make newly compelling the otherwise clichéd message of how ghettoized thinking perpetuates itself, how an underclass connives at its own entrapment. Thus closeted homosexuality functions here as the symbol of one kind of immigrant situation—or perhaps just the ghetto experience (for the narrator does not explicitly characterize himself, his mother, or his father as immigrants). Trapped in a condition he refuses to acknowledge, he embraces the exitlessness that, according to his twisted logic, constitutes honor, the keeping of an obscure faith.

However sketchy and resentful and unreliable, the remarks of the narrator afford a glimpse of an alternative to the prison of impotence and bad faith in which he languishes—an alternative to machismo's cultural straitjacket. Beto, whose delinquency apparently did not extend to cutting school (101–2), saw the ghetto for what it was and aspired, early on, to escape. Here, too, that first remark about him, "He's a pato now" (91), invites the deconstructive turn. The reader eventually understands that, with regard to sexuality, Beto has discarded macho pretense, come out of whatever closet a ghetto adolescence (and porn-addled father) had forced him into. Pathetically, meanwhile, the narrator associates social mobility with faggotry. Trapped by his appalling notion that the one connotes the other, the narrator seems to think that one can escape the barrio only by "sucking dick." He will presumably remain in his airless ghetto of body and spirit. Although he may at one time have liked books, he discards, inscription unread, the book Beto gives him on his departure. As the title suggests, the narrator will drown. He has already drowned. He was always drowning.

Elsewhere in this collection, the metaphor of the closet reconfigures itself in the metaphor of the mask. In "Ysrael" and "No Face," the collection's two stories of disfigurement and masking, the author/narrator/protagonist seems half to recognize himself in the pathetic figure of the boy whose face was eaten, in infancy, by a pig. Baiting the disfigured boy is as cruel to the self as to the ostensible target. Told that "if we were to look on his face we would be sad for the rest of our lives" (9), the narrator fails to see something discernible by the reader: that one must number immigrants—the narrator and his family—among those who suffer a lifelong sadness. As an immigrant, the adult who remembers and writes about Ysrael knows what it is to inspire disgust in his neighbors; it is the powerful subtext of his story.

"Ysrael" and "No Face" comprehend a number of intertexts, both literary and cinematic. Indeed, masks and the disfigurements beneath them were quite a presence in the movie culture of Díaz's youth. Perhaps, at a young and impressionable age, the author saw David Lynch's *The Elephant Man*, which came out in 1980 (as did *Friday the 13th*). Peter Bogdonovich's *Mask* appeared in 1985. The horrific Leatherface of Tobe Hooper's *The Texas Chainsaw Massacre* (1974), incidentally, was played by Gunnar Hansen, who had immigrated from Iceland at the age of five. On the literary side is the biblical story of Jacob, renamed Israel when he looks upon an awful visage and lives to tell about it (Gen. 32, 30). In Díaz's story, of course, the awful visage is that of Ysrael, not God, but the name is appropriate to the first in a series of stories about a diaspora. The most important analogue to the central figure in Díaz's strangely moving mask stories, however, is that seriocomic creation the Laughing Man, whose odd *nom de pègre* provides the title to one of the most memorable fictions in J. D. Salinger's debut collection, *Nine Stories* (1953). Victim of severe cranial deformation in childhood (his head was put into a vise), the Laughing Man nonetheless becomes the resourceful foe of evildoers of every stripe. Nothing daunted by his early disfigurement, he "grew into manhood with a hairless, pecan-shaped head and a face that featured, instead of a mouth, an enormous oral cavity below the nose. The nose itself consisted of two flesh-sealed nostrils. . . . Strangers fainted dead away at the sight of the Laughing Man's horrible face."[10]

The connection is more than fanciful, because of Ysrael's touching fantasy life as superhero gifted with "FLIGHT" (153), "INVISIBILITY" (155), and "STRENGTH" (156). Like the Laughing Man, he devotes himself to "fighting evil" (160) and wears a mask to spare the sensibilities of those around him. But Ysrael lacks the helper or sidekick that is standard issue for superheroes. No one will play Tonto to his Lone Ranger. By the same token, the prurience of Yunior and his brother Rafa, who go to brutal lengths to render Ysrael unconscious, unmask him, and view the hideous visage, contrasts with the delicacy of the Laughing Man's faithful confederate Omba, who in a memorable scene avoids violating his master's privacy, redraping the poppy-petal mask over the features of the unconscious man.

Salinger's story is, among other things, an allegory of the artist's transformation of his own experience—often his suffering—into art. The Laughing Man is the invention of a likeable but ill-featured young law student who runs a one-man after-school program, a kind of mobile day care. He projects his own ugliness as the Laughing Man's disfigurement; his own intelligence, industry, and creativity as the Laughing Man's resourceful super-heroism. Even as it captures the escapist transport of comic books and other pulp fiction, in other words, the story reflects incisively on the mysterious alchemy of art. But it takes an unsettling turn. As in Díaz's stories, boy loses girl. When things go wrong between John Gedsudski and the lovely Mary Hudson (the reader does not learn what, the better to preserve the mystified child's-eye view of these matters), the heartbroken storyteller kills off his hero, thereby violating the most basic convention of such tales. In destroying the Laughing Man, John Gedsudski thoughtlessly and prematurely thrusts his young listeners into an adult world that will systematically crush all such fantasies of transcendence. His naïve and innocent charges are devastated, terribly shaken by this blindsiding of their childhood's privileged island of magical agency. For as much as he was the projection of John Gedsudski's passionately creative sense of himself, the Laughing Man was also, in imagination, the collective imago of his young listeners. Thus the narrator remembers, in the aftermath of the Laughing Man's demise, being nearly undone by a bit of red tissue blowing down the street.

Salinger's children must always emigrate from the country of childhood to the country of adulthood—a painful maturation revisited in the fictions of Junot Díaz, where the children must also survive the wrenching passage out of one culture and into another. Nor do the years bring to them much in the way of certainty and security—at least not these poorest of immigrants. This insight constitutes the disguised thematic baggage of "No Face," in which the reader wonders why the narrator represents Ysrael's prospective emigration and deliverance through cosmetic surgery as little more than delusions, fresh cruelty. This element makes sense, in fact, only if one recognizes the maimed boy as a complex, proleptic figure of the immigrant.

Ysrael's disfigurement seems to distill the very ugliness of third-world poverty. Yet he also anticipates and reifies the facelessness of the immigrant, so often relegated to a kind of invisibility among the native-born. Many an immigrant goes doubly masked in the new world: sometimes one retreats behind a mask, sometimes the mask is effectively imposed by neighbors unable or unwilling to look beyond one's pathetic exterior. External prejudice and stereotyping, in other words, weave a veil that precludes recognition of the immigrant face, the immigrant humanity. At the same time, immigrants—at least as depicted by Díaz—are at pains to mask themselves, to avoid being seen in their vulnerability, their pain. They feel that only a front of indifference or toughness will shield them from the circumambient hostility or contempt.

Race and Class

Just as machismo calls up the iconoclast in Díaz, so does he dispense with the standard pieties regarding race and class. In "Boyfriend," "How to Date," "Edison, New Jersey," and "Drown," he explores working-class racism at its most insidious, for his characters despise the African in themselves. Gottlieb declares that "Díaz's achievement as a writer lies in the fluency with which he crosses aesthetic borders, roughs up literary distinctions between 'high' and 'low,' and marries documentary realism to the artistic requirements of his craft. . . . Díaz has provided us with an exemplary chapter in the novel of American Empire, showing us both the literal impoverishments produced by colonialism, and—perhaps more difficult to accomplish—the excruciatingly subtle ways in which that colonialism can be internalized and allowed a second life." But such pronouncements risk making Díaz's work one-dimensional. In fact, one gets only an occasional glimpse of the American presence in the Dominican Republic (two passing references to the 1965 invasion)—no doubt heavy-handed at one time but not necessarily the *fons et origo* of this nation's shortcomings or the sufferings of its emigrants. Colonialism per se is surely incidental to the woes of Díaz's characters (though Yunior's mother, Virta, bears the scars of ordnance from the 1965 invasion). Díaz aspires less to cheap politics than to literary discrimination.

One feels compelled, then, to propose a more precise term or terms for the subject matter here, for Díaz is concerned not so much with the history of systematic, state-sponsored exploitation of pigmented populations and their lands (one definition of colonialism) as with the forms of discrimination specific to immigrants in the here and now. Díaz scrutinizes the more or less xenophobic—and frequently racist—tendency of a dominant ethnic group to despise and exploit the immigrant, especially if differently colored. Yet he emphasizes the overt racism of Anglos less than the more insidious and destructive racism that is homegrown and often internalized. One need not go to America to learn this kind of racism: at home in the Dominican Republic, Yunior's brother reviles him for his hair and skin color, calling him "the Haitian" (5).

Díaz touches often on the mixed ethnicity of his characters. The reader hears on more than one occasion about un-Caucasian hair: "Run a hand through your hair like the whiteboys do," the narrator of "How to Date" counsels himself—"even though the only thing that runs easily through your hair is Africa" (145). Yunior, too, mentions Afro hairstyles (his own and that of an uncle), and he has learned to be sensitive to shades of skin color. More emphatic is the little disquisition on racially valenced romantic preferences in a story such as "Boyfriend," in which two doomed couples must deal with the complications of racialized desire (though only the narrator seems fully cognizant of these). The "dark-skinned" title character "liked to get down on the white girls" (114), and the abandoned girlfriend, notwithstanding her use of "straighteners" (116), seems not to have been white enough for him. By the same token, the narrator, though assured by his friends "how light you are" (115), has lost his own girlfriend to a presumably lighter Italian. The story ultimately concerns the narrator's coming to terms with his misunderstanding of the "barrio rules." As the narrator of "Drown" remarks the proscription of whites at the local swimming pool (94), so has this narrator fondly imagined the existence of a racial and cultural understanding: "Latinos and blacks in, whites out—a place we down cats weren't supposed to go" (114). Supposedly, in other words, romantic pursuit of whites would be widely condemned as an appalling admission of their greater value in the erotic marketplace. "Boyfriend" centers, in fact, on the recognition that any such shibboleth remains chimerical, that, as the witty and sympathetic narrator of "How to Date" admits, "the white ones are the ones you want the most" (145). To gratify that desire, "tell her that you love her hair, that you love her skin, her lips, because, in truth, you love them more than you love your own" (147). Against this kind of racism, the betrayal within or by one's own, one cannot prevail.

Race, class. "Edison, New Jersey" concerns the second term in this notorious duo: class in America as experienced by a couple of consumerism's minor functionaries, men who deliver high-end pool tables (as Díaz himself once did). Rather than emphasizing the modicum of skill required to set them up, the narrator dwells on the boredom and frustrations of the work, especially when no one is present to take delivery. Big and heavy, the commodity itself offers a double symbolism: historically an upper-class pastime, snooker or billiards becomes, in America, a working-class game: pool. Poor layabouts proverbially squander time in pool halls, playing a game they could not afford at home (nor is there room in a poor person's home for the table). A fine cue, the narrator observes, can run nearly a thousand dollars. The equipment can, however, be purchased by the rich, and the delivery men spend their days observing just how far they are from real prosperity (the narrator takes bitter pleasure in calculating how many years it would take, on his pay, actually to buy one of the tables he delivers). The narrator has enough education, however, to be observant and to bring in the occasional sophisticated comparison. Thus he admires things that last, whether fine pool tables, the Roman sewers of Bath, England, or the masonry of the ancient Incas. Similarly, he refers to the brain scientist Paul Broca in commenting on the impressive cranium visible in a picture of the man, Pruitt, who has arranged for delivery of a pool table. The narrator seems unsure whether such a "dome" (134) suggests a preposterous big-headedness or some more or less legitimate mental dominance by the cultural elite: "Pruitt. Most of our customers have names like this, court case names: Wooley, Maynard, Gass, Binder, but the people from my town, our names, you see on convicts or coupled together on boxing cards" (130). Amusingly, these names do in fact figure in various law cases. In 1977 the Supreme Court ruled, in *Wooley v. Maynard,* that a New Hampshire husband and wife had the right to cover up the state motto on their license plate, "Live Free or Die." Inscribing their names in case law, privileged Anglos seem to lay exclusive claim to justice itself. Literally made in their image, the system serves their interests and renders justice problematic for those with the wrong surnames. Even here, ironically, in the delivery man's passing observation, the convicts and boxers remain preterite, unnamed.

As college dropout, the pool table deliverer finds himself perennially behind the eight ball, as it were. Like other narrators in *Drown* (or like Salinger's John Gedsudski), he struggles to recover from the loss of a girlfriend, Jeva, which has left him emotionally damaged. Along with love, he loses the prospect of social mobility, for Jeva came from suburbia: her home had a lawn for mowing, a father who offers the narrator a job in "utilities" (as, famously, Dustin Hoffman was once told to think "plastics"). The narrator's interest now in Pruitt's Quisqueyana maid/mistress suggests that, warming to another woman, he is at least—like the similarly lorn narrator of "Boyfriend"—coming out of his breakup numbness. But the Quisqueyana ignores his overtures, preferring her own suburbanite, Pruitt, and the world of privilege he represents. In returning to Pruitt, she in fact does what the narrator and his partner do: as delivery men they return, over and over, to the home of the master, the home of the gallingly rich and superior Anglo for whom, now and forever, they labor.

An instinct for economy and for circumventing cliché manifests itself in what the author does not include in these chronicles, these monologic *tajadas de vida.* Díaz describes his characters at two ends of the spectrum, alternating pictures of *aguantando* (waiting to be sent for) with sketches of slum life in America—all the while postponing any account of the actual immigration, Dominican Republic to United States. A certain emotional climax attends, then, on the depiction, in "Negocios" (the last story in the collection), of the difficult life of an immigrant following his arrival in "this freezing hell of a country" (179). Here the author puts Yunior's father, Ramón de las Casas Sr., under the microscope, describing experiences so filled with hardship as almost to excuse his dereliction. To know all, as the French saying has it, is to pardon all; consequently, by the end, Yunior interviews his father's other wife in an atmosphere of passion spent, fires of resentment banked. *Drown* ends with the departure of Ramón Sr. for the Dominican Republic, whence he will at long last escort his original "familia" to a new life in the United States.

Rather than telling the story of his own arrival in America at the age of nine, Yunior tells that of his father, which involves a significant narrational remove, a narrative displacement that complements the geographical displacement. This may be simply because the father's experiences are the more arduous and compelling, but one senses something else here, a Telemachiad that frames rather than merely complements the father's odyssey. Readers do not find out whether Ramón Sr. is still alive in the present—though they learn that at a certain point, like the Odysseus of Dante and Tennyson, "he had left us for good" (206). But like any other son, Díaz's Telemachus internalizes his father, passes through phases of yearning for and idealizing him. Back in the Dominican Republic, he and his brother think of him, as the reader sees in "Aguantando," as the deliverer who will come for them "in the night, like Jesus" (87). This notion has its complement in the odd remark, in "Drown," about the Raritan's being "so low and silty that you don't have to be Jesus to walk over it" (102), for Beto, who crosses the Raritan to go to Rutgers, is another older male who decamps, another version of the absconding father for whom, nonetheless, one watches and waits, as for a deliverer.

In "Negocios" the curious embedding of Ramón Sr.'s story in that of his son suggests that the filial identity subsumes the paternal. It may also be related to the son's sense of a doubly tenuous connection to the new country, given that his father became a citizen through a bigamous marriage (The conceit noted elsewhere in this study—homeland as mother, America as bride—here undergoes a subtle variation.) The narrative culminates as Yunior—Ramón Jr.—visits Nilda, who displays a photograph of another Ramón, his half-brother. Contemplating this image, Yunior looks as it were into a flawed mirror, and he makes a curious observation: "We were brothers all right, though his face respected symmetry" (206). What does this statement mean? What ought to be most unambiguously symmetrical, one imagines, is paternity: the young men should to some degree or other share a father's features. The "though," however, suggests otherwise. Does the narrator mean that the half-brother's features register ("respect") the genetic presence of a different mother and so cannot be as near-specular as would a full brother's? Perhaps, but the simplest interpretation is the most convincing: for the first time, Yunior intimates that his own features are irregular—an admission (or claim) of no small psychological importance. If, as I am suggesting, a face that "respected symmetry" is one with features more regular than those of another, why is the less shapely visage that of Yunior? The outrageous answer—facial "symmetry" is reserved to the native-born—takes the reader back to the symbolism of "Ysrael" and "No Face." The immigrant's face must bear some blemish, however attenuated; Yunior's facial imperfection, real or fancied, is the marker of his alien origin, the mask of embattled subjectivity. In his encounters with and reflections on paternal and fraternal versions of himself, in fact, Yunior momentarily resembles the highly fragmented speaker in *The Waste Land*: "Musing upon the king my brother's wreck / And on the king my father's death before him."[11] Researching the story of Ramón the immigrant father, Ramón the immigrant son briefly regards the picture of Ramón the American-born brother, and in this proliferation of Ramóns, Díaz suggests at once the coalescence and the progressive refraction of immigrant identity.

The paradoxes of unity and division manifest themselves at every level of this book. Its discontinuities of form seem to coexist with teasing intimations of larger coherence. Its tonally undifferentiated voices may, after all, mask a single narrator. These jugglings of the many and the one, of unity and fragmentation, ultimately rehearse the perennial problematics of psychological wholeness ("identity") and cultural assimilation. What makes the assimilation conundrum especially moving in *Drown* is that all the shoring of fragments here effects only the prolegomenon to any larger integration into American life.

≋ Conclusion

We, Them, Us

I have the documents. Documents, proof, evidence, photograph, signature. One day you raise the right hand and you are American. They give you an American Pass port. The United States of America.

—Theresa Hak Kyung Cha, *DICTEE*

In reading immigrant writers, one naturally considers questions of national identity, both individual and collective. One distinguishes immigrants from the exiles and expatriates who look always to their homeland, no matter how remote the prospects of a return. Thus Joyce, an expatriate through most of his adult years, remains always Irish. However long she resides in France, Gertrude Stein remains an American. Nor does a D. H. Lawrence or Ernest Hemingway or F. Scott Fitzgerald ever change his actual nationality. Although W. H. Auden came to this country and became a citizen, he never really became an American. Exiled to America, Alexander Solzhenitsyn eventually repatriated, as did the Australian Cristina Stead (author of *The Man Who Loved Children*). Not that everyone falls into an easy and obvious category. Vladimir Nabokov became a United States citizen and wrote that paean to the American social and cultural landscape, *Lolita*, but spent his last years in Switzerland. A lifelong exile, he never succeeded in letting go of Russia. Thomas Mann became an American citizen but continued to write in German; Isabel Allende, also a citizen, is a somewhat different case: though she continues to write in Spanish, that tongue is increasingly recognized as a language of the United States.

In the earlier decades of the twentieth century, comparatively few immigrants became successful English-language writers—though Anzia Yezierska, Abraham Cahan, Mary Antin, Henry Roth, Ayn Rand, and Carlos Bulosan showed that it could be done. But historical circumstance precluded literary aspirations for most immigrants; usually poor and uneducated, they had little hope of becoming writers. Why, then, so many now? It cannot be that the numbers of already educated or English-speaking immigrants have suddenly gone up; after all, enormous numbers of Scots and Irish, in the past, effected no such literary efflorescence. No, more is at work here than the prior education or enhanced opportunities for literary apprenticeship among the newly naturalized. What has changed is the perception of ethnicity: from a quality needing to be burned away in some refiner's fire of cultural homogenization, it has acquired distinction, cachet, and a quite literal marketability. Increasingly congenial to evolving literary taste, the fictions of immigrant literati fill display tables in bookstores and often vie for space on college syllabi with the literary fruit of homegrown ethnicity: books, stories, and poems by Chicana/o, Latino/a, Native American, and African American authors. Whether they distill America on the printed page or spin tales of an exotic homeland, immigrant writers compel the attention of a burgeoning readership.

But one credits more than academic or cultural fashion for the simple ubiquity, in recent years, of English-language novels, memoirs, and other literary works by immigrant authors. One credits also the freshness of their vision and the extraordinary quality of their writing. Among the best in contemporary American letters, these new talents seem to spend hardly a season in that limbo of the obscure and under-read; rather, they move swiftly to the American Book Award (Chang-rae Lee, Shirley Geok-lin Lim), the National Book Critics Circle Award (Bharati Mukherjee), PEN/Hemingway recognition (Walter Abish, Chang-rae Lee, Akhil Sharma, Jhumpa Lahiri, Ha Jin), the National Book Award (Ha Jin), the Pulitzer Prize (Jhumpa Lahiri, Charles Simic, Frank McCourt), MacArthur fellowships (Charles Simic, Walter Abish, Aleksandar Hemon), the Nobel Prize (Singer, Bellow, Brodsky, Walcott), and—if I may be permitted a little bathos—the sweet fruition of the Oprah Book Club (Ursula Hegi).

My interest in these authors began with simple curiosity about their perceptions of and feelings for a country that often brutalizes newcomers. Would they regard the United States as haven or vale of tears? Would they resent the manifold ways "we" discriminate against those insufficiently like ourselves? These questions, I found, were predicated on a naïve premise: that immigrant authors, naturally telling stories shaped by and depicting their own race, ethnicity, and postcolonial hybridity, must as naturally foreground the *politics* of this subject matter. Not so. To be sure, one of the things immigrants take to is the American privilege of criticizing American institutions. Nowhere is it written that one must wait a generation or two before joining that critical chorus. But immigrant novelists—even the acerbic Jamaica Kincaid—tend to qualify criticism by interposing flawed or immature narrators (or viewpoint characters) between themselves and their readers. Unlike some of their first-generation cousins, these writers seem more in tune with the reality principle that governs the relationship between a societal center and its margins. Whatever America's shortcomings in the past or present, immigrants nearly always have an acute awareness (and often personal, firsthand experience) of social, political, and historical horrors on a much larger scale. This knowledge and the perspective it fosters lend any criticism they do level a good deal of authority.

The point is that these writers identify themselves as artists first, immigrants second. If in fact they seldom disparage their new country, neither do they simply sing its praises—at least not as part of any expression one would recognize as literary. After all, as Matthew Arnold long ago suggested, literature remains committed to a more or less refined mediation of real and ideal, a "criticism of life." Insofar as these authors chiefly interest themselves in their craft, they bristle, in interviews, at attempts to put them in a political box, which they rightly fear as a kind of artistic ghetto (see, in the chapter on *Jasmine*, Mukherjee's repudiation of the victim theme).

The present study, then, has primarily concerned immigrant authors who write in English and set their fictions in the new homeland. Generally speaking, of course, the younger the author at the time of immigration, the greater the American focus. Of authors who grew to maturity before coming to America, some write only of their native countries; others divide their literary attention between old haunts and new. Most commonly, immigrant protagonists resemble their creators: born in another country, they come to America with their parents, as do Garcia's Pilar, Díaz's Yunior, Cao's Mai, and Alvarez's García girls. Others arrive alone: Mukherjee's Jasmine, Kincaid's Lucy, Law-Yone's immigrant siblings, Hegi's Stefan Blau. All proceed through a *Bildung* that culminates in more or less successful acculturation, but at times one encounters a central or secondary character who, like Flannery O'Connor's Displaced Person, remains isolated and marginalized. One thinks of the narrator's doomed brother in Law-Yone's *The Coffin Tree* and, to some degree, Aleksandar Hemon's Josef Pronek; Mukherjee occasionally depicts immigrants (Professorji and his circle, for example, in *Jasmine*) who gravitate to some ghetto or ethnic enclave and permanently postpone immigration of the heart, mind, and spirit.

As the fictions examined here show, few immigrants completely abandon their prior national identity. However heartfelt the naturalization and whatever the scale of brutality, suffering, and poverty left behind in the old country, the self remains sporadically subject to often painful nostalgia. All the more remarkable, then, the extent to which this yearning is subordinated to—or allowed no more than equal place among—the various standard mythemes of the immigration story. Indeed, I have suggested that a semiotics of immigrant fiction reveals itself in certain characteristic topoi: narrative fragmentation, for example, or remembered scenes of awkwardness in the American classroom, or the reversal of generational roles (as children, more swiftly becoming adept at the language and customs of the new country, take on responsibility for their suddenly infantilized elders). Often, as in these examples, the motifs group themselves as pictures of America as seen through the eyes of the immigrant. On the other hand, a number of these shared features concern more or less nostalgic representation of the country of origin: a parent left behind, along with ancestral graves; real and factitious old-country folktales; the occasional glimpse of village life and old world mores. Still others bridge the gap: the sensation of "double consciousness," a narrator's anthropological detachment, and marriage customs problematically translated from one world to another.

Commonly some feature or features may play a more prominent role than others, and often those receiving special emphasis announce larger thematic developments. Thus the retrieval of old-country folktales proves especially important to Keller's *Comfort Woman*, just as narrative fragmentation and temporal reversal seem meaningfully overdetermined in *Drown* and *How the García Girls Lost Their Accents*. The post-Confucian themes of *Monkey Bridge* emerge in the marriage of certain motifs: the parent left behind (the Vietcong grandfather) and the young person who must serve as translator and factotum for a mother rendered helpless by her arrival on these shores. The narrator also comments on her own "anthropologist's eye," though that conceit seems less central here than in, say, Mukherjee's *Jasmine*, where the occasional comparison of old and new world mores makes the observant and perceptive immigrant an amateur social scientist of no small perspicacity. In Danticat's *Breath, Eyes, Memory*, by contrast, the full semiotic—including generational conflict (notably over the old-country obsession with female chastity), a serious eating disorder, and travail in school (with French the language of instruction, rather than English)—serves retrospection almost exclusively, constantly referring backward, to Haiti, rather than forward, to America. The most pronounced element is also the most regressive in this sense: the host of Haitian folktales that, illustrating character, action, and destiny, prove at once immensely appealing and highly evocative of all that makes the homeland unlivable. In their selection of and emphasis on certain features of immigration's matrix story, then, authors signal the extent to which their characters embrace American experience—or fixate on their past in a lost world, its difficulties or unlivability perceptually transformed, sometimes, by the metastasizing mendacity of retrospect.

Historically and sociologically, immigration has always been important to the character of this country, and any study of contemporary American immigrant writing intersects with much that defines the national experience, literary and otherwise. As I noted early on, even the poorest of today's literary immigrants have much in common with those figures who once had the opening pages of our anthologies to themselves—the John Winthrop, John Smith, William Bradford, Anne Bradstreet, and Edward Taylor who have only in recent years admitted other voices, commonly in translation, to their exclusive club: not only Native Americans but also selected New World Spaniards, a couple of Frenchmen, and that famous Genoese. Indeed, this late diversification takes its place amid a full-blown politics of the anthology, some publishers still associated with a conservative canonicity, others with radical expansion of the canon.

The reader will have recognized this critic's political valence before now. Let me admit formally to the bias. Though I would shudder to be lumped together with those shrill right-wing commentators who reproach liberal conscience for an ethics of blame-America-first, I have little patience with the school of absolutist cultural critique that neglects to historicize the nation's occasional failures to live up to the ideals expressed in the Declaration of Independence, the Constitution, the Bill of Rights, and the body of civil rights legislation that made explicit what was always implicit in those documents. One test of the liberal sensibility (if, as Robert Frost says, it will take the soft impeachment from a friend) is whether it is willing to learn from the downtrodden it tends guiltily to idealize. In other words, can those who indict America for various forms of racist or colonial exploitation actually listen to and respect what the elsewhere-oppressed have to say on these subjects?

Derrida, who died as these pages were being written, famously argued that writing, ostensibly speech at a remove (and so less immediate, less the vehicle of "presence"), is really, in its economy of signification, the model for speech. By the same token, one might imagine the immigrant as petitioner for a subject position as American, where in fact the American subject was always already an immigrant. I began this book expecting to find some differences between the imaginative expression of immigrants and that of other Americans—especially, perhaps, Americans of the first generation. Instead, I have found that immigrant desire in its most current form proves, once again, that America remains, first and last, "the country"—in that Richard Powers line I have quoted before—"of the universally displaced."[1] Whatever distinctions one makes regarding the perceptual freshness of immigrant as opposed to first-generation writers, one finds that the concerns with identity, the toil-filled personal history, the passionate insistence that America live up to its ideals, and other such classic themes are as likely to figure in the writings of one group as the other. Certainly both groups strive to negotiate assimilation on terms agreeable to their sense of ethnic integrity.

The introductory chapter of this book, a couple of hundred pages back, bears an epigraph from the essay in which Bharati Mukherjee describes the naturalization ceremony at which, in 1988, she herself became an American citizen. By way of concluding, I would like to return to that essay and note, again, Mukherjee's engaging demolition of certain stereotypes:

> The old pieties of immigration no longer hold. A Norman Rockwell would have been hard-pressed to find the immigrant icons of an earlier era—the hollow-eyed and sunken-cheeked were not in evidence. There was a notable lack of old ladies in black babushkas, with wrinkled, glistening cheeks. (Their closest ethnic embodiment, a beautiful Russian woman sitting in front of me, was reading Nabokov's *Speak, Memory* during the long waiting period.) A Dominican man next to me joked as we sat down after pledging allegiance, "Hey, now we can make a citizen's arrest!" Behind me, Chinese teen-agers passed copies of *The New Yorker.* I don't think we're on Ellis Island any more.[2]

Arriving in Oz with her dog, Dorothy declares, "Toto, I have a feeling we're not in Kansas any more." Mukherjee's little nod toward that moment reminds readers of the perspectival switch that naturalization effects. According to the metaphor, the contemporary immigrant officially crosses the American threshold not in drab, black-and-white Ellis Island but in some bright heartland courtroom, its waiting area replete with magazines that those about to become citizens already know how to read. The sophisticated immigrants Mukherjee describes probably know already that Kansas and Oz were always the same, the prairie reality merely transformed into a child's Technicolor dream. They probably know, too, that the American Oz contains its colorless, tornado-plagued places as well as its jeweled, versicolor cities. Indeed, as it stretches from Ellis Island to Angel Island, America subsumes fifty versions of the Kansas that Dorothy and Toto now share with José and Nguyen and Kyoko and Stefan and Guang-jin.

In my end is my beginning. The passage serving as epigraph to my first chapter bears repeating here in my last. Mukherjee, it will be recalled, invites readers to recognize how unstable the categories of "we" and "they" have become: "All around me I see the face of America changing. So do you, if you live in cities, teach in universities, ride public transport. But where, in fiction, do you read of it? Who, in other words, speaks for us, the new Americans from nontraditional immigrant countries? Which is another way of saying, in this altered America, who speaks for you?" With this double-barreled interrogative Mukherjee revises—in the African American community one would says she "signifies on"—the concluding line of the great novel that appeared at the middle of the last century, Ralph Ellison's *Invisible Man*: "Who knows but that, on the lower frequencies, I speak for you?"[3] I suspect that this modest echo signals something like an epistemic shift. If "the problem of the Twentieth Century," as W. E. B. Du Bois famously observed and iterated, "is the problem of the color-line," more and more we see that the great issue of the twenty-first will be another kind of liminality. Color still figures, but the "line" is the border or frontier or threshold or *līmes* that the immigrant crosses, like the hero of old, in the quest for freedom, opportunity, and, presently, citizenship in a great nation.

≋ **Notes**

Introduction

1. Bharati Mukherjee, "Immigrant Writing: Give Us Your Maximalists!" *New York Times Book Review*, August 28, 1988, p. 28.

2. Vladimir Nabokov, *Pnin* (Garden City, N.Y.: Doubleday, 1957), p. 183. Subsequent quotations are cited parenthetically in the text.

3. Julia Alvarez, *Something to Declare* (Chapel Hill, N.C.: Algonquin Books, 1998), p. 22.

4. Ibid., pp. 63–64.

5. Ibid., pp. 28–29.

6. Richard Rodriguez, *An Autobiography: Hunger of Memory: The Education of Richard Rodriguez* (Boston: D. R. Godine, 1982), p. 26.

7. Ibid., p. 150.

8. Gerald Howard, "The American Strangeness: An Interview with Don DeLillo," *Hungry Mind Review* 43 (1997): 16.

9. Rey Chow, *Women and Chinese Modernity: The Politics of Reading between West and East* (Minneapolis: University of Minnesota Press, 1991), p. xvii.

10. Rey Chow, *Writing Diaspora: Tactics of Intervention in Contemporary Cultural Studies* (Bloomington: Indiana University Press, 1993), p. 16.

11. Ibid., p. 35.

12. Shirley Geok-Lin Lim, "The Ambivalent American: Asian American

Literature on the Cusp," in *Reading the Literatures of Asian America*, ed. Lim and Amy Ling (Philadelphia: Temple University Press, 1992), pp. 18, 22.

13. Bharati Mukherjee, *Jasmine* (New York: Grove Weidenfeld, 1989), p. 77.

14. Mukherjee, "Immigrant Writing," p. 28.

15. T. S. Eliot, "Tradition and the Individual Talent," in *The Sacred Wood* (London: Methuen, 1950), p. 51.

1. Slavs of New York

1. Private interview quoted in James Atlas, *Bellow: A Biography* (New York: Random House, 2000), p. 14.

2. I take these examples from the "Non-English Writings" section of volume 18 of *The Cambridge History of English and American Literature*, 18 vols. (Cambridge: Cambridge University Press, 1907–21).

3. Lorraine Adams, *Harbor* (New York: Knopf, 2004), p. 65.

4. For a comparison of these two novels, see Ruth Essex, "Bellow's Sammler and Kosinski's Kosky in New York," *New Voices in an Old Tradition: Studies in American Jewish Literature* 13 (1994): 85–92.

5. Charles Berryman, "Saul Bellow: Mr. Sammler and King Lear," *Essays in Literature* 10.1 (1983): 85. Barbara Tepa Lupack, *Plays of Passion, Games of Chance: Jerzy Kosinski and His Fiction* (Bristol, Ind.: Wyndham Hall, 1988), p. 141.

6. Vladimir Nabokov, *Pnin* (Garden City, N.Y.: Doubleday, 1957), pp. 144, 104.

7. Eva Hoffman, *Lost in Translation: A Life in a New Language* (New York: Dutton, 1989), p. 198. Hereafter cited parenthetically in the text.

8. Geoffrey Stokes and Eliot Fremont–Smith, "Jerzy Kosinski's Tainted Words," *Village Voice*, June 22, 1982, pp. 1, 41–43. Correcting some minor details in their exposé, James Park Sloan confirms its most damaging elements in *Jerzy Kosinski: A Biography* (New York: Dutton, 1996), pp. 385–93.

9. Paul R. Lilly Jr., *Words in Search of Victims: The Achievement of Jerzy Kosinski* (Kent, Ohio: Kent State University Press, 1988), p. 66.

10. Jerzy Kosinski, *Being There* (New York: Harcourt Brace Jovanovich, 1971), p. 77. Hereafter cited parenthetically in the text.

11. Certain points here are also made by Jack Hicks, *In the Singer's Temple* (Chapel Hill: University of North Carolina Press, 1981), p. 236, and Lupack, *Plays of Passion*, pp. 145–47. See also Ivan Sanders, "The Gifts of Strangeness: Alienation and Creation in Jerzy Kosinski's Fiction," *Polish Review* 19.3–4 (autumn–winter 1974): 171–89; and Norman Lavers, *Jerzy Kosinski* (Boston: Twayne, 1982).

12. George Plimpton and Rocco Landesman, "The Art of Fiction XLVI–Jerzy Kosinski," in *Conversations with Jerzy Kosinski*, ed. Tom Teicholz (Jackson: University Press of Mississippi, 1993), p. 31. Another working title, he remarks here, was *Dasein*, the Heidegger term that Kosinski took to "mean the

state in which one *is* and *is not* at the same time." One might better apply the concept, so defined, to Eva Hoffman's novel *The Secret*.

13. Saul Bellow, *Mr. Sammler's Planet* (New York: Viking, 1970), p. 135. Hereafter cited parenthetically in the text.

14. Jean Baudrillard, "The Precession of Simulacra," in *Simulations*, trans. Paul Foss, Paul Patton, and Philip Bleitchman (New York: Semiotext[e], 1983), pp. 12, 11.

15. Byron L. Sherwin, *Jerzy Kosinski: Literary Alarmclock* (Chicago: Cabala Press, 1981), p. 38.

16. Sloan, *Jerzy Kosinski*, p. 290.

17. Don DeLillo, *Americana* (Boston: Houghton Mifflin, 1971), pp. 137–38.

18. Don DeLillo, "The Power of History," *New York Times Magazine*, September 7, 1997, p. 62.

19. *Andy Warhol* (Stockholm: Moderna Museet, 1968), n.p.

20. I have taken these details from James Atlas, *Bellow: A Biography* (New York: Random House, 2000), pp. 6–7, 14.

21. Richard Powers, *Operation Wandering Soul* (New York: William Morrow, 1993), p. 296.

22. Thomas Pynchon, *Gravity's Rainbow* (New York: Viking, 1973), p. 737.

23. Henry Adams, *The Education of Henry Adams* (Boston: Houghton Mifflin, 1961), p. 330.

24. Alfred Kazin, *Bright Book of Life: American Novelists and Storytellers from Hemingway to Mailer* (London: Secker & Warburg, 1974), pp. 136–37.

25. Philip Larkin, "If, My Darling," in *Collected Poems*, ed. Anthony Thwaite (New York: Farrar, Straus, Giroux, 1989), p. 41.

26. Vladimir Nabokov, *Strong Opinions* (New York: McGraw-Hill, 1973), p. 83.

27. Aldous Huxley, "Appendix," in Tomorrow and Tomorrow and Tomorrow (New York: Harper & Row, 1956), p. 289.

28. Sigmund Freud, *Civilization and Its Discontents*, trans. James Strachey, in *The Standard Edition of the Complete Psychological Works of Sigmund Freud*, 24 vols., ed. Strachey (London: Hogarth Press, 1953–74), 21:97.

29. Kazin, *Bright Book of Life*, pp. 136, 138. Critics who agree with Charles Berryman that "Bellow does know how to maintain a critical difference from his fictional character" (85) include Gloria L. Cronin, "Searching the Narrative Gap: Authorial Self–Irony and the Problematic Discussion of Western Misogyny in *Mr. Sammler's Planet*," in *Saul Bellow: A Mosaic. Twentieth–Century American Jewish Writers*, vol. 3 (New York: Lang, 1992), pp. 97–122; Susan Glickman, "The World as Will and Idea: A Comparative Study of *An American Dream* and *Mr. Sammler's Planet*," *Modern Fiction Studies* 28.4 (1982–83): 569–82; and Allen Guttman, "Saul Bellow's Mr. Sammler," *Contemporary Literature* 14.2 (1973): 157–66.

30. Thomas Pynchon, *Vineland* (New York: Little, Brown, 1990), p. 28.

31. Daniel Fuchs, *Saul Bellow: Vision and Revision* (Durham: Duke University Press, 1984), pp. 229–30.

32. Ellen Pifer, *Saul Bellow Against the Grain* (Philadelphia: University of Pennsylvania Press, 1990), pp. 13, 25.

33. Sarah Blacher Cohen, *Saul Bellow's Enigmatic Laughter* (Urbana: University of Illinois Press, 1974), p. 186. "In an early draft excerpted in *The Atlantic Monthly*," notes Atlas, Sammler imagines "the white of semen on her mouth" (*Bellow*, 387).

34. James Joyce, *Ulysses*, corrected text, ed. Hans Walter Gabler with Wolfhard Steppe and Claus Melchior (New York: Random House, 1986), p. 169.

35. Adams, *Education*, p. 383.

36. Quotations are from *The Complete Works of William Shakespeare*, ed. Hardin Craig (Chicago: Scott, Foresman, 1961).

37. Berryman characterizes Sammler as "eccentric, touched with lunacy, endearing, and indestructible." See Berryman, "Saul Bellow: Mr. Sammler and King Lear," p. 91.

38. The word appears in the fifth volume of Toynbee's *A Study of History*. Thomas Docherty, "Postmodernism: An Introduction," in *Postmodernism: A Reader*, ed. Docherty (New York: Columbia University Press, 1993), p. 1.

2. Immigration and Primal Scene

1. Joan Hoffman, "'She Wants to Be Called Yolanda Now': Identity, Language, and the Third Sister in *How the García Girls Lost Their Accents*," *Bilingual Review/La Revista Bilingüe* 23.1 (January–April 1998): 22.

2. Abraham Cahan, *The Rise of David Levinsky* (1917; reprint, New York: Harper, 1960), p. 86.

3. Jacqueline Stefanko, "New Ways of Telling: Latinas' Narratives of Exile and Return," *Frontiers: A Journal of Women's Studies* 17.2 (1996): 51.

4. Julia Alvarez, *How the García Girls Lost Their Accents* (Chapel Hill: Algonquin Books, 1991), p. 83. Hereafter cited parenthetically in the text.

5. B. J. Leggett, *Early Stevens: The Nietzschean Intertext* (Durham: Duke University Press, 1992), p. 170.

6. Julia Alvarez, *Something to Declare* (Chapel Hill: Algonquin Books, 1998), pp. 222, 259. Hereafter cited parenthetically in the text.

7. Miryam Criado, "Lenguaje y Otredad Sexual/Cultural en *How the García Girls Lost Their Accents*," *Bilingual Review/La Revista Bilingüe* 23.3 (September–December 1998): 203.

8. Gilbert H. Muller, *New Strangers in Paradise: The Immigrant Experience and Contemporary American Fiction* (Lexington: University Press of Kentucky, 1999), p. 124.

9. Ibis Gómez-Vega, "Hating the Self in the 'Other'; Or, How Yolanda Learns to See Her Own Kind in Julia Alvarez's *How the García Girls Lost Their Accents*," *Intertexts* 3.1 (spring 1999): 85.

10. Ludmila Kapschutschenko-Schmitt, "Julia Alvarez y Cristina García: Hibridación cultural en la novela exílica hispano-estadounidense," in *Proyec-*

ciones sobre la novela, ed. Linda Gould Levine and Ellen Engelson Marson, Inca Garcilaso series 604 (Hanover, N.H.: Ediciones del Norte, 1997), p. 116.

11. Maribel Ortiz-Márquez, "From Third World Politics to First World Practices: Contemporary Latina Writers in the United States," in *Interventions: Feminist Dialogues on Third World Women's Literature and Film*, ed. Bishnupriya Ghosh and Brinda Bose (New York: Garland, 1997), p. 242, n. 17.

12. Thomas Pynchon, *The Crying of Lot 49* (Philadelphia: Lippincott, 1966), p. 175.

13. Jean Rhys, *Wide Sargasso Sea* (New York: Dutton, 1966), p. 47.

14. Edwidge Danticat also tells this story—in *The Farming of Bones* (1998). Rita Dove, in a note to her poem on this incident, says that it was the rolled Spanish "r" that the Haitians could not pronounce.

15. Ezra Pound, *Selected Poems* (New York: New Directions, 1949).

16. Marny Requa, "The Politics of Fiction" (interview with Alvarez), *Frontera*, no. 5, http://www.fronteramag.com/issue5/Alvarez/ (last accessed March 25, 2002).

17. Marie Arana, *American Chica: Two Worlds, One Childhood* (New York: Delta, 2001), p. 37.

18. María Inés Lagos, "Deconstrucción del estereotipo hispánico en narraciones de Julia Alvarez, Cristina García y Esmeralda Santiago,"in *Studies in Honor of Myron Lichtblau*, ed. Fernando Burgos, Homenajes series 16 (Newark, Del.: Juan de la Cuesta, 2000), p. 208.

19. Philip Larkin, "Annus Mirabilis," in *Collected Poems* (New York: Farrar, Straus, Giroux, 1989), p. 167.

20. William Luis, *Dance between Two Cultures: Latino Caribbean Literature Written in the United States* (Nashville: Vanderbilt University Press, 1997), p. 268.

3. Survival on the Tangled Bank

1. Aleksandar Hemon, "Blind Jozef & Dead Souls" in *The Question of Bruno* (New York: Doubleday, 2000), pp. 170, 171.

2. Werner Sollors, *Beyond Ethnicity* (New York: Oxford University Press, 1986), p. 7.

3. Ursula Hegi, *The Vision of Emma Blau* (New York: Simon & Schuster, 2000), p. 240. Hereafter cited parenthetically in the text.

4. In her March 6, 2000, Salon.com review, Sarah Harrison Smith reproaches Hegi as "sometimes too simplistic in her characterization of German attitudes"; that is, the German American characters would be more plausible if their "responses to Hitler were complicated and fluctuating—shame mixed with pride in Hitler's autobahns, or something like that." http://cobrand.salon.com/books/review/2000/03/06/hegi/ (last accessed July 8, 2003).

5. F. Scott Fitzgerald, *The Great Gatsby*, ed. Matthew J. Bruccoli (1925; reprint, New York: Cambridge University Press, 1996), p. 6.

6. Vladimir Nabokov, *Pnin* (Garden City, N.Y.: Doubleday, 1957), p. 25.

7. Diana Postlethwaite, "100 Rms, Lake Vu," *New York Times Book Review*, February 13, 2000, http://www.nytimes.com/books/00/02/13/reviews/000213 .13postlt.html (last accessed July 8, 2003).

8. Bharati Mukherjee, *Jasmine* (New York: Grove Weidenfeld, 1989), p. 12. Hereafter cited parenthetically in the text.

9. Kathryn Hume, *American Dream, American Nightmare: Fiction since 1960* (Urbana: University of Illinois Press, 2000), p. 33.

10. Bharati Mukherjee, "Two Ways to Belong in America," *New York Times*, September 22, 1996, 4:13.

11. See Abdul JanMohammed, "Worldliness-without-World, Homelessness-as-Home: Toward a Definition of the Specular Border Intellectual," in *Edward Said: A Critical Reader*, ed., Michael Sprinker (Oxford: Basil Blackwell, 1992), pp. 96–120.

12. Kathleen Hendrix, "Vision of a Brave New World: Bharati Mukherjee Writes about the New Americans, the Non-European Immigrants Who She Says Are Changing the Nation," *Los Angeles Times*, November 12, 1989, p. 1. Eva Hoffman makes a similar point: "I've heard American expatriates and other immigrants to Western Europe complain that the societies of England or France are stratified, closed, and impregnable from the outside. When I begin the process of my Americanization, I find myself in the least snobbish of societies." See Eva Hoffman, *Lost in Translation* (New York: E. P. Dutton, 1989), p. 195.

13. Nicholas A. Basbanes, interview with Bharati Mukherjee, http://www .georgejr.com/oct97/mukerjee.html (last accessed March 22, 1998).

14. Jamaica Kincaid, *Lucy* (New York: Farrar, Straus, Giroux, 1990), p. 41. For an essay-length comparison of *Lucy* and *Jasmine*, see Rosanne Kanhai, " 'Sensing Designs in History's Muddles': Global Feminism in the Postcolonial Novel," *Modern Language Studies* 26.4 (fall 1996): 119–30. Kanhai reads Mariah's observation as "cultural appropriation," which is "a form of imperialism" (124).

15. Mukherjee made these remarks in a spring 1994 interview in *Mosaic*, the online Asian Studies journal at the University of Pennyslvania. It was no longer available at the time of publication (my notes date from 1998). The *Mosaic* Web site, http://dolphin.upenn.edu/mosaic/, advised that decisions regarding archived material were pending.

16. In the lengthy, fascinating interview in *Jouvert*, Mukherjee shows herself an accomplished polemicist, remarkably knowledgeable about postcolonial theory and remarkably candid in skewering it: "The mission of postcolonial studies seems to be to deliberately equate Art and journalism, to reduce novels to specimens for the confirming of their theories. If an imaginative work doesn't fit the cultural theories they approve of, it's dismissed as defective. The relationship between the artist and the postcolonial scholar has become adversarial." See Tina Chen and S. X. Goudie, "Holders of the Word: An Interview with Bharati Mukherjee," *Jouvert* 1.1 (1997), http://social.chass.ncsu.edu/jou vert/viii/bharat.htm (last accessed August 31, 2003).

17. Samir Dayal, "Creating, Preserving, Destroying: Violence in Bharati

Mukherjee's *Jasmine*, in *Bharati Mukherjee: Critical Perspectives*, ed. Emmanuel S. Nelson (New York: Garland, 1993), pp. 66, 67, 76.

18. Deepika Bahri, "Always Becoming: Narratives of Nation and Self in Bharati Mukherjee's *Jasmine*," in *Women, America, and Movement: Narratives of Relocation*, ed. Susan L. Roberson (Columbia: University of Missouri Press, 1998), p. 143.

19. Michael Connell, Jessie Grearson, and Tom Grimes, "An Interview with Bharati Mukherjee," *Iowa Review* 20.3 (1990): 8.

20. John K. Hoppe, "The Technological Hybrid as Post-American: Cross-Cultural Genetics in *Jasmine*," *Melus* (winter 1999): 139, http://www.findarticles.com/cf_0/m2278/4_24/63323864/print.jhtml (last accessed August 25, 2003).

21. As Kristin Carter-Sanborn reminds us, however, Mukherjee can also, as in "Immigrant Writing: Give Us Your Maximalists!," valorize "duality" and "split subjectivity" as artistically enabling. See Kristin Carter-Sanborn, " 'We Murder Who We Were': *Jasmine* and the Violence of Identity," in *Subjects and Citizens: Nation, Race, and Gender from "Oroonoko" to Anita Hill*, ed. Michael Moon and Cathy N. Davidson (Durham: Duke University Press, 1995), p. 440.

22. Scott London, "Crossing Borders: An Interview with Richard Rodriguez," http://www.scottlondon.com/interviews/rodriguez.html (last accessed August 29, 2003).

23. See, for example, Uma Parameswaran, review of *Jasmine*, *World Literature Today* 64.4 (1990): 699. Inderpal Grewal, in "Reading and Writing the South Asian Diaspora: Feminism and Nationalism in North America," in *Asian-American Writers*, ed. Harold Bloom (Philadelphia: Chelsea House, 1999), 187–99, criticizes the novel as "written for Euro-American audiences with the gaze of a Euro-American tourist" (198). Grewal reproaches Mukherjee for representing middle-class American life as the sole locus of a life peaceful and whole. "Instead of dismantling the hegemony of the term, 'American,' she wants to be included in it" (194).

24. Frederick Jackson Turner, "The Significance of the Frontier in American History," in *The Frontier in American History* (New York: Holt, Rinehart, Winston, 1962), pp. 2–3.

25. I have cited this familiar reference work because the iconography it sketches coincides more closely with Mukherjee's image of the vengeful Jyoti/Jasmine than do the more detailed representations of standard studies of the goddess and her place in the Hindu pantheon. These mention fetus earrings, a belt of severed arms, and other gory details. See David Kinsley, *The Sword and the Flute: Kālī: and Krsna: Dark Visions of the Terrible and the Sublime in Hindu Mythology* (Berkeley: University of California Press, 1975), or the essays in Rachel Fell McDermott and Jeffrey J. Kripal, *Encountering Kālī: In the Margins, at the Center, in the West* (Berkeley: University of California Press, 2003).

26. Carmen Wickramagamage, "The Empire Writes Back: Bharati Mukherjee's *Jasmine* as Post-Colonial Feminist Text," in *Literary Studies East*

and West, vol. 12, ed. Cristina Bacchilega and Cornelia N. Moore (Honolulu: University of Hawaii Press, 1996), p. 74.

27. Joseph Campbell, *The Hero with a Thousand Faces* (New York: Meridian, 1956), p. 115.

28. Clark Blaise and Bharati Mukherjee, *Days and Nights in Calcutta* (Garden City, N.Y.: Doubleday, 1977), p. 170.

29. Chang-rae Lee, *Native Speaker* (New York: Riverhead Books, 1995), p. 267.

30. Runar Vignisson, "Bharati Mukherjee: An Interview," *SPAN: Journal of the South Pacific Association for Commonwealth Literature and Language Studies* 34–35 (1992–93): 160, http://wwwmcc.murdoch.edu.au/ReadingRoom/litserv/ SPAN/34/Vignisson.html (last accessed August 18, 2003).

31. Sybil Steinberg, "Immigrant Author Looks at U.S. Society," *Publishers Weekly,* August 25, 1989, p. 46.

4. Language, Dreams, and Art in Cristina Garcia's *Dreaming in Cuban*

1. Achy Obejas, *Memory Mambo* (Pittsburgh: Cleis, 1996), p. 13.

2. Edwidge Danticat, *Breath, Eyes, Memory* (New York: Soho Press, 1994), p. 154.

3. Oscar Wilde, *The Importance of Being Earnest,* in *The Complete Works of Oscar Wilde* (New York: Perennial Library, 1989), p. 373.

4. Cristina Garcia, *Dreaming in Cuban* (New York: Knopf, 1992), p. 134. Hereafter cited parenthetically in the text.

5. Allan Vorda, "I Come from a Place That's Very Unreal: An Interview with Jamaica Kincaid," in *Face to Face: Interviews with Contemporary Novelists,* ed. Vorda (Houston: Rice University Press, 1993), p. 105.

6. Maribel Ortiz-Márquez, "From Third World Politics to First World Practices: Contemporary Latina Writers in the United States," in *Interventions: Feminist Dialogues on Third World Women's Literature and Film,* ed. Bishnupriya Ghosh, Brinda Bose, and Chandra Talpade Mohanty (New York: Garland, 1997), p. 234.

7. "A Prayer for My Daughter," in *The Collected Poems of W. B. Yeats* (New York: Macmillan, 1956), p. 186.

8. "Gacela de la Huida," trans. Stephen Spender and J. L. Gill, in *The Selected Poems of Federico García Lorca,* ed. Francisco García Lorca and Donald M. Allen (New York: New Directions, 1955), p. 167. Hereafter cited in the text.

9. Mary S. Vásquez, "Cuba as Text and Context in Cristina Garcia's *Dreaming in Cuban,*" *Bilingual Review/La revista bilingüe* 20.1 (January–April 1995): 23.

10. See Juan Nunez, "In Lecture, Mexican Author Carlos Fuentes Shares 10 Tips for Aspiring Writers," *Brown Daily Herald,* April 19, 2001, http://www .browndailyherald.com/stories.cfm?ID=4588 (last accessed December 12, 2002).

11. Jacqueline Stefanko, "New Ways of Telling: Latinas' Narratives of Exile and Return," *Frontiers: A Journal of Women's Studies* 17.2 (1996): 51.

12. Wallace Stevens, "Man Carrying Thing," in *The Palm at the End of the Mind: Selected Poems and a Play* (New York: Vintage, 1990), p. 281.

13. "Four Writers Sitting Around Talking," http://www.oregonlive.com/books/index.ssf 1997–1998.

14. Allan Vorda, "A Fish Swims in My Lung: An Interview with Cristina Garcia," in *Face to Face: Interviews with Contemporary Novelists*, ed. Vorda (Houston: Rice University Press, 1993), pp. 65, 76.

15. Wallace Stevens, "Someone Puts a Pineapple Together," in *The Palm at the End of the Mind: Selected Poems and a Play* (New York: Vintage, 1990), p. 295. Subsequent quotations are from this text.

16. Dick Hebdige, *Subculture: The Meaning of Style* (New York: Methuen, 1977), p. 7. Hereafter cited parenthetically in the text.

17. Adriana Méndez Rodenas, "En búsqueda del paraíso perdido: La historia natural como imaginación diaspórica en Cristian García," *MLN* 116.2 (2001): 394. Several critics emphasize the ingenuity with which Garcia makes family dynamics and personal psychology the vehicles of geopolitical meanings. See, for example, Stefanko's observation that "the historical events of colonization, revolution, and threatened invasion entwine around the personal issue of family separation and exile" ("New Ways of Telling," 56) or, more broadly, David Mitchell's argument that the national is pervasively subsumed in the familial. David T. Mitchell, "National Families and Familial Nations: Communista Americans in Cristina Garcia's *Dreaming in Cuban*," *Tulsa Studies in Women's Literature* 15.1 (spring 1996): 51–60. My only quarrel with these readings is that, constantly foregrounding the problematics of what the critics themselves admit is a chimera of essentialist *Cubanismo*, they tend to neglect the story's simultaneous questioning of American identity.

18. "Unguarded Gates," in *The Poems of Thomas Bailey Aldrich*, vol. 2 (Cambridge: Riverside Press, 1897), pp. 71–72.

19. Bharati Mukherjee, *Desirable Daughters* (New York: Hyperion, 2002), p. 17

20. Mitchell, "National Families and Familial Nations," p. 58.

21. Ernest Hemingway, *Death in the Afternoon* (New York: Scribner's, 1932), p. 192.

5. Korean Connection

1. Nora Okja Keller, *Comfort Woman* (New York: Viking, 1997), p. 71. Hereafter cited parenthetically in the text.

2. Theresa Hak Kyung Cha, *DICTEE* (1982; reprint, Berkeley: University of California Press, 2001), p. 21.

3. Ibid., p. 45.

4. Chung-Hei Yun, "Beyond 'Clay Walls': Korean American Literature,"

in *Asian-American Writers*, ed. Harold Bloom (Philadelphia: Chelsea House, 1999), p. 184.

5. Chang-rae Lee, *A Gesture Life* (New York: Riverhead Books, 1999), p. 95. Hereafter cited parenthetically in the text.

6. Rainer Maria Rilke, "Herbsttag," in *Das Buch der Bilder* (New York: Frederick Ungar, n.d.), p. 51.

7. Matthew Arnold, "Stanzas from the Grande Chartreuse," in *Selected Poetry and Prose* (New York: Holt, Rinehart and Winston, 1953), p. 77.

8. Chang-rae Lee, *Native Speaker* (New York: Riverhead Books, 1995), p. 134. Hereafter cited parenthetically in the text.

9. These examples are all from *White Noise* (New York: Viking, 1985), except for the last, which is from *Running Dog* (New York: Knopf, 1978).

10. Salar Abdoh, *The Poet Game* (New York: Picador, 2000), pp. 181, 66.

11. Richard Powers, *Operation Wandering Soul* (New York: William Morrow, 1993), pp. 33, 35.

12. Crystal Parikh, "Ethnic America Undercover: The Intellectual and Minority Discourse," *Contemporary Literature* 43.2(2002): 279.

13. Tina Chen, "Impersonation and Other Disappearing Acts in *Native Speaker* by Chang-rae Lee," *Modern Fiction Studies* 48.3 (fall 2000): 650.

14. Ralph Ellison, *Invisible Man* (New York: Random House, 1952), p. 500.

15. Joe Porcelli, *The Photograph* (Charleston, S.C.: Wyrick & Company, 1997), p. 143. Hereafter cited parenthetically in the text.

16. Thomas De Quincey, *Antigone*, in *Collected Writings*, ed. David Mason, vol. 13 (London: A. & C. Black, 1896–97), p. 220.

17. Walt Whitman, "The Sleepers," *Leaves of Grass*, ed. Jerome Loving (New York: Oxford University Press, 1990), p. 328.

18. Harold Bloom, *The Ringers in the Tower: Studies in the Romantic Tradition* (Chicago: University of Chicago Press, 1971), p. 99.

19. Percy Bysshe Shelley, *Prometheus Unbound*, in *The Complete Poetical Works of Percy Bysshe Shelley*, ed. Thomas Hutchinson (London: Oxford University Press, 1934).

20. According to the *OED*, the racial epithet actually originated earlier, in the Philippines.

21. F. Scott Fitzgerald, *The Great Gatsby* (New York: Cambridge University Press, 1991), p. 138.

22. Mary Jane Hurst, "Language, Gender, and Community in American Fiction at the End of the Century," *Southwest Journal of Linguistics* 17.1 (1998): 12.

23. John C. Hawley, "Gus Lee, Chang-rae Lee, and Li-Young Lee: The Search for the Father in Asian American Literature," in *Ideas of Home: Literature of Asian Migration*, ed. Geoffrey Kain (East Lansing: Michigan State University Press, 1997), p. 189.

24. Tim Engles, "'Visions of Me in the Whitest Raw Light': Assimilation and Doxic Whiteness in Chang-rae Lee's *Native Speaker*," *Hitting Critical Mass* 4.2 (summer 1997): 44–45.

6. Haitian Persephone

1. W.E.B. Du Bois, *The Souls of Black Folk*, in *Writings* (New York: Library of America, 1986), p. 364.

2. The line is spoken by Francesca da Rimini in canto 5 of the *Inferno:* "No greater anguish than to recall, in a time of misery, happier days."

3. Edwidge Danticat, *Breath, Eyes, Memory* (New York: Vintage, 1994), pp. 151, 234. Hereafter cited parenthetically in the text.

4. Junot Díaz, *Drown* (New York: Riverhead Books, 1996), p. 179.

5. Marilyn Halter, *Shopping for Identity: The Marketing of Ethnicity* (New York: Schocken, 2000), p. 119. Delia Caparoso Konzett historicizes these concerns with reference to the reception of Anzia Yezierska, Zora Neale Hurston, and Jean Rhys. Noting in these writers "a high degree of awareness concerning the commodity value of ethnic narratives," she defends them against perceptions that they might be "pandering in some way to the lurid tastes of the foreign and exotic." Konzett calls for "institutional practices" that will not "reduce ethnicity to a marketable stereotype . . . but preserve it as a complex compound of inherited legacies and elected affiliation, of partially fixed and partially open identities." See Delia Caparoso Konzett, *Ethnic Modernisms: Anzia Yezierska, Zora Neale Hurston, Jean Rhys, and the Aesthetics of Dislocation* (New York: Palgrave Macmillan, 2002), pp. 167, 168.

6. Werner Sollors, *Beyond Ethnicity: Consent and Descent in American Culture* (New York: Oxford University Press, 1986), p. 19.

7. Renee H. Shea, "The Dangerous Job of Edwidge Danticat: An Interview, *Callaloo* 19.1 (1996): 386.

8. Ibid., 385.

9. Nancy F. Gerber, "Binding the Narrative Thread: Storytelling and the Mother-Daughter Relationship in Edwidge Danticat's *Breath, Eyes, Memory*," *Journal of the Association for Research on Mothering* 2.2 (2000): 188–99.

10. Gloria Anzaldúa, *Borderlands/La Frontera: The New Mestiza* (San Francisco: Aunt Lute, 1987), pp. 16, 22.

7. Assimilation and Adolescence

1. Jamaica Kincaid, *A Small Place* (New York: New American Library, 1988), p. 31. Hereafter cited parenthetically in the text.

2. Allan Vorda, "I Come from a Place That's Very Unreal: An Interview with Jamaica Kincaid," in *Face to Face: Interviews with Contemporary Novelists*, ed. Vorda (Houston: Rice University Press, 1993), p. 98.

3. Maya Jaggi, "Kincaid in Revolt," Johannesburg *Mail & Guardian*, November 5, 1997, http://www.mg.co.za/mg/books/kincaid.htm (last accessed October 9, 2002. Also available at http://www.eng.fju.edu.tw/worldlit/carib bean/rebel.htm (last accessed October 4, 2005).

4. Kay Bonetti, "An Interview with Jamaica Kincaid," *Missouri Review* 15.2

(1992), http://www.missourireview.org/index.php?genre=Interviews&title=An+Interview+with+Jamaica+Kincaid (last accessed October 11, 2002).

5. I borrow this term from Robert Stepto's theory of African American literature, which contrasts narratives of "ascent" (from slavery or Jim Crow) and "immersion" (in ethnic experience). The ex-slave, achieving literacy, ascends (often cartographically, by moving north) and becomes, through literacy, an "articulate survivor"—a person empowered and free but deracinated, estranged from the community from which she or he sprang. See Robert B. Stepto, *From Behind the Veil: a Study of Afro-American Narrative*, 2nd ed. (Urbana: University of Illinois Press, 1991).

6. Jamaica Kincaid, *Lucy* (New York: Farrar, Straus, Giroux, 1990), p. 96. Hereafter cited parenthetically in the text.

7. Gary E. Holcomb, "Travels of a Transnational Slut: Sexual Migration in Kincaid's *Lucy*," *Critique* 44 (spring 2003): 297.

8. Moira Ferguson, "*Lucy* and the Mark of the Colonizer," *Modern Fiction Studies* 39.2 (summer 1993): 256.

9. Helen Tiffin, "Cold Hearts and (Foreign) Tongues: Recitation and the Reclamation of the Female Body in the Works of Erna Brodber and Jamaica Kincaid," *Callaloo* 16.4 (fall 1993): 919.

10. Ibid., 920.

11. For a friendlier analysis of the novel's "odor paradigm," including its treatment of such olfactory motifs as sweet-smelling Maria and "perfumed Gauguin" (who, in his autobiography, makes much of the earthy redolence of Tehura, his Tahitian bride), see Holcomb, "Travels of a Transnational Slut," pp. 300, 307–8, 309.

12. Gilbert H. Muller, *New Strangers in Paradise: The Immigrant Experience and Contemporary American Fiction* (Lexington: University Press of Kentucky, 1999), p. 160.

13. Diane Simmons, *Jamaica Kincaid* (New York: Twayne, 1994), p. 122.

14. Ferguson, "*Lucy* and the Mark of the Colonizer," 241–42. I find attempts to go beyond the circumstantial collocation of Lucys unconvincing.

15. Muller, *New Strangers in Paradise*, p. 160. Muller explains that "the United States from Kincaid's perspective has an imperial history and a hegemonic place in the hemisphere, and the large-scale arrival of non-Europeans in the country after World War II serves to create a postcoloniality that permits an interrogation of the Anglo-American narrative of Empire" (159).

16. Ibid., p. 158.

17. As Kincaid told Kay Bonetti, "I was forced to memorize John Milton and that was a very painful thing. But I'm not going to make myself forget John Milton because it involves a painful thing. I find John Milton very beautiful, and I'm glad that I know it. I'm sorry that the circumstances of how I got to know it were so horrid, but, since I know it, I know it and I claim every right to use it" ("An Interview"; see note 4).

18. "I detest everything about England, except the literature." Vorda, "I Come from a Place," p. 79.

19. She told Bonetti that she read *Jane Eyre* when she was "about ten years old" ("An Interview"; see note 4).

20. Jade Ngoc Quang Huýnh, *South Wind Changing* (St. Paul, Minn.: Gray-wolf Press, 1994), p. 275. Hereafter cited parenthetically in the text.

21. Martine Silber, "Chang-rae Lee ou les figures grimaçantes du passé," *Le Monde des Livres*, August 31, 2001, http://www.lemonde.fr/article/0,5987, 3260—218409–,00.html (last accessed September 18, 2002).

22. T. S. Eliot, "Tradition and the Individual Talent," in *The Sacred Wood* (London: Methuen, 1950), p. 50.

23. Lan Cao, *Monkey Bridge* (New York: Penguin Putnam, 1997), p. 15. Hereafter cited parenthetically in the text.

24. Mirinda J. Kossoff, "Visiting Law Professor Lan Cao's Vietnam Memories Turned into Praised Work of Fiction," http://www.bowiestate.edu/academics/english/freshcomp/lcarticle.htm (last accessed December 1, 2004).

25. Lisa Lowe, *Immigrant Acts* (Durham: Duke University Press, 1996), p. 9. Hereafter cited parenthetically in the text.

26. Carlos Bulosan, *America Is in the Heart* (1943; reprint, Seattle: University of Washington Press, 1973), pp. 189–90.

8. Ethnicity as Pentimento

1. Mylène Dressler, *The Deadwood Beetle* (New York: BlueHen, 2001), p. 4. Hereafter cited parenthetically in the text.

2. Werner Sollors, *Beyond Ethnicity: Consent and Descent in American Culture* (New York: Oxford University Press, 1986), pp. 6, 4.

3. Richard Eder, "Exploring a Present That Is Invaded by the Past," *New York Times*, May 22, 2000, E8.

4. Vladimir Nabokov, *Lectures on Literature*, ed. Fredson Bowers (New York: Harcourt Brace Jovanovich, 1980), p. 280.

5. Ibid., pp. 266, 260.

6. Steven G. Kellman, "The Truth under the Table," *Texas Observer*, October 12, 2001, http://www.texasobserver.org/showArticle.asp?ArticleID=453 (last accessed May 31, 2002).

7. Sigmund Freud, *Beyond the Pleasure Principle*, trans. James Strachey, in *The Standard Edition of the Complete Psychological Works of Sigmund Freud*, ed. Strachey, vol. 18 (London: Hogarth Press, 1953–74), pp. 16, 23, 36.

8. J. D. Salinger, *For Esmé with Love and Squalor and Other Stories* (London: Hamish Hamilton, 1953), pp. 115–16.

9. Immigration as *Bardo*

1. Wendy Law-Yone, *The Coffin Tree* (New York: Knopf, 1983), p. 167. Hereafter cited parenthetically in the text.

2. Janie C. Har, "Food, Sexuality, and the Pursuit of a Little Attention," *Hitting Critical Mass: A Journal of Asian American Cultural Criticism* (fall 1993): 85.

3. Francis Kingdon-Ward, *Burma's Icy Mountains* (London: Jonathan Cape, 1949), pp. 268, 241, 270, 268–69. In addition to a thorough account of the economics of finding and harvesting *Taiwania cryptomerioides*, Kingdon-Ward explains the importance of an especially sturdy coffin: "There is a good and proper reason why the mandarin wishes to own a coffin of durable timber. For the Chinese after death is first buried and then burned; and the interval between burial and cremation may be two or three years. Nay, the interval between death and burial may likewise be long. According to Chinese belief, it is important for the body (or at least the skeleton) to be complete at the time of cremation; otherwise it will be incomplete at the resurrection also and enter the shadow world a cripple. Unless the coffin can be guaranteed to hold together, which it can do only if made of some resistant, usually scented, wood, there is every likelihood that some of the bones will be lost, as almost invariably happens with the poorer classes who are buried in cheap coffins" (268).

4. Vladimir Nabokov, *Pnin* (Garden City, N.Y.: Doubleday, 1957), pp. 81–82.

5. Stuart Gilbert, *James Joyce's Ulysses* (London: Faber, 1930), p. 263n. See also Georges Contenau, *La civilisation phénicienne* (Paris: Payot, 1926), p. 108.

6. Wendy Law-Yone, "The Outsider," *Time*, August 18–25, 2003, http://www.time.com/time/asia/2003/journey/burma.html_(last accessed May 12, 2004).

7. Bharati Mukherjee, *Jasmine* (New York: Grove Weidenfeld, 1989), p. 185.

8. Interview with Tamara Ho and Nancy Yoo, in *Words Matter: Conversations with Asian American Writers*, ed. King-Kok Cheung (Honolulu: University of Hawaii Press, 2000), pp. 301–2.

9. Ebony Adams, "Wendy Law-Yone," Voices from the Gaps (University of Minnesota), http://voices.cla.umn.edu/newsite/authors/LAWYONEwendy .htm (last accessed June 23, 2004).

10. For the argument that the reader should resist the narrator's judgment on this score, see Rachel C. Lee, "The Erasure of Places and the Re-siting of Empire in Wendy Law-Yone's *The Coffin Tree*," originally in *Cultural Critique* 35 (winter 1996–97): 149–78, consulted on-line, December 1, 2004, http://www .english.ucla.edu/faculty/rlee/Lee-Erasure.html. Lee's article contains an error or two: the narrator is not tortured in Rangoon; carceral language and imagery are not limited to the 3 East sequence; and one doubts that Shan contracts malaria in the United States. But she persuasively contests readings that deny this novel's postcolonial specificity: "Under the discourse of the 'universal' subject . . . double consciousness and a sense of dislocation belong firstly to the modern subject, with the refugee only entering into that modern and now postmodern stage with his/her emigration to the First World." Lee sees in such readings a tendentious " 'politics of placelessness' wherein locational and temporal markers that render this story specifically about the traumatic dislocation of Asian refugees are deemed peripheral to readers' assessments of value."

11. As Tamara Ho observes, "Readers of *The Coffin Tree* should consider how it is that Law-Yone's construction of madness comments on or critiques different cultural conditions that cause the characters to abandon reason in both Asia and the United States." See Tamara C. Ho, "*The Coffin Tree* by Wendy Law-Yone," in *A Resource Guide to Asian American Literature*, ed. Sau-ling Cynthia Wong and Stephen H. Sumida (New York: MLA, 2001), p. 114.

12. William Cowper, "The Castaway," in *Cowper: Verse and Letters*, ed. Brian Spiller (Cambridge, Mass.: Harvard University Press, 1968), p. 140.

13. Interview with Tamara Ho and Nancy Yoo, p. 292.

14. *The Tibetan Book of the Dead*, trans. Lāma Kazi Dawa-Samdup, ed. W. Y. Evans-Wentz, 3rd ed. (1927; reprint, London: Oxford, 1960), pp. 101–2. Hereafter cited by page in the text. I have also consulted the translations by Frank J. MacHovec (New York: Peter Pauper Press, 1972) and Francesca Fremantle and Chögyam Trungpa (London: Shambhala, 1975).

15. Kathryn VanSpanckeren, "The Asian Literary Background of *The Woman Warrior*, in *Approaches to Teaching Kingston's "The Woman Warrior*," ed. Shirley Geok-lin Lim (New York: MLA, 1991), p. 51.

16. Thomas Pynchon, *The Crying of Lot 49* (Philadelphia: Lippincott, 1966), pp. 170, 180, 182.

17. Interview with Tamara Ho and Nancy Yoo, p. 295

18. Ibid., p. 294.

19. Lee, "Erasure of Places."

20. Edmund Ronald Leach, *Political Systems of Highland Burma* (Boston: Beacon Press, 1964), p. 217.

21. Leslie Milne and Wilbur Willis Cochrane, *Shans at Home* (London, 1910), cited in Leach, *Political Systems of Highland Burma*, p. 216n12.

22. I am indebted here to one of my students, Jonathan Sedberry, who suggested the analogy between Law-Yone's hanged man and Eliot's.

10. Closet and Mask

1. Junot Díaz, *Drown* (New York: Riverhead Books, 1996), p. 29. Hereafter cited parenthetically in the text.

2. "Rencontre avec Aleksandar Hemon," unsigned interview in *Zone littéraire*, http://www.zone-litteraire.com/entretiens.php?art_id=45 (last accessed February 12, 2003).

3. Kathleen Hendrix, "Vision of a Brave New World Books: Bharati Mukherjee Writes about the New Americans, the Non-European Immigrants Who She Says Are Changing the Nation," *Los Angeles Times*, November 12, 1989, p. 1.

4. "Rencontre avec Aleksandar Hemon."

5. Maximo Zeledón, "Dominican Dominion," *La Frontera*, no. 5, http:www.fronteramag.com/issue5/Díaz/index.htm (last accessed April 10, 2002).

6. Ibid.

7. Ibid.

8. Eli Gottlieb, "Review of *Drown* by Junot Díaz," *Boston Review* 21.6 (December–January 1996–97), http://bostonreview.mit.edu/BR21.6/prose.html #gottlieb (last accessed December 2, 2004).

9. Evelyn P. Stevens, "Marianismo: The Other Face of Machismo in Latin America," in *Female and Male in Latin America*, ed. Ann Pescatello (Pittsburgh: University of Pittsburgh Press, 1973), pp. 94–95. Díaz has argued (in the interview with Zeledón) against the notion that machismo is unique or specific to Latino cultures: "When everybody is saying Machismo, I'm like, suck my d— [Laughs], because this is not common to Latinos. It's common to everybody who belongs to a hyper-patriarchal society, very much like the one in the United States."

10. J. D. Salinger, "The Laughing Man," in *Nine Stories* (New York: Little, Brown, 1953), pp. 58–59.

11. T. S. Eliot, *The Waste Land*, in *Collected Poems, 1909–1962* (London: Faber, 1963), p. 70.

Conclusion

1. Richard Powers, *Operation Wandering Soul* (New York: William Morrow, 1993), p. 296.

2. Bharati Mukherjee, "Immigrant Writing: Give Us Your Maximalists!" *New York Times Book Review*, August 28, 1988, p. 28.

3. Ralph Ellison, *Invisible Man* (New York: Random House, 1952), p. 581.

≋ Works Cited

Abdoh, Salar. *The Poet Game*. New York: Picador, 2000.

Adams, Ebony. "Wendy Law-Yone." Voices from the Gaps. University of Minnesota. http://voices.cla.umn.edu/newsite/authors/LAWYONEwendy.htm (last accessed June 23, 2004).

Adams, Henry. *The Education of Henry Adams*. 1918. Boston: Houghton Mifflin, 1961.

Adams, Lorraine. *Harbor*. New York: Knopf, 2004.

Aldrich, Thomas Bailey. *The Poems of Thomas Bailey Aldrich*. Vol. 2. Cambridge: Riverside Press, 1897.

Alvarez, Julia. *How the García Girls Lost Their Accents*. Chapel Hill: Algonquin, 1991.

——. *Something to Declare*. Chapel Hill: Algonquin, 1998.

Andy Warhol. Exhibition catalogue. Stockholm: Moderna Museet, 1968.

Anzaldúa, Gloria. *Borderlands/La Frontera: The New Mestiza*. San Francisco: Aunt Lute, 1987.

Arana, Marie. *American Chica: Two Worlds, One Childhood*. New York: Delta, 2001.

Arnold, Matthew. "Stanzas from the Grande Chartreuse." In *Selected Poetry and Prose*. New York: Holt, Rinehart and Winston, 1953.

Atlas, James. *Bellow: A Biography*. New York: Random House, 2000.

Bahri, Deepika. "Always Becoming: Narratives of Nation and Self in Bharati Mukherjee's *Jasmine*." In *Women, America, and Movement: Narratives of Relocation*, ed. Susan L. Roberson. Columbia: University of Missouri Press, 1998.

Basbanes, Nicholas. "Interview with Bharati Mukherjee." http://www.georgejr.com/oct97/mukerjee.html (last accessed March 22, 1998).

Baudrillard, Jean. "The Precession of Simulacra." In *Simulations*, trans. Paul Foss, Paul Patton, and Philip Bleitchman. New York: Semiotext[e], 1983.

Bellow, Saul. *Mr. Sammler's Planet*. New York: Viking, 1970.

Berryman, Charles. "Saul Bellow: Mr. Sammler and King Lear." *Essays in Literature* 10.1 (1983): 81–92.

Blaise, Clark, and Bharati Mukherjee. *Days and Nights in Calcutta*. Garden City, N.Y.: Doubleday, 1977.

Bloom, Harold. *The Ringers in the Tower: Studies in the Romantic Tradition*. Chicago: University of Chicago Press, 1971.

Bonetti, Kay. "An Interview with Jamaica Kincaid." *Missouri Review* 15.2 (1992). http://www.missourireview.org/index.php?genre=Interviews&title=An+Interview+with+Jamaica+Kincaid (last accessed October 11, 2002).

Bulosan, Carlos. *America Is in the Heart*. 1943. Seattle: University of Washington Press, 1973.

Cahan, Abraham. *The Rise of David Levinsky*. 1917. New York: Harper, 1960.

Cambridge History of English and American Literature. 18 Vols. Cambridge: Cambridge University Press, 1907–21.

Campbell, Joseph. *The Hero with a Thousand Faces*. New York: Meridian, 1956.

Cao, Lan. *Monkey Bridge*. New York: Penguin Putnam, 1997.

Carter-Sanborn, Kristin. " 'We Murder Who We Were': *Jasmine* and the Violence of Identity." In *Subjects and Citizens: Nation, Race, and Gender from "Oroonoko" to Anita Hill*, ed. Michael Moon and Cathy N. Davidson. Durham: Duke University Press, 1995.

Cha, Theresa Hak Kyung Cha. DICTEE. 1982. Berkeley: University of California Press, 2001.

Chen, Tina. "Impersonation and Other Disappearing Acts in *Native Speaker* by Chang-rae Lee." *Modern Fiction Studies* 48.3 (fall 2000): 637–67.

Chen, Tina, and S. X. Goudie. "Holders of the Word: An Interview with Bharati Mukherjee." *Jouvert* 1.1 (1997). http://social.chass.ncsu.edu/jouvert/viii/bharat.htm (last accessed August 31, 2003).

Cheung, King-Kok, ed. *Words Matter: Conversations with Asian American Writers*. Honolulu: University of Hawaii Press, 2000. 283–302.

Chow, Rey. *Women and Chinese Modernity: The Politics of Reading between West and East*. Minneapolis: University of of Minnesota Press, 1991.

Chow, Rey. *Writing Diaspora: Tactics of Intervention in Contemporary Cultural Studies*. Bloomington: Indiana University Press, 1993.

Cohen, Sarah Blacher. *Saul Bellow's Enigmatic Laughter*. Urbana: University of Illinois Press, 1974.

Connell, Michael, Jessie Grearson, and Tom Grimes. "An Interview with Bharati Mukherjee." *Iowa Review* 20.3 (1990): 7–32.

Contenau, Georges. *La civilisation phénicienne*. Paris: Payot, 1926.

Cowper, William. *Cowper: Verse and Letters*. Ed. Brian Spiller. Cambridge: Harvard University Press, 1968.

Criado, Miryam. "Lenguaje y Otredad Sexual/Cultural en *How the García Girls Lost*

Their Accents." Bilingual Review/La Revista Bilingüe 23.3 (September–December 1998): 195–205.

Cronin, Gloria L. "Searching the Narrative Gap: Authorial Self-Irony and the Problematic Discussion of Western Misogyny in Mr. Sammler's Planet." In Saul Bellow: A Mosaic. Twentieth-Century American Jewish Writers. Vol. 3. New York: Lang, 1992.

Danticat, Edwidge. Breath, Eyes, Memory. New York: Soho, 1994.

Dayal, Samir. "Creating, Preserving, Destroying: Violence in Bharati Mukherjee's Jasmine." In Bharati Mukherjee: Critical Perspectives, ed. Emmanuel S. Nelson. New York: Garland, 1993. 65–88.

DeLillo, Don. Americana. Boston: Houghton Mifflin, 1971.

——. "The Power of History." New York Times Magazine, September 7, 1997, 60–63.

——. Running Dog. New York: Knopf, 1978.

——. White Noise. New York: Viking, 1985.

De Quincey, Thomas. Antigone. Vol. 13 of Collected Writings. Ed. David Masson. 14 Vols. London: A. & C. Black, 1896–97.

Díaz, Junot. Drown. New York: Riverhead, 1996.

Docherty, Thomas. "Postmodernism: An Introduction." In Postmodernism: A Reader, ed. Thomas Docherty. New York: Columbia University Press, 1993.

Dos Passos, John. Manhattan Transfer. 1925. Boston: Houghton Mifflin, 1953.

Dressler, Mylène. The Deadwood Beetle. New York: BlueHen, 2001.

Du Bois, W. E. B. The Souls of Black Folk. In Writings, ed. Nathan Huggins. New York: Library of America, 1986.

Eder, Richard Eder. "Exploring a Present That Is Invaded by the Past." Review of Vertigo by W. G. Sebald. New York Times, May 22, 2000, E:8.

Eliot, T. S. "Tradition and the Individual Talent." In The Sacred Wood. London: Methuen, 1950.

——. The Waste Land. In Collected Poems, 1909–1962. London: Faber, 1963.

Ellison, Ralph. Invisible Man. New York: Random House, 1952.

Engles, Tim. "'Visions of Me in the Whitest Raw Light': Assimilation and Doxic Whiteness in Chang-rae Lee's Native Speaker." Hitting Critical Mass 4.2 (summer 1997): 27–48.

Essex, Ruth. "Bellow's Sammler and Kosinski's Kosky in New York." New Voices in an Old Tradition: Studies in American Jewish Literature 13 (1994): 85–92.

Ferguson, Moira. "Lucy and the Mark of the Colonizer," Modern Fiction Studies 39.2 (summer 1993): 237–59.

Fitzgerald, F. Scott. The Great Gatsby. 1925. Ed. Matthew J. Bruccoli. New York: Cambridge University Press, 1996.

"Four Writers Sitting Around Talking." http://www.oregonlive.com/books/index.ssf 1997–1998.

Freud, Sigmund. Beyond the Pleasure Principle. Trans. James Strachey. Vol. 18 of The Standard Edition of the Complete Psychological Works of Sigmund Freud. 24 vols. Ed. Strachey. London: Hogarth Press, 1953–74.

——. Civilization and Its Discontents. Trans. James Strachey. Vol. 21 of The Standard Edition of the Complete Psychological Works of Sigmund Freud. 24 vols. Ed. James Strachey. London: Hogarth Press, 1953–74.

Fuchs, Daniel. Saul Bellow: Vision and Revision. Durham: Duke University Press, 1984.

Garcia, Cristina. *Dreaming in Cuban.* New York: Knopf, 1992.

García Lorca, Federico. *The Selected Poems of Federico García Lorca.* Ed. Francisco Garcia Lorca and Donald M. Allen. Trans. Stephen Spender and J. L. Gill. New York: New Directions, 1955.

Gerber, Nancy F. "Binding the Narrative Thread: Storytelling and the Mother-Daughter Relationship in Edwidge Danticat's *Breath, Eyes, Memory.*" *Journal of the Association for Research on Mothering* 2.2 (2000): 188–99.

Gilbert, Stuart. *James Joyce's "Ulysses."* London: Faber, 1930.

Glickman, Susan. "The World as Will and Idea: A Comparative Study of *An American Dream* and *Mr. Sammler's Planet.*" *Modern Fiction Studies* 28.4 (1982—83): 569—82.

Gómez-Vega, Ibis. "Hating the Self in the 'Other'; Or, How Yolanda Learns to See Her Own Kind in Julia Alvarez's *How the García Girls Lost Their Accents.*" *Intertexts* 3.1 (spring 1999): 85–96.

Gottlieb, Eli. Review Of *Drown* by Junot Díaz. *Boston Review* 21.6 (December–January 1996–97). http://bostonreview.mit.edu/BR21.6/prose.html#gottlieb (last accessed December 2, 2004).

Grewal, Inderpal. "Reading and Writing the South Asian Diaspora: Feminism and Nationalism in North America." In *Asian-American Writers,* ed. Harold Bloom. Philadelphia: Chelsea House, 1999.

Guttman, Allen. "Saul Bellow's Mr. Sammler." *Contemporary Literature* 14.2 (1973): 157–66.

Halter, Marilyn. *Shopping for Identity: The Marketing of Ethnicity.* New York: Schocken, 2000.

Har, Janie C. "Food, Sexuality, and the Pursuit of a Little Attention." *Hitting Critical Mass: A Journal of Asian American Cultural Criticism* (fall 1993): 83–92.

Hawley, John C. "Gus Lee, Chang-rae Lee, and Li-Young Lee: The Search for the Father in Asian American Literature." In *Ideas of Home: Literature of Asian Migration,* ed. Geoffrey Kain. East Lansing: Michigan State University Press, 1997.

Hebdige, Dick. *Subculture: The Meaning of Style.* New York: Methuen, 1977.

Hegi, Ursula. *The Vision of Emma Blau.* New York: Simon & Schuster, 2000.

Hemingway, Ernest. *Death in the Afternoon.* New York: Scribner's, 1932.

Hemon, Aleksandar. *The Question of Bruno.* New York: Doubleday, 2000.

Hendrix, Kathleen. "Vision of a Brave New World: Bharati Mukherjee Writes about the New Americans, the Non-European Immigrants Who She Says Are Changing the Nation." *Los Angeles Times,* November 12, 1989, p. 1.

Hicks, Jack. *In the Singer's Temple.* Chapel Hill: University of North Carolina Press, 1981.

Ho, Tamara. "*The Coffin Tree* by Wendy Law-Yone." In *A Resource Guide to Asian American Literature,* ed. Sau-ling Cynthia Wong and Stephen H. Sumida. New York: MLA, 2001.

Ho, Tamara, and Nancy Yoo. "Wendy Law-Yone." In *Words Matter: Conversations with Asian American Writers,* ed. King-Kok Cheung. Honolulu: University of Hawaii Press, 2000.

Hoffman, Eva. *Lost in Translation: Life in a New Language.* New York: E. P. Dutton, 1989.

——. *The Secret*. New York: Public Affairs, 2002.

Hoffman, Joan. "'She Wants to Be Called Yolanda Now': Identity, Language, and the Third Sister in *How the García Girls Lost Their Accents*." *Bilingual Review/La Revista Bilingüe* 23.1 (January–April 1998): 21–27.

Holcomb, Gary E. "Travels of a Transnational Slut: Sexual Migration in Kincaid's *Lucy*." *Critique* 44 (spring 2003): 297–312.

Hoppe, John K. "The Technological Hybrid as Post-American: Cross-cultural Genetics in *Jasmine*." *Melus* (winter 1999): 137–56.

Howard, Gerald. "The American Strangeness: An Interview with Don DeLillo." *Hungry Mind Review* 43 (1997): 13–16.

Hume, Kathryn. *American Dream, American Nightmare: Fiction since 1960*. Urbana: University of Illinois Press, 2000.

Hurst, Mary Jane. "Language, Gender, and Community in American Fiction at the End of the Century." *Southwest Journal of Linguistics* 17.1 (1998): 1–13.

Huxley, Aldous. "Appendix." In *Tomorrow and Tomorrow and Tomorrow*. New York: Harper & Row, 1956.

Huỳnh, Jade Ngoc Quang. *South Wind Changing*. Saint Paul: Graywolf, 1994.

Jaggi, Maya. "Kincaid in Revolt." *Mail & Guardian* (Johannesburg), November 5, 1997. http://www.mg.co.za/mg/books/kincaid.htm (last accessed October 9, 2002).

JanMohammed, Abdul. "Worldliness-without-World, Homelessness-as-Home: Toward a Definition of the Specular Border Intellectual." In *Edward Said: A Critical Reader*, ed. Michael Sprinker. Oxford: Basil Blackwell, 1992.

Joyce, James. *Ulysses*. Corrected text. Ed. Hans Walter Gabler with Wolfhard Steppe and Claus Melchior. New York: Random House, 1986.

Kanhai, Rosanne. "'Sensing Designs in History's Muddles': Global Feminism in the Postcolonial Novel." *Modern Language Studies* 26.4 (fall 1996): 119–30.

Kapschutschenko-Schmitt, Ludmila. "Julia Alvarez y Cristina García: Hibridación cultural en la novela exílica hispano-estadounidense." In *Proyecciones sobre la novela*, ed. Linda Gould Levine and Ellen Engelson Marson. Hanover, N.H.: Ediciones del Norte, 1997.

Kazin, Alfred. *Bright Book of Life: American Novelists and Storytellers from Hemingway to Mailer*. London: Secker & Warburg, 1974.

Keller, Nora Okja. *Comfort Woman*. New York: Viking, 1997.

Kellman, Steven G. "The Truth under the Table." *Texas Observer*, October 12, 2001. http://www.texasobserver.org/showArticle.asp?ArticleID=453 (last accessed May 31, 2002).

Kincaid, Jamaica. *Lucy*. New York: Farrar, Straus, Giroux, 1990.

——. *A Small Place*. New York: New American Library, 1988.

Kingdon-Ward, F[rancis]. *Burma's Icy Mountains*. London: Jonathan Cape, 1949.

Kinsley, David. *The Sword and the Flute: Kālī and Krsna: Dark Visions of the Terrible and the Sublime in Hindu Mythology*. Berkeley: University of California Press, 1975.

Konzett, Delia Caparoso. *Ethnic Modernisms: Anzia Yezierska, Zora Neale Hurston, Jean Rhys, and the Aesthetics of Dislocation*. New York: Palgrave Macmillan, 2002.

Kosinski, Jerzy. *Being There*. New York: Harcourt Brace Jovanovich, 1971.

Kossoff, Miranda J. "Visiting Law Professor Lan Cao's Vietnam Memories Turned into

Praised Work of Fiction." http://www.bowietstate.edu/academics/artsci/english/ freshcomp/lcarticle.htm (last accessed July 17, 2003).

Lagos, María Inés. "Deconstrucción del estereotipo hispánico en narraciones de Julia Alvarez, Cristina García y Esmeralda Santiago." In *Studies in Honor of Myron Lichtblau*, ed. Fernando Burgos. Newark, Del.: Juan de la Cuesta, 2000.

Larkin, Philip. *Collected Poems*. Ed. Anthony Thwaite. New York: Farrar, Straus, Giroux, 1989.

Lavers, Norman. *Jerzy Kosinski*. Boston: Twayne, 1982.

Law-Yone, Wendy. *The Coffin Tree*. New York: Knopf, 1983.

——. "The Outsider." *Time*, August 18– 25, 2003. http://www.time.com/time/asia/2003/ journey/burma.html (last accessed May 12, 2004).

Leach, Edmund Ronald. *Political Systems of Highland Burma*. Boston: Beacon Press, 1964.

Lee, Chang-rae. *A Gesture Life*. New York: Riverhead, 1999.

——. *Native Speaker*. New York: Riverhead, 1995.

Lee, Rachel C. "The Erasure of Places and the Re-siting of Empire in Wendy Law-Yone's *The Coffin Tree*." *Cultural Critique* 35 (winter 1996–97): 149–78.

Leggett, B. J. *Early Stevens: The Nietzschean Intertext*. Durham: Duke University Press, 1992.

Lilly, Paul R. *Words in Search of Victims: The Achievement of Jerzy Kosinski*. Kent, Ohio: Kent State University Press, 1988.

Lim, Shirley Geok-Lin. "The Ambivalent American: Asian American Literature on the Cusp." In *Reading the Literatures of Asian America*, ed. Shirley Geok-Lin Lim and Amy Ling. Philadelphia: Temple University Press, 1992.

London, Scott. "Crossing Borders: An Interview with Richard Rodriguez." http://www .scottlondon.com/interviews/rodriguez.html (last accessed August 29, 2003).

Lowe, Lisa. *Immigrant Acts*. Durham: Duke University Press, 1996.

Luis, William. *Dance Between Two Cultures: Latino Caribbean Literature Written in the United States*. Nashville: Vanderbilt University Press, 1997.

Lupack, Barbara Tepa. *Plays of Passion, Games of Chance: Jerzy Kosinski and His Fiction*. Bristol, Ind.: Wyndham Hall, 1988.

McDermott, Rachel Fell, and Jeffrey J. Kripal, eds. *Encountering Kālī: In the Margins, at the Center, in the West*. Berkeley: University of California Press, 2003.

Méndez Rodenas, Adriana. "En búsqueda del paraíso perdido: la historia natural como imaginación diaspórica en Cristian García." *MLN* 116.2 (2001): 392–418.

Milne, L[eslie], and W[ilbur] W[illis] Cochrane. *Shans at Home*. London, 1910.

Mitchell, David. T. "National Families and Familial Nations: Communista Americans in Cristina Garcia's *Dreaming in Cuban*." *Tulsa Studies in Women's Literature* 15.1 (spring 1996): 51–60.

Moon, Michael, and Cathy N. Davidson, eds. *Subjects and Citizens: Nation, Race, and Gender from "Oroonoko" to Anita Hill*. Durham: Duke University Press, 1995.

Mukherjee, Bharati. *Desirable Daughters*. New York: Hyperion, 2002.

——. "Immigrant Writing: Give Us Your Maximalists!" *New York Times Book Review*, August 28, 1988, pp. 28–29.

——. "Interview with Bharati Mukherjee." *Mosaic* (spring 1994). http://dolphin.upenn .edu/~mosaic/.

———. *Jasmine*. New York: Grove Weidenfeld, 1989.

———. "Two Ways to Belong in America." *New York Times*, September 22, 1996, 4:1.

Muller, Gilbert H. *New Strangers in Paradise: The Immigrant Experience and Contemporary American Fiction*. Lexington: University Press of Kentucky, 1999.

Nabokov, Vladimir. *Lectures on Literature*. Ed. Fredson Bowers. New York: Harcourt Brace Jovanovich, 1980.

———. *Lolita*. New York: Putnam's, 1955.

———. *Pnin*. 1957. New York: Anchor Press, 1984.

———. *Strong Opinions*. New York: McGraw Hill, 1973.

Nunez, Juan. "In Lecture, Mexican Author Carlos Fuentes Shares Ten Tips for Aspiring Writers." *Brown Daily Herald*, April 19, 2001. http://www.browndailyherald.com/stories.cfm?ID=4588 (last accessed December 12, 2002).

Obejas, Achy. *Memory Mambo*. Pittsburgh: Cleis, 1996.

Ortiz-Márquez, Maribel. "From Third World Politics to First World Practices: Contemporary Latina Writers in the United States." In *Interventions: Feminist Dialogues on Third World Women's Literature and Film*, ed. Bishnupriya Ghosh, Brinda Bose, and Chandra Talpade Mohanty. New York: Garland, 1997.

Parameswaran, Uma. Review of *Jasmine* by Bharati Mukherjee. *World Literature Today* 64.4 (1990): 699.

Parikh, Crystal. "Ethnic America Undercover: The Intellectual and Minority Discourse." *Contemporary Literature* 43.2 (2002): 249–84.

Pifer, Ellen. *Saul Bellow Against the Grain*. Philadelphia: University of Pennsylvania Press, 1990.

Plimpton, George, and Rocco Landesman. "The Art of Fiction XLVI—Jerzy Kosinski." In *Conversations with Jerzy Kosinski*, ed. Tom Teicholz. Jackson: University Press of Mississippi, 1993.

Porcelli, Joe. *The Photograph*. Charleston, S.C.: Wyrick & Company, 1997.

Postlewaite, Diana. "100 Rooms, Lake Vu." *New York Times Book Review*, February 13, 2000. http://www.nytimes.com/books/00/02/13.13postlt.html (last accessed July 8, 2003).

Pound, Ezra. *Selected Poems*. New York: New Directions, 1949.

Powers, Richard. *Operation Wandering Soul*. New York: William Morrow, 1993.

Pynchon, Thomas. *The Crying of Lot 49*. Philadelphia: Lippincott, 1966.

———. *Gravity's Rainbow*. New York: Viking, 1973.

———. *Vineland*. New York: Little, Brown, 1990.

"Rencontre avec Aleksandar Hemon." *Zone littéraire*. http://www.zone-litteraire.com/entretiens.php?art_id=45 last accessed February 12, 2003).

Requa, Marny. "The Politics of Fiction." *Frontera* 5.25. http://www.fronteramag.com/issue5/Alvarez/ (last accessed March 2002).

Rhys, Jean. *Wide Sargasso Sea*. New York: Dutton, 1966.

Rilke, Rainer Maria. "Herbsttag." In *Das Buch der Bilder*. New York: Frederick Ungar, n.d.

Rodriguez, Richard. *An Autobiography: Hunger of Memory: The Education of Richard Rodriguez*. Boston: D. R. Godine, 1982.

Salinger, J. D. *For Esmé with Love and Squalor and Other Stories*. London: Hamish, Hamilton, 1953.

Sanders, Ivan. "The Gifts of Strangeness: Alienation and Creation in Jerzy Kosinski's Fiction." *Polish Review* 19.3–4 (autumn–winter 1974): 171–89.

Shakespeare, William. *The Complete Works of William Shakespeare.* Ed. Hardin Craig. Chicago: Scott, Foresman, 1961.

Shea, Renee H. "The Dangerous Job of Edwidge Danticat: An Interview." *Callaloo* 19.2 (1996): 382–89.

Shelley, Percy Bysshe. *Prometheus Unbound.* In *The Complete Poetical Works of Percy Bysshe Shelley,* ed. Thomas Hutchinson. London: Oxford University Press, 1934.

Sherwin, Byron L. *Jerzy Kosinski: Literary Alarmclock.* Chicago: Cabala Press, 1981.

Silber, Martine. "Chang-rae Lee ou les figures grimaçantes du passé." *Le Monde des Livres,* August 31, 2001. http://www.lemonde.fr/article/0,5987,3260—218409-,00 .html (last accessed September 18, 2002).

Simmons, Diane. *Jamaica Kincaid.* New York: Twayne, 1994.

Sloan, James Park. *Jerzy Kosinski: A Biography.* New York: Dutton, 1996.

Smith, Sarah Harrison. "Review: The Vision of Emma Blau. http://cobrand.salon.com/ books/review/2000/03/06/hegi/ (last accessed July 8, 2003).

Sollors, Werner. *Beyond Ethnicity: Consent and Descent in American Culture.* New York: Oxford University Press, 1986.

Stefanko, Jacqueline. "New Ways of Telling: Latinas' Narratives of Exile and Return." *Frontiers: A Journal of Women Studies* 17.2 (1996): 50–69.

Steinberg, Sybil. "Immigrant Author Looks at U.S. Society." *Publishers Weekly,* August 25, 1989, pp. 46–47.

Stepto, Robert B. *From Behind the Veil: a Study of Afro-American Narrative.* 2nd ed. Urbana: University of Illinois Press, 1991.

Stevens, Evelyn P. "Marianismo: The Other Face of Machismo in Latin America." In *Female and Male in Latin America,* ed. Ann Pescatello. Pittsburgh: University of Pittsburgh Press, 1973.

Stevens, Wallace. *The Palm at the End of the Mind: Selected Poems and a Play.* New York: Vintage, 1990.

Stokes, Geoffrey, and Eliot Fremont-Smith. "Jerzy Kosinski's Tainted Words." *Village Voice,* June 22, 1982, pp. 1, 41–43.

Tibetan Book of the Dead. 1927. Ed. W. Y. Evans-Wentz. Trans. Lāma Kazi Dawa-Samdup. 3rd ed. London: Oxford University Press, 1960.

Tibetan Book of the Dead. Trans. Francesca Fremantle and Chögyam Trungpa. London: Shambala, 1975.

Tibetan Book of the Dead. Trans. Frank J. MacHovec. New York: Peter Pauper Press, 1972.

Tiffin, Helen. "Cold Hearts and (Foreign) Tongues: Recitation and the Reclamation of the Female Body in the Works of Erna Brodber and Jamaica Kincaid." *Callaloo* 16.4 (fall 1993): 909–21.

Turner, Frederick Jackson. "The Significance of the Frontier in American History." In *The Frontier in American History.* New York: Holt, Rinehart, Winston, 1962.

VanSpanckeren, Kathryn. "The Asian Literary Background of *The Woman Warrior.* In *Approaches to Teaching Kingston's "The Woman Warrior,"* ed. Shirley Geok-lin Lim. New York: MLA, 1991.

Vásquez, Mary S. "Cuba as Text and Context in Cristina Garcia's *Dreaming in Cuban*." *Bilingual Review/La revista bilingüe* 20.1 (January–April 1995): 22–27.

Vignisson, Runar. "Bharati Mukherjee: An Interview." *SPAN: Journal of the South Pacific Association for Commonwealth Literature and Language Studies* 34–35 (1992–93): 153–68.

Vorda, Allan. "A Fish Swims in My Lung: An Interview with Cristina Garcia." In *Face to Face: Interviews with Contemporary Novelists*, ed. Allan Vorda. Houston: Rice University Press, 1993.

——. "I Come from a Place That's Very Unreal: An Interview with Jamaica Kincaid." In *Face to Face: Interviews with Contemporary Novelists*, ed. Allan Vorda. Houston: Rice University Press, 1993.

Whitman, Walt. "The Sleepers." In *Leaves of Grass*, ed. Jerome Loving. New York: Oxford University Press, 1990.

Wickramagamage, Carmen. "The Empire Writes Back: Bharati Mukherjee's *Jasmine* as Post-colonial Feminist Text." In *Literary Studies East and West*, vol. 12, ed. Cristina Bacchilega and Cornelia N. Moore. Honolulu: University of Hawaii Press, 1996.

Wilde, Oscar. *The Importance of Being Earnest*. In *The Complete Works of Oscar Wilde*. New York: Perennial Library, 1989.

Yeats, W. B. *The Collected Poems of W. B. Yeats*. New York: Macmillan, 1956.

Yun, Chung-Hei. "Beyond 'Clay Walls': Korean American Literature." In *Asian-American Writers*, ed. Harold Bloom. Philadelphia: Chelsea House, 1999.

Zeledón, Maximo. "Dominican Dominion." *La Frontera*, no. 5. http:www.fronteramag.com/issue5/Díaz/index.htm. (last accessed April 10, 2002).

≋ Index